STAGES OF IDENTITY: A STUDY OF ACTORS

In memory of my mother

THELMA MAST

1921 - 1984

who loved life and theatre

Stages of Identity: A Study of Actors

SHARON MAST
Senior Lecturer in Sociology,
Victoria University of Wellington,
New Zealand

Published for the London School of Economics and Political Science by

Gower

Published by
Gower Publishing Company Limited,
Gower House, Croft Road, Aldershot, Hants GU11 3HR,
England

Gower Publishing Company
Old Post Road
Brookfield
Vermont 05036
USA

British Library Cataloguing in Publication Data

Mast, Sharon
   Stages of identity : a study of actors.
   1. Acting——Social aspects
   I. Title
   792'.028   PN2071.S6

   ISBN 0-566-00872-6

Printed in Great Britain by Paradigm Print,
Gateshead, Tyne and Wear

Contents

Tables

Preface

This book, which is based on the research I submitted as a PhD thesis to the London School of Economics in 1980, owes its existence to the work and goodwill of many people.

In their supervision of the original research, Paul Rock and David Downes provided a perfect balance of intellectual challenge and emotional support, thereby making an inestimable contribution to the study. That they were exemplary supervisors has been of continuing value to me as I have tried to help my students with their research. Paul Rock and, at a later stage, PDC Davis of the LSE Publications Committee were instrumental in finding a suitable publisher for the study, and for their efforts on my behalf I am extremely grateful. Professor Edward Sagarin, who first kindled my interest in the sociology of everyday life, read with great care the many drafts of this work which I sent to him over the years, and for his constructive criticism and encouragement, I thank him. I am also grateful for the helpful comments of Ken Plummer and Peter Melser.

Irving Mast and the late Thelma Mast played the intangible but crucial role of supportive parents throughout the entire research period, as well as offering more tangible and equally crucial financial support during those lean graduate school years. By virtue of her professional interest in filmmaking and screenwriting, my sister, Bernice Mast, provided a valuable sounding board for my ideas. I am even more indebted to her for her continuing enthusiasm and encouragement. In his capacity as proofreader, critic, colleague, friend and supporter, my husband, Chris Else, demonstrated unerring patience and sensitivity. For his unreserved support and love, I am profoundly grateful. And, for providing necessary diversion and welcome refreshment from the potentially all-consuming research enterprise, I wish to thank my good friends Anne Aylor, Florence Carter, Judy Hayter, Gill King, Donna Sturm, Evelyn Tavarelli, Nancy Teufel and Anna Tomsich-Swain.

Thanks are also due to the University of London Central Research Fund for assisting with field work expenses and to my colleagues in the VUW Department of Sociology and Social Work for graciously allowing me the time to complete the research when I first arrived in New Zealand. Ruth Mansford, Miria Clements and Christine Morgan of the VUW Computing Services Centre did an admirable job of preparing the camera-ready copy and were a pleasure to work with. The JAI Press kindly consented to the inclusion in this book of material from my article, 'Working for Television: The Social Organization of TV Drama', which was originally published in Symbolic Interaction. For her administrative expertise and warm concern, I thank Ann Trowles of the LSE Department of Sociology.

Finally, to the many actors, directors, producers, and teachers who generously participated in interviews and allowed me to observe them at work, I give my deepest thanks. They took a keen interest in helping an outsider to understand their world. I sincerely hope that they find this account of that world an accurate and insightful one.

Sharon Mast,
Wellington, July 1985.

1 Introduction

DEFINING THE PROBLEM

This book is a study of dramatic actors. It was prompted by an interest in the differences between interaction in theatre and in everyday life. At first these differences seemed to involve theoretical matters which could be clarified by reference to writing in the fields of theatre and sociology, but it soon became apparent that the only satisfactory approach was an empirical study of the training and work of actors. The development of the research project is therefore reflected in the plan of the book. This introductory chapter outlines briefly the sociological perspectives which informed the study and discusses the problems I encountered as the research progressed. Chapter 2 presents the case studies which are based on my observation of actors in drama school, theatre and television. In Chapter 3 I discuss the general problem of the formation and maintenance of the actor's occupational identity, returning to the issues which inspired this study – the nature of acting, life and theatre – in Chapter 4. The conclusion suggests parallels between dramatic acting and the potential for freedom of action in everyday life.

Two theoretical frameworks in sociology are particularly valuable to a study of dramatic actors: interactionism and the dramaturgical perspective. Interactionism stresses the importance of the interpretation of situations to an individual's assessment of goals and choice of goal directed behaviour as well as the interplay between the constructions of self-identity and social reality. The dramaturgical perspective rests on the analogy between life and theatre, emphasising that the concern to present oneself favourably to others is important to an understanding of the dynamics of social interaction. Since these frameworks guided my study of actors, a brief introduction to them is necessary.

The interactionist perspective grew from the ideas of a University of Chicago philosopher named George Herbert Mead. His writings were posthumously collected by his students under the title, Mind, Self and Society: From the Standpoint of a Social Behaviorist, published in 1934. The term 'symbolic interactionism' was coined by one of Mead's students, Herbert Blumer, who continues to be one of the major proponents of this perspective which views interaction as crucial to an understanding of self and society.

Self is the central concept in the interactionist perspective. According to Blumer, its importance lies in the fact that:

> In declaring that the human being has a self, Mead had in mind chiefly that the human being can be the object of his own actions. He can act toward himself as he might act toward others ... Mead regards this ability of the human being to act toward himself as the central mechanism with which the human being faces and deals with his world [1].

The fact that individuals can be objects to themselves means that they are aware of their relationship to the external world. In the internal world of the mind, one can evaluate various courses of action and choose between them. One then acts in the external world, usually in interaction with others, and the outcomes of these interactions are privately assessed, thus influencing the formulation of future plans. The self, for Mead, was a process consisting of the phases of the 'I' and the 'me'; the 'I' is the impulsive, innovative phase; the 'me' is the reflective phase of action, the attitudes we take towards our own actions. These attitudes are learned from specific (significant) others like parents, teachers and peers, as well as from generalised others or the groups and communities to which we belong. Clarifying the difference between the 'I' and the 'me', Mead writes, 'we distinguish that individual who is doing something from the "me" who puts the problem up to him' [2]. Our actions in the social world are thus a blend of idiosyncratic and shared features; the notion of self as consisting of an 'I' and a 'me' mirrors the relationship between the individual and society. The self-identity or reflexive self is the sum total of reflections which we entertain about our thoughts and actions in both the private (internal) and social (external) worlds.

If social life consists of social interaction, individuals must fit their independent lines of action together [3]. To do this, they must be able to predict roughly both the reactions of others to their own actions and the likely actions of these others ('take the role of the other'). Sharing meanings and values (or culture) enables such prediction to occur, for while selves are partly idiosyncratic ('I') they also contain common features ('me'). For this reason, social interaction is somewhat, but never wholly predictable [4].

The situation is an important variable in understanding the course which interaction takes. Within a culture there are usually numerous roles, or 'cluster[s] of related meanings and values that guide and direct an individual's behavior in a given social setting' [5]. When interacting individuals interpret their own and each other's roles in similar ways, they are said to share the definition of the situation. Again, this does not ensure complete predictability, for interaction consists of both 'behaviors that are routinely organized and those that are actively constructed in a self-conscious and interpretive fashion' [6]. The situation and our role within it place certain constraints on our behaviour; yet, in fulfilling what we take to be the situational or role requirements, we invariably add a personal touch. By doing this, we are actually creating and modifying the roles themselves, or 'role-making' [7].

By definition, interaction requires that both partners to the encounter (or 'ego' and 'alter') simultaneously engage in role-taking and role-making. This opens up the possibility of considerable innovative activity, as each individual both anticipates the reactions of others and constructs a role on the basis of his or her own interpretation and idiosyncratic style.

An interactionist view of social relations stresses the dynamic, interpretive view of social reality and the interrelation of individual and society. We are born into a particular social world and are taught by family, peers, teachers, work associates and the mass media how one in our various social positions should act; yet, social life is neither a static nor determined enterprise with society or others as dictators and individuals as obedient servants. Individuals react to these influences - interpreting their relevance to themselves - and by acting, act back on society (the sum of interactions between individuals and groups), thus modifying its structure.

The dramaturgical perspective, while also concerned with interaction, has a somewhat different emphasis. Although the concept of role obviously 'carries a message from the drama' [8], the use of theatrical terminology has not always signified a dramaturgical view of social life [9]. The term appeared in sociological literature long before Erving Goffman, the originator of the dramaturgical perspective in sociology, published The Presentation of Self in Everyday Life in 1956. Goffman was influenced by the writings of the literary critic, Kenneth Burke [10], who argued that an adequate description of a social act requires an account of the act (what took place), the scene (the background situation), the agent (who performed the act), the agency (what means were used to execute the act) and the purpose of executing the act. Goffman reformulated this dramatistic description of individual action in sociological terms by emphasising the group effort required to sustain an individual performance. He noted that performances require a supporting cast (teamwork), that the convincing staging of a performance relies upon the separation of 'front' and 'back' regions, that the discrepant role adopted by any one performer can jeopardise the performance of the team, and so on.

By stressing the performance features of interaction, the dramaturgical perspective, like interactionism, can be seen to stress the dynamic quality of social relations. The affinity between the dramaturgical and interactionist perspectives rests on an evaluation of the former as:

> the most persistent application of Blumer's view that meaning is a construction, a building process in which outcomes depend not on what is (construed either as psychological or sociological structures), but on what is going on or processes in the interaction itself .[11]

Yet, while the dramaturgical perspective focuses attention on 'what is going on', its view of the backdrop against which interaction occurs diverges from that of the interactionist:

> Clearly, in Goffman's work the social situation consists primarily of the existence of social norms, symbols and conventions (generically, frameworks) as objective conditions of interaction. This treatment contrasts rather sharply with the view of norms, symbols, and conventions as a product of interaction, achieved through a collective negotiating process.[12]

> [The] dramaturgical model refers to the team of stage actors who night after night seek to create an acceptable illusion, rather than to the drama itself, with its plot line and evolving, relatively unpredictable, sequence of transactions.[13]

Thus, there are both similarities and differences between the two perspectives. Both are employed in the case studies in Chapter 2 as means of interpreting the interaction under observation, and the implications of each perspective for an understanding of the differences between theatre and everyday life are taken up in later chapters.

Both the interactionist and dramaturgical perspectives are necessary for an understanding of actors and dramatic reality. Although the interactionist perspective might be fruitfully applied to the investigation of any occupation, the symbolic process of reality and identity construction is nowhere as evident as in the case of the dramatic actor. In the course of enacting the 'given' roles of dramatic scripts, actors must, by virtue of their interpretation of these roles, create new ones. Dramatic reality, like everyday reality, is thus socially constructed. The self-identity of the dramatic actor on the everyday plane both informs and is transformed by role performance on the dramatic plane. The interactionist perspective provides the tools needed to analyse the essential nature of this occupation. Moreover, the examination of dramatic acting, compared to other occupations, affords the unique advantage of investigation of dual levels of interaction; I will continually shift my focus from the actor as creator of career on the everyday plane to the actor as creator of character on the dramatic plane.

The interactionist perspective is often criticised for confining itself to the study of small groups [14]. Yet, the case studies will show that it is a useful framework for the examination of organisations - particularly those of the drama school and television production which took place within formal organisations. The study of the drama school will demonstrate how organisations modify their members' self-identities, how the subworld of an occupational group imparts its worldview (or system of meanings) to prospective members, and how the acceptance of that worldview influences both self-identity and action choices, which are themselves mutually modifying. The case studies of professional actors in theatre and television will show that, contrary to criticism [15], the interactionist perspective does not portray self-identity as totally free-floating and ever changing, but rather that people become committed to certain paths of action as they 'lodge' their self-identities in careers [16].

The efficacy of the dramaturgical analogy as a description of everyday social interaction ultimately rests on the difference between staged and everyday life. Sociological treatment of this problem has often suffered from a lack of familiarity with the business of acting. Mangham and Overington note that, 'little knowledge of what is the theater has yet entered the use of the

theatrical perspective in the social sciences' while Wilshire says
that 'role theorists seldom have any idea of what actually occurs
when artists play roles onstage, and this is an important
limitation of their theorizing' [17]. Most of us know about
acting from the standpoint of the audience; the view from the other
side of the footlights which I approximated in my role as
participant observer revealed a very different picture.

Generally, the actual everyday performance is contrasted with the
ideal theatrical performance; Burns, for example, assumes that the
artistic control of theatrical action overcomes the problems of
everyday interaction, in which:

> there is a certain amount of unpredictability, clumsiness and
> recalcitrance, among actors and audience. Climaxes do not
> always occur; scenes do not 'come off'; appropriate lines are
> not spoken; relationships often disintegrate, because, as in an
> improvisation, the actors dry up.[18]

The artistic control assumed of theatre neglects the fact that
the dramatic actors are human beings subject to the same less than
perfect performances on stage as they are in their everyday
conduct. Theatrical action is often characterised as given,
scripted or determined, and it is on this basis that the analogy is
made to the scripted nature of everyday social life. But Plummer
notes[19] that if the sociologist is to make use of the
dramaturgical analogy, it should be with a conception of drama
based on improvisation rather than classical drama. What I am
contending and will show in the following chapters is that, even
within theatre, the actual enactment of the scripted drama is very
much like improvisation and so leads to a view of both dramatic and
everyday reality as essentially dynamic and interpretive. The
dramaturgical analogy is only a metaphor, not a strict equation of
one thing with another, and if carried too far, can be misleading.
We are more than players on a stage.

The interactionist concerns of reality definition and
interpretation, role-making and role-taking, will be most apparent
whenever character construction and play production are discussed.
But clearly, the dramaturgical perspective must feature as an
important part of the analysis of dramatic actors, for these are
people whose occupation requires them to stage theatrical
performances. Furthermore, both their training and the organisation
of their occupation lead them to attend diligently to the staged or
dramaturgical features of their performances on the level of
everyday interaction. Just as the interactionist perspective alerts
us to the process of creating dramatic reality, so the
dramaturgical perspective sensitises us to the actor's attempts to
sustain an identity or manage the impressions he or she makes on
others, whether as actor or character.

Given my dual concerns of theatre and everyday life, several of the terms which I will use throughout this study must be defined. Goffman confronts this problem in Frame Analysis:

> the problem is that we tend to use the term "role" to refer to Gielgud's professional occupation, to the character Hamlet (being a part available to Gielgud), and even to the special capacity of Hamlet as son or as prince ...[20]

and I will follow Goffman's chosen usage:

> I shall use the term "role" as an equivalent to specialized capacity or function, understanding this to occur both in offstage real life and its staged version; the term "person" will refer to the subject of a biography, the term "part" or "character" to a staged version thereof.[21]

In this study, the term drama is used in the sense of 'a story of life and action for representation by actors' [22], whereas theatre will refer to that venue of produced drama consisting of a live performance before an audience, in contrast to other media for dramatic presentation such as radio, television and film.

I accord with Tyrone Guthrie's definition of acting :

> in general we use the word to signify pretending to be somebody else in the particular context of drama, a character in a play, of which the theme, the sequence of events (or plot), the nature of the persons and the very words which they speak have all been previously conceived by an author, then written down, then rehearsed (or repeated over and over) by actors.[23]

Finally, the most ambiguous term is actor. I use the term social actor to refer to the participant in a non-dramatic social situation (including the participant in drama, when discussing his or her attendance to non-dramatic aspects of the work situation). I use the term dramatic actor to refer to the person engaged in a dramatic production and/or to refer to the individual who considers dramatic acting to be his or her occupation. The 'and/or' is important in this context since some dramatic actors, unlike other professionals, spend a great deal of time doing other kinds of work. In such cases, I take the subjective identification with the occupation as the defining feature, rather than actual participation in the activity of acting, provided that the actor in question has either trained or worked professionally. When using the term dramatic actor, I do not, however, necessarily include only those individuals who have trained in an accredited drama school, although empirically this is usually the case. Finally, when for simplicity I use the term actor alone, it should be clear from the context whether I am referring to dramatic actors or social actors.

RESEARCHING THE PROBLEM

Although the interactionist perspective has sometimes been accused of failing to provide clear methodological prescriptions [24], it lends itself to the selection of participant observation and intensive interviewing as appropriate techniques. If we accept that:

> man creates at least some of the conditions for his own actions, then it can be presumed that he acts in his own world, at the very place and time that he is. The researcher himself must be at the location, not only to watch but also to listen to the symbolic sounds that characterize this world. A dialogue with persons in their natural situation will reveal the nuances of meaning from which their perspectives and definitions are continually forged.[25]

As in any dialogue, the researcher as participant must engage in role-taking, anticipating the other's reaction to jointly observed events, in order to comprehend the other's view. The study of actors is interesting in this respect, for the researcher tries to understand the actor in much the same way that the actor tries to understand the character. Of course, the goals are different, for the goal of the researcher is not portrayal, but understanding. The actor finds out what is going on on the dramatic level by participating in and observing the production's development; the researcher finds out what is going on on the everyday level by observing the unfolding social reality which the participants create.

Before discussing the techniques of participant observation and interviewing, it must be said that this style of research differs markedly from its scientific counterpart:

> it differs from the somewhat pretentious posture of the research scholar who under established scientific protocol is required in advance of his study to present a fixed and clearly structured problem, to know what kinds of data he is to collect, to have and hold to a prearranged set of techniques, and to shape his findings by previously established categories.[26]

The qualitative researcher cannot clearly structure the problem at the outset, for its ultimate shape will be affected by the unpredictable course of events which constitute the data. The techniques I used to understand my subject matter included not only observation and interviewing, but the study of books and articles about and for actors; psychological and sociological studies of actors, other artists and occupational roles; even ordinary theatregoing triggered thoughts about the study as I inevitably became the twenty-four hour a day researcher.

Clearly, when one wishes to test hypotheses derived from a rigorous theory, more controlled techniques like the experiment or survey may be appropriate. Although the qualitative researcher may not work with explicitly stated hypotheses, especially in the early stages of research:

> the researcher will surely pose many hypotheses informally at several points in his work, since almost every observation he makes will confirm, deny or modify a guess, a conjecture, speculation, or assumption in his own thinking.[27]

These working hypotheses are gradually supported or discarded as one moves from what Blumer calls the stage of exploration to the stage of inspection [28]. After a period of remaining open to all possible interpretations of the observed events, one subjects selected hypotheses to more careful scrutiny to find out if what one has vaguely assumed to be the case is confirmed by further observation.

If my interpretive framework leads me to reject a rigid, predetermined method, my own reactions to the research process will be influenced accordingly. The confidence and control of the experimental researcher who imposes a situation on subjects and then monitors their reactions will be replaced in the case of the qualitative researcher by the ambiguity and consequent anxiety which a natural setting invites. Again, my experience paralleled that of the actors I studied insofar as my fears of an unconstructable interpretation of their behaviour mirrored their fears of an unconstructable interpretation of their characters. Thus, the flexibility which is the advantage of qualitative research can produce the psychological insecurity in its practitioners which Gans has so clearly described [29]. Psychological insecurity and the possibility of failure stem from the fact that qualitative techniques require a personal relationship between researcher and participants. This will become evident from a discussion of participant observation and interviewing.

Participant observation has been defined by Becker and Geer as:

> that method in which the observer participates in the daily life of the people under study, either openly in the role of

researcher or covertly in some disguised role, observing things that happen, listening to what is said, and questioning people, over some length of time.[30]

The decision to function as a known or unknown observer is dictated both by what one wants to know and the nature of the group one wants to know about. Objections to covert observation usually concern the ethics of the situation, but there are practical disadvantages as well; Lofland and Lofland discuss the problem of devoting attention to the real role one takes up in the group at the expense of attention to the research problem [31]. It was clearly impractical in my case to function as an unknown observer, for the available real roles in theatre and television require the special skills of actor, director, stage manager or technician. The drama school case study required the special skills of the teacher or the unlikelihood of being selected as a student (a role which, even if miraculously achieved, would have required extraordinary attention). Clearly, the characteristics of one's research case must be considered when choosing the appropriate observational role.

As a known observer, I encountered a different set of difficulties. First, I had to gain entry to the field settings I wanted to observe. In the cases of the organisational settings of drama school and television, this meant winning acceptance of both the officials and of all the other members concerned. Informal contacts were essential in these cases. The theatre case was somewhat different; being a fringe (semiprofessional) theatre production, the organisation was far less formal. I attended the publicised audition, explained my intentions and was given permission to sit in on rehearsals.

Once inside, however, the researcher must win the cooperation of all participants, especially those (if any) who have not been consulted in the initial decision. The right to remain present is continually negotiated, and Gans remarks that:

The participant-observer also functions like an actor, for he lives a role rather than his own life, and his participation is always, at least to some extent, a performance.[32]

Thus, impression management was as much my concern as the actors'; I had to maintain a position of neutrality in the face of attempts by various internal factions to co-opt me to their side; I had to affect a stance which was unobtrusive without calling attention to myself by virtue of abnormal passivity; I had to be willing to listen to the views of the participants without appearing too offensive in my unwillingness to offer them advice and criticism; in short, I had to exercise as much diplomacy as possible without contracting the diplomat's disease of obvious artificiality.

If one succumbs to the allegiances encouraged by the participants, then bias may enter into one's study. The theatre and television cases each had two 'sides' - the actors and the production staff. Here, I had to establish neutrality since it was from the producers that I first had to seek permission to observe. The potential problem was far more pronounced in the drama school case, given the greater power differential between teachers and students. Considering my age at the time I did this study, I could have been taken for either one of the older students or one of the younger teachers, and age definitely engendered some of the ambiguity of my status. Becker et al. discuss the problems which can arise when one attempts an understanding of the student perspective [33], noting that the adoption of this perspective need not necessarily imply a biased viewpoint. Discussions with teachers can increase one's understanding of the student perspective, but the students may not see things this way. They may demand allegiance, as when I, taking a coffee break on the staff side of the canteen, was half-jokingly called 'traitor' by a student on the other side of the counter. I tried to resolve this problem by taking lunch and coffee breaks with the students, while openly lingering after classes for discussions with the teachers.

The qualitative researcher's methodology may also lead to bias. If one is required to take the role of the participants in an effort to understand them, the danger arises of accepting their worldview completely. Nevertheless, as Fred Davis comments [34], the acquired intersubjective view of the participants' world is not the same thing as the participants' view. Another parallel with the actors emerges here: as I will discuss later, actors are still themselves when they play dramatic roles - they do not become their characters. In the same way, seeing the world through the eyes of the participants did not mean that I forfeited my own vision or capacity to criticise them. Nor was I doomed to fall prey to the occupational hazard of 'going native' - renouncing one's research role and, in this case, becoming an actor. Nevertheless, field work does create pressures towards involvement.

Gans says that participants make sense of the observer's presence by attempting to accord him or her a conventional role within the group [35]. I found that in the drama school, since I was neither teacher nor student, I was treated like a critic of sorts with both students and teachers trying to elicit aesthetic judgements from me. In the theatre group, I was sometimes viewed as an assistant stage manager and expected to pitch in as even the actors must do in a semiprofessional setting. In the television production with its complex array of technical personnel, I was least expected to participate, thus taking up the conventional role of TV viewer.

Despite the occasional attempts by participants to involve the
researcher, 'the external pressure to participate is much weaker
than the internal pressure and desire to become involved' [36].
This need for involvement can exert an insidious influence on the
observer of dramatic actors, for without anyone's knowledge, one
can slip into the mental role of theatrical spectator. While this
is enjoyable, it means that for the time being, one has dropped the
observational stance. Similarly, the desire to exist within the
situation rather than on its margins can lead to negligence in
note-taking. My failure at times to note observations provided the
temporary comfort of pretending to be just another of the listening
participants. Of course, the moment I regained consciousness of my
actual role, I paid the price for temporary solace with the guilt
and regret of possibly unrecoverable, unrecorded insights.

Although most, if not all, people who undertake participant
observation probably feel the need for involvement, perhaps this
desire afflicts the observer of actors more strongly. After all, I
spent my days watching (usually) talented artists carving out
alternative realities in a conscious fashion. The attractiveness of
everyday reality seemed to diminish even though I felt myself an
outsider to the more enveloping and seemingly more valuable world
of theatre. Again my experience may have paralleled that of the
actor for whom everyday life may seem dreary in comparison to its
intensified portrayal in drama.

So far I have spoken only of my observation of actors although I
also conducted interviews with them at the close of each field
case. By conducting interviews after the period of observation had
ended, I hoped that the actors would feel they could speak more
freely than they might were I to remain in the field setting after
the interviewing. Whether or not respondents conceal or distort
information is an ever present problem in research. This problem of
impression management is perhaps heightened in the case of the
actor who can be expected to have special skills in this area [37].
The apparent cooperation I obtained may simply represent the
actors' competence at playing the role of respondent as though it
were any other role they were required to adopt in the course of
their work. Such an influence is perhaps unavoidable, for in
seeking an interview with them as actors I may have unwittingly
activated the 'star image' with responses affected accordingly.
Still, having spent considerable time with these people before
conducting the interviews, I felt that we had developed as much
mutual trust as might be expected from an interviewing
relationship.

Informal interviews were conducted in the course of changing
classes, having lunch, travelling from rehearsal to home; formal
interviews were conducted in the equally unlikely locations of

changing rooms, cafeterias and piers (where one actor had elected to spend his day off sunning). Researchers of deviant groups[38] and artistic occupations[39] have remarked upon the necessity of following their respondents to the far reaches of their natural settings in order to obtain the desired data. This is consistent with the decision to reject the research style which Blumer described, in which researchers not only impose analytical categories on their subjects, but usually administer tests on their own territory, replete with scientific apparatus and its authoritative symbolism. In contrast to this, Schatzman and Strauss describe the interviewing strategy of the qualitative researcher:

> The interviewer does not use a specific, ordered list of questions or topics because this amount of formality would destroy the conversational style. He may have such a list in mind or actually in hand, but he is sufficiently flexible to order it in any way that seems natural to the respondent and to the interview situation. ... Far from becoming disorganized by this state of affairs, the interviewer builds upon what has apparently become a shared event. Conversation implies this very property.[40]

This form of interviewing illuminates the way in which respondents subjectively structure reality. By stressing the conversational aspect of the interview and minimising the imposition of the interviewer's own constructs, respondents are forced to describe their situations in their own terms. For this reason, the rather vague questions which appear in the interview schedules (see the Research Appendix) such as 'feelings about the production', do not reflect laziness on my part, but were part of a conscious research strategy. Even in the case of apparently straightforward questions, I found a fascinating dissimilarity between the respondents' interpretations of these questions; the interpretations themselves became valuable data which brought me closer to the actors' experience.

Just as the ease with which entry to field settings is achieved reveals features of those settings themselves, so do the unanticipated and surprising remarks of respondents (often made before or after the interview has been implicitly acknowledged by the pair to have begun or ended) reveal features of reality of which the researcher may be unaware. In the drama school, for example, the extreme interest expressed by many respondents in the responses of others revealed that the training, though undergone collectively, was in its own way a very private affair. Secondly, a rather bold respondent concluded our interview with a look of disbelief, saying, 'Don't you want to know anything about my personal life?!' and proceeded to tell me about his girlfriend. While such information may not have seemed germane to my enquiry, his own surprise indicated that interest in the 'whole person' might not be the forte of the drama school, despite its personalised instruction.

The interviews were a vital part of the study insofar as they provided a check on my own hypotheses about the experience of the actor. For example, after becoming familiar with small scale theatre productions, I started the television case study and found the trappings of a large commercial TV production quite astounding. There was a danger of overestimating the influence of the organisational and technical aspects of TV on the actors involved in the production. The interviews with the TV actors helped me to gauge the fit between my reactions and theirs, and in fact proved that my speculations about the importance of these factors to the actors' experience were not exaggerated.

Throughout this discussion of research methods, I have drawn parallels between my experiences and the actors' wherever applicable. These parallels should come as no surprise, given that the observer is also in some ways a participant; in fact, it is the sharing of this role which gives the researcher the way in to the experience of the true participants. Two examples from the TV case study come to mind. First, some of the TV play's outside filming sequences were shot before the entire cast met for a read-through of the scripts of all the episodes. This meant that they were acting parts of the play in front of the cameras before having the complete picture of the story in their minds. Except for their preliminary reading of the scripts and previous experience of working in this out of sequence way, their apparent confusion about the play was the same as mine at this stage. Later in the case study, I noticed that I was less enthusiastic about this field case than I had been about the other two, and I wondered whether the lengthy task I had set myself had become prematurely routine. However, once it became clear that this was a feature of the actors' own work experience - that they also missed the 'electricity' of theatre - I realised that their attitude to the production had coloured my feelings toward it; through this realisation I learned more about them, and so my interest was renewed.

A word about the cases chosen is in order. The problem of gaining access to research sites is frequently referred to in the methodological literature. During the early stages of my research, the formal settings for theatre and television work sometimes seemed impenetrable; in some cases, neither direct approaches by me nor indirect approaches to various organisations by helpful contacts and 'connections' managed to result in permission to take up a field work role. Nevertheless, access was finally negotiated with the three cases which are discussed in Chapter 2; and while they were chosen, as I imagine is often the case, largely on the basis of availability, this does not detract from their usefulness as examples of actors' work settings from which theoretical insights emerge.

The activities described all took place in London[41] and each case has been used to highlight a different aspect of the actor's career. I focus on the transformation of self-identity in the Drama School; the negotiation of dramatic and everyday reality in the Theatre Company; and the problems of sustaining an occupational identity in the face of role conflict in the TV Group. I do not wish to imply that the issues raised in each case study apply to that setting alone; modifications of identity continue throughout the course of the actor's career and do not cease with formal training; many work situations, in drama school, theatre, TV and film present an opportunity for intensive characterisation work, just as any of these work settings may produce the role conflict which I characterise as television related. The conflict here was between the occupational value of money, which is available in TV and that of artistic excellence, which is missing from the drama typically produced for TV. But this same conflict might arise in commercial theatre. I will show that it is impossible to predict which situation will provoke which response in any particular individual. Some activities will fit neatly into actors' conceptions of their own careers, and therefore go unnoticed, while others will be discrepant with their expectations and thus emerge as problematic. Each case is used to highlight the aspect of career which generally surfaces in that setting, although its salience is not necessarily applicable to the case of every participant.

Similarly, although a biographical approach is used in the sequencing of the studies, I cannot assume that all participants will have experienced these activities in that particular order. Most, though not all, actors attend drama school, and this is dealt with first. A six to twelve month interim period between graduation from drama school and the acquisition of professional status (in the form of provisional union membership) is common, during which time many graduates seek work in the semiprofessional sector of fringe theatre, although this field is exploited by fully professional actors without current paid employment. This is the second case I discuss. Finally, although television is often, though not always, an option which presents itself later in one's career, requiring, for various reasons to be discussed, some length of experience in the occupation, there are obviously young actors who find work in this sector. Thus, the sequencing of cases can only be a vague approximation of the actor's career path, since the career path itself and its stages of progress are ambiguous.

In the following chapters, I will make statements about the career experience of the actor without having investigated large scale professional theatre or the film industry [42]. The two work settings which I did investigate are often devalued by the actor, each for different reasons. Only professional theatre or film - or perhaps nothing short of leading roles in each - would be congruent with at least the novice's expectations. Yet, the actors I observed are 'normal'; they devote time to semiprofessional theatre and television as well as to the occasional West End (fully professional) theatre production, although the latter is not a major work outlet for those with financial obligations. These are the 'middle range' [43] actors and the anxieties engendered by the work opportunities available to them are themselves typical. Thus, while I have not investigated, and so cannot speak for, either the chronically unemployed actor (the person who is virtually an actor by identification only) or the star, I feel that intensive analysis of the cases chosen yields an understanding of that typical actor who defies the extremes of the popular stereotype.

Any sociological account is selective in two respects. First, as participant observer one's own values and interests necessarily influence perception of the social setting. I could not observe all that happened in each setting or catch every conversation, and what I did observe was seen through my own personal and analytical lenses. Secondly, in writing up one's field work, one inevitably selects from the range of recorded observations in order to construct a coherent account. I sincerely hope that this view disadvantages neither the reader nor the participants who so kindly cooperated in this study.

I will conclude this introduction with one final comment on the research process which gave rise to this book. Gans provides us with a provocative suggestion:

> Soon, someone must do a study of participant-observers, to find out what kinds of people take to this research method and why, and particularly to learn what personality types are drawn to the marginal social relationships which are the essence of participant-observation. [44]

The reader may wish to bear this comment in mind while examining, in the following chapters, the case of the dramatic actor - a person who, like the participant observer, is in but not of the events in which he or she participates - in this case, the events of a scripted dramatic reality.

NOTES:

[1] H. Blumer, 'Society as Symbolic Interaction'.

[2] G. Mead, Mind, Self and Society, p. 177.

[3] See H. Blumer, 'Society as Symbolic Interaction', p. 184.

[4] See R. Turner, 'Role Taking: Process vs. Conformity', p. 35.

[5] A. Rose, 'A Systematic Summary of Symbolic Interaction Theory', p. 10.

[6] N. Denzin, 'Symbolic Interaction and Ethnomethodology: A Proposed Synthesis', p. 923.

[7] See R. Turner, 'Role-Taking', p. 22.

[8] E. Loudfoot, 'The Concept of Social Role', p. 134.

[9] See K. Davis, Human Society.

[10] See K. Burke, A Grammar of Motives.

[11] C. Edgley and R. Turner, 'Masks and Social Relations: An Essay on the Sources and Assumptions of Dramaturgical Social Psychology', p. 6.

[12] R. Lauer and W. Handel, Social Psychology, p. 444.

[13] B. Glaser and A. Strauss, 'Awareness Contexts and Social Interaction', p. 675.

[14] See N. Denzin, mentioned in B. Meltzer, et al., Symbolic Interactionism, p. 89.

[15] See B. Meltzer, et al., ibid., Ch. 3. See also P. Rock, The Making of Symbolic Interactionism for a critique of (and rebuttal to criticisms of) interactionism.

[16] See K. Plummer, Sexual Stigma, p. 16.

[17] I. Mangham and M. Overington, 'Performance and Rehearsal: Social Order and Organizational Life', p. 207; B. Wilshire, Role Playing and Identity, p. 261.

[18] E. Burns, Theatricality, p. 139.

[19] See K. Plummer, Sexual Stigma, p. 19.

[20] E. Goffman, Frame Analysis, p. 129.

[21] Ibid.

[22] Chambers 20th Century Dictionary, p. 392.

[23] T. Guthrie, Tyrone Guthrie on Acting, pp. 7-8.

[24] See B. Meltzer, et al., Symbolic Interactionism, Ch. 3.

[25] L. Schatzman and A. Strauss, Field Research, pp. 5-6.

[26] H. Blumer, 'The Methodological Position of Symbolic Interactionism', in Symbolic Interactionism, pp. 40-41.

[27] L. Schatzman and A. Strauss, Field Research, p. 12.

[28] See H. Blumer, 'The Methodological Position of Symbolic Interaction'.

[29] See H. Gans, 'The Participant Observer as a Human Being: Observations on the Personal Aspects of Field Work'.

[30] H. Becker and B. Geer, 'Participant Observation and Interviewing: A Comparision', p. 28.

[31] See J. Lofland and L. H. Lofland, Analyzing Social Settings, p. 49.

[32] H. Gans, 'The Participant Observer as a Human Being', p. 313.

[33] See H. Becker, et al., Boys in White, p. 110.

[34] See F. Davis, 'The Martian and the Convert', p. 339.

[35] See H. Gans, 'The Participant Observer as a Human Being', p. 305.

[36] Ibid., pp. 305-6.

[37] I am indebted to Peter K. Manning for this point.

[38] See N. Polsky, Hustlers, Beats and Others, p. 135.

[39] See C. Ryser, 'The Student Dancer', p.100.

[40] L. Schatzman and A Strauss, Field Research, p. 73.

[41] A pilot study was conducted in New York City during the summer of 1975.

[42] Limitations of time and access prevented me from including such cases in my study.

[43] See D. Layder, 'Occupational Careers in Contemporary Britain: with Special Reference to the Acting Profession'.

[44] H. Gans, 'The Participant Observer as a Human Being', p. 317.

2 The case studies

A. BECOMING AN ACTOR

Introduction

Sixty-three students were registered at the Drama School during the term in which I did most of my field work. The training programme is divided into seven terms, and the School admits a new intake of students every other term. That term, 22 students were in the 2nd term, 19 were in the 4th term, and 22 were in the 6th term. Those in their 6th and 7th terms are called senior students since it is in the last two terms of training that students perform regularly before a paying public.

The students participate in an extremely demanding programme, attending classes from 10.00 to 5.30 Monday to Friday, at the very least; often, there are evening classes or weekend rehearsals to attend as well as evening performances from the 4th term onward. In this study, I will describe the students' experience from selection through to graduation.

The Drama School audition

Of the more than 600 people who apply and reach the audition and interview stage, only 14 males and 7 females are accepted (reflecting the ratio of male to female roles in theatre). To

audition for the school, each applicant performs two pieces for the
selection committee which consists of the permanent staff of four
teaching directors (no specialist teachers - teachers of voice,
movement or speech - are included on this board). If any one
auditioner thinks that the applicant should be selected, that
applicant is given a second audition before the principal, whose
decisions are final. About half the applicants, according to the
principal, are eliminated through consensus among the auditioners.
Very few generally receive the approval of all members of the
committee and there is a wide ranging middle group of those who are
passed by some but not by others. Although the auditioners vote
independently, it appears that there is some attempt to arrive at a
joint decision - probably because of the impracticality of sending
all possible acceptances through to the second audition. Finally,
twenty-one or twenty-two students are chosen each term.

Apart from the number of applicants, the number selected and the
central facts about the selection procedure, the issue of selection
is fairly subjective. Unlike so many occupations in which the
applicant's skills can be objectively judged, the occupation of
acting and the opportunity to train for it are in the hands of
people who often describe their own decision making as an intuitive
process. Several interesting issues emerge from interviews with
auditioners: first, the terms in which they describe what it is
that they are looking for in an applicant; second, the difficulty
they have in making the distinction between the actor as actor and
as person; and third, the way in which they justify their selection
decisions in the light of the later achievements of the students
they previously chose.

The essentially intuitive nature of casting decisions has been
commented on by a professional casting director:

> It's all subjective, but people keep trying to operate as
> though it were not. In the end, it always comes down to this: I
> like him or I don't like him.[1]

This was similarly noted by the School auditioners when asked what
it was that they were looking for when an applicant auditioned:

> You can put words on it ... but they remain words, ultimately,
> because ultimately you sit there and think, 'Here comes this
> again, I know it' ... At the crudest and lowest point, it's
> what person wakes you up.[2]

> I'm trying to justify after the event what I know happens
> instinctively.

It's a very subjective and intuitive selection process and can't be subjected to measurement.

When pressed, the auditioners were able to describe the criteria they apply, but this is still an elaboration upon a subjective process:

You can say that what you're looking for is that what the person shows is unusual, individual, fresh, and it reveals the text that they are speaking.

It's got to be that you see how they are using that, imaginatively, in the situation that they're playing.

In a 5 minute audition, if they speak two or three lines truthfully and illuminatingly, I think they've probably got something.

What I am looking for is people who would make interesting actors.

These same auditioners were aware of the ambiguous nature of this selection process (or, indeed, of professional auditions): is the person chosen because of observable acting talent, potential, or ability, or, rather, for qualities which inhere in the self - and how far can the two be distinguished? In other words, there is evidence of a belief that something about the person contains the innate quality of an actor. This emerges strongly in the following auditioners' remarks:

A person may never have been on a stage in his life, and yet he may look right there.

'It's a magic, it's something that makes them special ... Sometimes someone can seem terrible but you know that the magic is there. If they do their piece quite nicely and you say no, and the applicant asks what he did wrong, you can't say, 'You're not a very exciting person', or you didn't come over as that ... Sometimes someone will come on stage and you'll say, 'Isn't she marvellous - but no'[3].

I think you look for what I would call acting animals - people who come on and interest you, arrest your attention somehow - although some do that without in any way being actors ... The number of people who come along to audition whom you instinctively know to be actors is very small indeed[4].

A belief in the innateness of an acting 'quality' engenders the attitude that training cannot make an actor, but can only develop the talent of one. Only one student said, when asked why he decided to become an actor, that he was, essentially, an actor, but this belief may have lain behind students' more general statements such as, 'I was selected because I was good' or 'because they thought I was good'.

The third issue which emerges from the discussion of selection procedures is the way in which the auditioners use the later achievements of students to justify their selection decisions:

> We all know what it is that we're doing and somehow we must be doing it right because the people who come here, by and large, manage to get through the course and develop into reasonable actors - so what is it that we're all saying yes to, we should be able to pin down.

> With experience, I have become more accurate in my choices - that is, I've made fewer mistakes in that someone I thought would be good turned out to be hopeless.

What the auditioners don't mention (or don't appear to be aware of) is the fact that the same group of teaching directors/auditioners who make the initial selection decision make the later appraisal of the developing student. Thus, not only are they necessarily subjective evaluations, but they are made by the same people at two points in time, the latter appraisal viewed as a justification of the former. Of course, a fairly objective test of both selection and training outcomes is the future employability of those trained - except that the employment of actors is not based on ability alone.

When I asked the students about their reactions to the selection audition, the large majority recalled the experience as a terrifying or nerve racking one. Several recalled that they had not been as nervous as they had expected to be, or that the occasion was an enjoyable one; several others spoke of the effect which other applicants had had upon their own composure. They were nervous because others were, and this was apparently the appropriate reaction to the situation; or, the nervousness of others had a calming effect on them; or, the confidence of others had a belittling effect. The students who felt their own chances of success minimised by the glamorous or theatrical appearance of other candidates showed some awareness of the possible personal criteria used by the auditioners apart from the criterion of ability[5]. In relating the horrors of the audition, two students said:

> I went on stage, and all I could see was a pair of glasses in the back of this dark theatre, and I just played the whole thing to the glasses.

It's black, you can't see anything but the lights - they tell you not to be scared, but it's like the Gestapo.

One of the auditioners remarked that most of the applicants 'haven't got an idea at all', which meant not 'realising that part of acting is that you're trying to say something to somebody else, so that maybe you'd better focus it'. The first of the two students quoted above was obviously aware of this, and treated the auditioner like an ordinary theatrical spectator. The second quote exemplifies the student's expectation that the audition will be like a face-to-face interview, in which case a rapid adjustment must be made when it turns out to be like a theatrical performance. The auditioner who spoke of students 'not having an idea' concluded that, 'really it's quite easy to get rid of a lot of them'. Evidently, one's chances of success at the audition depend a lot on defining the situation in the same way that the auditioners do.

Several students recalled gauging their chances of success at the Drama School audition in relation to the results of their auditions at other drama schools. The assumption was - and it is a fair one to make - that the School was one of the most prestigious of the London drama schools and therefore one of the most selective. A belief that the same selection criteria are used in different institutions is implied in the students' comments that, since they had already learned that they had not been accepted at a less prestigious institution, they judged their chances of being accepted at the School as less than they previously thought. If the students believe that the same selection criteria are used, they must feel that there is some identifiable quality - talent - which the skilled auditioner does or does not perceive.

When asked, 'Why do you think you were selected?', eight of the nineteen students interviewed attributed their success to the auditioners' discernment of objective skills, with remarks like, 'Because they thought I could act'; 'Because they saw I had skills'; 'Because my resume showed evidence of seriousness about acting'. Three students attributed their success to somewhat elusive, and at the same time personal characteristics, saying they were selected 'Because of a certain quality I have'; 'Because people find me interesting'; 'You later find out what qualities were saleable'.

First reactions to the training

Since my field work at the Drama School began in a term when there was no new intake, the most recent additions to the school were the 2nd termers. In order to get an idea of the initiate's reactions to training, I asked them (and those in more advanced terms) to try to

remember their first term at the School. The following account is
in part based on these recollections, although as recollections
they may contain some retrospective distortion. The remainder is a
result of direct observation.

I finished interviewing the students, as opposed to observing
them, during the following term when a new 1st term group had just
arrived. I witnessed their first day at the School, and this from
the viewpoint of some of the established students. This first day
of the new term, there was great excitement amongst these students
as they anticipated meeting the 1st termers - or, 'going in to look
them over', as their comments indicated. It seems that the 1st
termers' first day at the School recalled for the more advanced
students a difficult event in their own careers and so they happily
anticipated the opportunity to 'get their own back'. They seemed to
feel that their own status had been unquestionably raised by the
entry of a term below and talked as if they intended a rather harsh
initiation ceremony. In fact, this did not occur. Instead I
observed this group of what were now 3rd and 5th termers greeting
the newcomers with a mixture of curiosity and reserve.

Part of the initiate's difficulties of the first few days at the
School is perhaps caused by the apparent friendliness coupled with
an undercurrent of hostility which characterises the majority's
response. With a highly competitive selection process based on
criteria strongly related to personal characteristics, initiates
may well expect a warmer reception, for they have come to join the
ranks of the chosen. As one teacher remarked:

You come to the School feeling, I must have something in order
to get into [the School] coupled with this marvellous feeling
of, 'Here we go! I'm going to be able to do it all the time!'
When you come, you think, 'I can do anything!'

First termers, arriving with this feeling of specialness, must be
rather unsettled by the others' seeming indifference. More advanced
students, preoccupied with their own careers, see the first termers
simply as part of the institution's ongoing process.

More importantly, the initiates' sense of specialness influences
their relationships to two important groups of others: the student
body and the staff. It soon becomes clear that they cannot present
themselves in a favourable light to both groups at the same time.

Initiates quickly learn that student relationships are governed
by a norm of apparent uniformity. Although they are told by the
principal in his introductory talk that the reason they were chosen
was that 'something happened' when they came on stage - that there
was something special about them or their performance which

attracted the auditioners' attention - the students must necessarily conclude that there was something special about all twenty-one of them, and they therefore equally share this elite status. Of course, there is an inbuilt inadequacy to this conclusion. It is only when applicants have proven ability to a given standard on an objective skill that true uniformity is possible, and the notion of talent itself carries connotations of uniqueness.

A 2nd termer commented on the ill that could come of presenting oneself as a distinct personality, of becoming, for example, one of the 'comics' or 'funny people': 'If they want to, they can't really break out of that - they walk around with that identity'. Not only would this make one stand out from the crowd and violate the norm of uniformity, but in the world of the drama student, such a crystallised presentation of self carries a second meaning: since the social identity one presents is so closely related to the dramatic identities which one can portray, a typecast social identity carries with it the implication of a limited dramatic range. So, the pressures toward uniformity which result from the purportedly uniform status of the initiate at the School are exacerbated by the requirements of being a student in a school of dramatic art. Drama students learn very early on that in order to present themselves as actors to others and maximise their opportunities for varied dramatic roles, they must maintain the appearance of a fluid, neutral or muted identity.

There is the second problem of presenting oneself in a favourable light to one's teachers. Noting the dramaturgical care exercised by initiates, one teacher said:

> They start off very enthusiastically ... in some cases very ready to transmit an image of themselves as keen students or very alive people or as people who are riveted to the idea of truthful acting - then there's an easing out of initial postures, enthusiastic getting on with the work, and the process of discovery begins.

Students begin by self-consciously conveying their individuality to the teachers. However, one student with previous professional experience was careful to convey to her teachers an appearance of similarity to other students: 'I was over-humble, because I wanted not to seem as though I knew anything'. So, even so far as student/teacher relations are concerned, there is a tension between conveying sameness, and thus receptivity to training, and specialness, so that one's talent is recognised by teachers, attended to and developed.

those students off the stage'). In comparison to the initiates' own freshness and enthusiasm about the training they are about to undertake, the worry and self-doubt of more advanced students may make for a distorted perception of their own placement in the school as a whole - this worry and self-doubt being the outcome of the difficulties of the midpoint of the student career, or senior students' concerns about imminent (un)employment. Initiates may be given walk-on parts in senior productions, in which case the discrepancy between their own and the senior students' abilities may loom large. First termers, then, draw conclusions about their own status from a variety of highly visible 'facts', and their necessarily limited understanding of the reasons behind the appearances produces a specific initiate perspective on the training programme. The initiate's perspective will change as familiarity with the School and experience of its programme increases; however, while this perspective is held, it constitutes the initiate's real experience.

In discussing the 1st termer's reactions to the training, I have not yet focused on the training itself. In the 1st and 2nd terms the technical, as opposed to production, aspects of the course are emphasised. As students progress through the seven terms, they spend more and more time rehearsing for actual productions until in the 6th and 7th terms, this is done to the exclusion of technical training (with the exception of one speech class per week that continues into the 7th term). Although several teachers mentioned the initiate's disappointment with the technical bias of the first half of the training, none of the students (again, giving retrospective accounts of their first reactions) remembered feeling this way.

One dimension which affects the students' orientation to the technical side of training is the extent to which they associate acting with theatre rather than television and film. The vast majority of students have acquired their ideas about professional acting from the latter sources even though their experience of acting, whether in school or amateur companies, is theatrical. In fact, only five of the 19 students interviewed cited enjoyment of previous acting experience as the reason for wanting to become an actor although 18 out of 19 had had previous acting experience. Several teachers felt that the students failed to associate acting with theatre and were therefore bewildered by the early, primarily technical, training; theatre acting appears a more artificial, less naturalistic enterprise than they had envisaged. This undoubtedly has serious implications for the student's conception of characterisation, as a speech teacher described:

Students say, 'But I want to do it naturally'. So I say, 'What's that? And are you going to be natural as an old lady or

- 29 -

a fat lady or a thin lady or a demanding lady?' Then we have to start to define what is acceptable and what is 'real'.

What I have been discussing here is the incipient occupational identity of the drama student. First, this entails the redefinition of activities legitimately associated with acting which include not only technical training, but also rehearsal as opposed to performance. Rehearsal is necessary and must therefore be defined as enjoyable if one is to survive the long hours spent doing it. The socialisation of the drama student is characterised by the tension between the increasing commitment to the occupation, stemming from increased activity within it, and the increasing demystification of the occupation stemming from the kinds of activities one does.

Secondly, a belief in the necessity of formal training is inculcated in these early stages and contributes to the growth of an occupational identity. Student acceptance of this perspective is evident in the remarks of the following three 2nd termers:

You can't start the programme thinking, 'I'm better than all the people that were refused'. That is true; however, you're not as good as you ought to be.

People make it without going to drama school, but if you've got something anyway, something like this can only increase it. It teaches you everything except experience.

I'd really thought that if a person really feels and knows what he's doing, you could take a person off the street and he could be a better actor than someone who's trained; I came with that kind of idea in mind. But it's not - you've got to learn craft, about [body] weight and working with other actors.

The official perspective on the necessity of formal training employs several metaphors. Entering students may or may not have had prior acting experience, whether professional or amateur. They may lack a 'way of working', be 'full of tricks', or suffer from 'bad habits'. For example, a teaching director remarked that, 'the 2nd termers don't actually have a way of working yet that a 5th termer will'. When I asked, 'What about the 2nd termer who comes in with an Equity (union) card?', she replied, 'It doesn't necessarily mean they'll have a way of working; they might be full of tricks and nonsense they've picked up in the professional theatre'. Because only those students with previous acting experience may have acquired tricks and ways of working while everyone may suffer from bad habits (of 'incorrect' body use in everyday life), the latter metaphor is most widely employed by teachers, and ultimately by students. Since bad habits reside in the most fundamental aspects of self, it becomes clear that the self must change if one is to acquire the occupational identity of the actor. (The debate between students and teachers over the evaluation of the familiar self will be discussed more fully later.)

This link between the transformation of self and occupational socialisation is the third element in the growth of occupational identity. When asked if the training changes the student's conception of self, this same teaching director quoted above replied:

> It must do, if it makes you look at yourself, which it does - I don't see how you could come out unchanged - if you do, nothing has happened.

Similarly, a 2nd term student was reassured by a teacher that this identity transformation would occur:

> He says that when you reach the 6th and 7th terms, and because you're rehearsing most of the day, you're virtually a professional - You grow, you look like an actor - some people grow beards, you just look different.

In the same interview, this student revealed that he had lost his confidence during the previous vacation. In other words, his occupational identity required the reinforcement of the school surroundings to sustain it at this stage in his career.

Two terms at the School provided sufficient professional pride for one 2nd termer to say, 'I hope I never need work so badly that I would accept just anything'. When asked if that meant she would rather work at something totally different, she replied, 'Yes, very much so'. Thus, at this very early stage of training, a paradox is apparent (though unrecognised by the student): In order to preserve one's identity as an actor, one must, at times, not act.

Of course, the growth of an occupational identity - the feeling that one is a professional - is strongly based on the acquisition of skills. In the case of actors, where the supply is high in relation to demand, the acquisition rather than practice of skills may be crucial to the maintenance of that identity. How does the drama student learn technique?

Learning technique

The teaching programme each term is modified by suggestions from students and staff. During the term in which I did my field work, the 2nd term programme was as described in Table 2.1 below:

Table 2.1
2nd Term Programme

Class	Hours per Week
Mime	2 (for 3 weeks)
Movement	7
Rehearsal	10
Singing	2
Speech	2
Stage Fights	1
Text	2 (for 3 weeks)
Voice	2
Voice and Movement	2

	26+ hours per week for 10 weeks

Several of these classes will be discussed below.

I observed two movement classes with two different teachers. In the first class, there were five students. The teacher discussed and demonstrated the positioning of the body relative to the social relationships being portrayed on stage, as well as the need to take the audience into account when positioning the body [7]. She demonstrated how the body would be held away from a second character on stage in order to denote a defensive attitude, and how one would walk and distribute one's weight in accordance with the motivation underlying the action. The students then attempted curved and straight moves around chairs as the teacher had demonstrated when discussing the physics of centrifugal force which affect the axis of the body. In criticising the students' attempts, the teacher said that they were not breathing in correspondence with the action, but against it. And, since they had failed to incorporate the appropriate wrist movement into their performance, the movement of the wrist was practiced alone. The teacher showed them the kinds of motivations which might underlie a particular wrist movement and finally accompanied this by the corresponding full body movement.

In the second 2nd term movement class I observed, the teacher tried to show the students how to change movement in relation to changes in tempo. They started the exercises with a running step but were stopped when the teacher noticed that, in concentrating on the leg movement, they had failed to control the rest of their bodies. The teacher was able to give each of the nine students in this class almost individual attention, particularly when they moved on to more strenuous exercises at the bar where the task was to coordinate arm and leg movements in opposite directions.

In the 2nd term movement classes (as in most 2nd term classes), there was greater variation in ability among students than was noticeable in later terms. Even when movement exercises appear to be wholly isolated from any application to actual acting, there are differences between students in attention to what can only be called aesthetic detail.

Movement training bears a further relation to acting ability than the simple improvement in body control; it no doubt accustoms the student to remembering sequences of physical actions. As such, it is essential for later production work in which the verbal side of the task is specifically noted in the script, but where a physical notation system is less developed. For example, the physical placement of actors' bodies on stage is easily noted ('downstage right') but actors must remember a director's instruction to move a part of the body a certain way.

From observation of other classes, it seems that some specialist teachers focus on the interrelation among various aspects of technique while others emphasise the importance of technique to acting in productions. Thus, the students gain a wide experience of specific movement training, movement in relation to breathing and voice, and movement in relation to acting. Since students at this stage are exposed to such different teaching approaches within one speciality and are aware of the need to integrate the technical training with dramatic performance, they are sometimes confused. For example, when in the 2nd term movement class the teacher reminded a student to monitor the separate parts of his body, he jokingly said, 'They keep telling me to act with the whole body!', here referring to the discrepancy between demands made by teaching directors and by specialist teachers. The training can be said to consist of a continual interplay between integrative and compartmentalising approaches.

One of the movement teachers I interviewed spoke of the difficulty she had distinguishing between the 2nd termers' inability to understand her instructions and their inability to produce the desired result. More often, she felt, the problem was that of producing the desired effect, and she cited the parallel example of understanding a written passage but being unable to convey its meaning through voice. Yet, students may say they understand the instruction when in fact they don't; here, the pressure to present oneself favourably in a competitive environment is apparent and actually impedes learning. Of course, in a case like this which requires the correct, overt physical response, the question arises whether understanding can truly be isolated from the ability to produce the action: it may only be in the correct production of the action that the student finds confirmation of understanding.

Problems of meaning and understanding are much more apparent in voice and speech classes, where an esoteric and metaphorical use of language prevails. Learning the language of a subculture, occupational or otherwise, enables an initiate to acquire the necessary skills and to adopt the appropriate subcultural identity.

For example, at the start of one 2nd term speech class, the teacher told the students to 'think' a certain part of the body in order to relax it. They were told to 'relax the neck' and then to 'relax the arms' as though one could 'send oneself a message', as a speech teacher said. The students were told to 'stretch the body upwards and outwards' without physically doing so.

In a 2nd term voice class, the students were told to 'check that you've got the space inside yourselves'. A number of misunderstandings are possible here. Students may never have performed these actions and so not know what the command refers to; they may have performed these actions without ever attaching a literal description to them; or they may have performed these actions and attached a different literal description to them ('expand the rib cage and extend the diaphragm'). Whatever the misunderstanding at the root of the incorrect response, only the teacher's definition of a response as correct enables the student to grasp the meaning of the command.

The teacher makes various attempts to ensure the student's understanding - to call forth in the student a response which can be defined as correct. For example, a student produced a sound in a voice class, and the teacher asked for 'more ah'. A second incorrect response from the student met with a repeat of the command. The student then said, 'I don't understand' and the teacher asked another student to demonstrate the correct response. After the third incorrect response from the first student, the teacher took her to a mirror where he had her observe her own production of the response. As she did this, he explained the physical mechanisms underlying the production of this sound. In other cases, he mimicked the incorrect responses so that the students could hear them and identify them as incorrect.

Evidently, the technical training proceeds partly by imitation. As one movement teacher said, although imitation is not the desired end it is used extensively in the 2nd term because it 'speeds things up so that the students can achieve the desired effect without experimenting aimlessly with all the possibilities'. Both teachers and students viewed the avoidance of trial and error as the principle underlying the training as a whole.

The ultimate aim of technical training is not imitation, but what I will call self-directed action. Students learn the mechanics of production - whether of body, speech or voice - by doing and by attaching verbal labels to their actions. The verbal labels enable them to instruct themselves, for language gives us the ability to react to our own commands as we would to others' [8]. Actors can treat their bodies as objects towards which they, in their minds and as selves, can orient their actions. As Strauss says in Mirrors and Masks:

> The act of identifying objects, human or physical, allows a person to organize his action with reference to those objects. Such overt action may consist of a series of smaller acts which add up to a line of activity, as for instance when you identify your pen as having run dry - The whole sequence of actions - observing that the pen ceases to write, pressing harder to test whether any ink remains ... constitutes the line of behavior 'released' by your definition of the pen as 'in need of ink'.[9]

Non-actors are rarely concerned with the way they use nonverbal cues (unless they are trying to create a particular impression) for people ordinarily convey to others the 'characters' they are. But actors will be quite concerned to convey the physical gestures appropriate to their characters and, since they cannot monitor these gestures without a mirror, they interpose a literal description of the mechanics of movement as a sort of remote control mechanism.

This objectification was evident in a 2nd term speech class in which students performed various vowel exercises and then turned to a textbook which included exercises with the sound of the letter 'L'. The teacher asked the students to tell her 'something about the letter "L"'; they described the placement of the tongue and the movement of air around it and gave other descriptive rules for the production of the sound. As with any mechanical skill, the objective description is only a preliminary phase of the training. Gradually, the knowledge is internalised and production becomes automatic.

In the Drama School, this process of self-objectification did not proceed without resistance from the students. The excessive joking which went on in the 2nd term speech class can be interpreted as an expression of role distance[10] - distance from the dehumanising role one is being asked to take in relation to oneself. Through this form of role distance, the student asserts the integrity of self. In describing the training as a whole, students and teachers sometimes refer to the process whereby students feel that teachers are 'breaking them down'. Whereas they have in mind a more general psychological process which will be discussed shortly, the technical training I have described is indeed a breaking down of

the self into categories for the purpose of analysis so that
ultimately one can direct one's own actions for dramatic ends.

The student in the first half of the course also hears of a later
stage of reintegration in the advanced terms. As one teacher
remarked, 'in senior terms, it all gels'. This term is used to
denote the integration of separate aspects of the training into a
competent dramatic performance as well as a 'reconstitution of
self' [11]. The actual gelling point occurs to different people
during different terms, but all who suffer through the
disintegrative stages of training have the assurance from others
that, sooner or later, the tide will turn. The elements of training
can be said to gel when the technical skills are used
unselfconsciously and are in harmony with the more creative aspects
of performance. The student who survives the transformation of self
which the technical training demands finds the reward in the
ability to act competently and confidently.

Learning to act

Although I am mainly concerned in this section with the drama
student's growing familiarity with the practice of acting and
workings of rehearsal, I must point out the link between learning
technique and learning to act.

Unlike the more advanced students, 2nd termers may find that
technical considerations are foremost in their own and their
directors' minds. One teaching director noted the interplay between
technical teaching and directing in his own work with 2nd termers.
He might pause in rehearsal to give a necessary technical tip to a
student; for example, during one rehearsal, he told a student to
convey displeasure by 'biting off' his consonants. Where, as in
this case, a director is especially directive, telling the actor
exactly how to speak and move, the actor's task is one of
imitation. This director provided the student with exemplary vocal
and physical moves because he did not feel that the 2nd termer had
yet learned, either intellectually or practically, the
correspondence between the vocal and physical gestures of any one
character. Other directors, however, urge the students to 'forget'
their technical training while rehearsing, saying:

> You have to trust that the physical work and voice work will
> actually pay off in the end, but you can't do that and try to
> be in the play at the same time.

Within one term a student may work with two directors who not
only have different ideas about technique and acting, but also
about the way to stage a play. Several teachers and students saw

this variety as the School's strength since it mirrors the situation in the professional world where the actor must adjust to different directors and their ways of working. For the novice, however, it undoubtedly adds to the confusion inherent in this stage of training.

One of the student's (or professional actor's) most important tasks is that of discovering, as early in the production as possible, the degree to which the director intends to share aesthetic decision making. Decisions of this sort must be made at various levels. (1) At the broadest level, the overall 'concept' of the play must be determined. The director usually decides this and many actors prefer to be responsible solely for the business of acting. They may even interpret a director's desire to share the creation of the overall concept with them as a sign of weakness or indecisiveness. Of course, individuals differ in the amount of power they wish to be given by a director, and it is likely that more general personality differences play a part here. (2) The director may explain the way a particular scene or sequence in a scene is to be played. At this level the director is often perceived as maintaining strong, but not excessive control of the situation while affording the actor a reasonable degree of latitude in creating the character. (3) Having conveyed the concept, message, or theme he or she intends to emphasise in the production or any one scene, the director may assume that the actors can deduce from this the nonverbal details of their own performances. In order to share decision making to this extent, the director must feel that the actor not only understands his or her intentions but can independently create and convey a characterisation which is consistent with it. The director who is perceived as the most directive is the one who specifies each nonverbal detail; this can amount to playing each part so that the actor can imitate it, as described earlier[12].

One of the 2nd term productions I observed was directed by the particularly directive director mentioned before. By describing several of the interactions between this director and his student actors, I hope to clarify the way that directorial style affects actors, and to point out some general features of rehearsal.

The first rehearsal began with the director asking the students to raise their hands as he called out the characters' names. He also told the students that he didn't know all of them by name, never having worked with this term before, but he did not ask them to introduce themselves. I mention this because it exemplifies the prominence of the object of the work (the character) over the subject (the actor), paralleling the neutralisation of self which occurs in technical training.

The director then asked the cast whether they liked the play, implying that they were to have read it before the first rehearsal (although some students told me that they never read the play in full). Since the only acceptable answer to the director's question is 'yes', what he is really requesting is ritualistic agreement to maintain a positive orientation to the production.

The students were asked to learn their lines by the end of the week. A 2nd term student once told me that senior students knew all their lines before they started to rehearse. From my observation of senior rehearsals, I knew this to be untrue, but the 2nd termer's remark was valuable to me, revealing as it did the initiate's awe of senior students and the standard he believed would be expected of him in later terms.

The director then said he was not accustomed to lengthy discussion of a play prior to its rehearsal and that those actors not involved in the scenes they would rehearse that day could leave. If the cast had not heard from more advanced students of this director's style, this might have been one of the first indications of his placement on the power sharing continuum. From his remark, they could deduce that he did not require much actor participation in the overall concept of the production, and secondly, that the actors would be expected to develop their characterisations in accordance with his ideas rather than in interaction with each other[13]. Had he subscribed to the other style of directing, he probably would have wanted them all to stay for the rehearsal in order to chart the progress of each other's roles. Some of the students left and actual rehearsal began.

The director started to block the play (setting out the broad physical movements of the actors on the set). This surprised some students who were accustomed to reading through the play with the director before moving around on the stage.

The rest of the rehearsals for this play took the customary form, while exhibiting the characteristics of rehearsal with a directive director. At one point a student explicitly voiced his dislike of such heavy direction. The director replied that the student was not yet 'ready' to take full charge of his dramatic role - that when 'he had achieved the discipline he would find the freedom'. When I later interviewed this director, he said that he modelled his teaching/director role on the master-apprentice relationship, which is another way of stating one's preference for minimal power sharing.

Directors at the other end of the scale may also come into conflict with their actors; they may devolve so much power to the actors that they feel lost. In one such case I observed, the student covertly challenged the very basis of his working relationship with the director by professing difficulty in learning his lines. His inability was real, but his excuse to the director ('If I could remember what happened in the scene, it would be easier to learn the lines') was a way of communicating his feeling that the director 'didn't know what he was doing', as that student later remarked in an interview. Thus, if the actor feels that the director cannot meet the requirements of a director's role in the production (providing a clear 'line' to follow), the actor's own role performance is impaired. I also found this to be true in the professional productions I observed.

In my discussion of technical training, I spoke of the need to learn the language of the subculture. Problems of language and meaning also arise in rehearsal in a somewhat different form. Here, the difficulty lies not in attaching labels to body movements, but in applying the same meaning to personality adjectives so that the director and actor can agree on characterisation.

For example, in one rehearsal the director described a character to the actor as 'bitchy, but never alienating - and always fascinating'. It must be assumed that these terms have a minimallly shared meaning for the director and actor. Stone writes that:

> According to Mead, meaning is established only when the response elicited by some symbol is the 'same' for the one who produces the symbol as for the one who receives it ... responses are <u>really</u> never the 'same' ... <u>meaning is always variable</u>.

> Meaning, then, is always a variable, ranging between non-sense on the one hand - the total absence of coincident responses - and what might be called boredom on the other - the total coincidence of such responses. Neither of these terminals can be approached very often in the duration of a transaction, for either can mean its end.[14]

One of the differences, then, between directors at the extremes of the power sharing continuum is the degree to which they demand that actors share their meaning of terms such as 'bitchy', 'alienating' or 'fascinating', rather than allowing the rehearsal to continue without correction despite the lack of such agreement. Sometimes the actor and director verbally negotiate the appropriate quality to enact. For example, in discussing her character, an actor remarked, 'I think her attitude is a little derogatory'. The director replied, 'I think it's positively demeaning'. The two agreed. By elaborating on the actor's own interpretation, the director convinced her to adopt the intensity of the quality he wanted and so achieved congruent meaning[15].

The problem of how congruence is identified and how it may be effectively demanded is much greater in drama school than in professional settings; in school, the director and actor may share meaning but the actor may not be able to formulate the response that would indicate such sharedness. Perhaps this is the main difference between drama school and professional productions: in the latter case, if the actor doesn't produce a response which indicates shared meaning, it is interpreted by the director as disagreement; in the former case, a student who wishes to disagree over the interpretation of a role must do so through verbal statements since failure to produce the required response is not always interpreted by the director as intentional. If this is the case, with increasing experience the actor may become able to use the occupational tools of body and voice, even within the dramatic role being played, to communicate to the director an opinion about the way the role should be played.

Obviously, as the students approach the end of their training, they define themselves and are defined by others as being nearer professional than student status. The 2nd termers' grievances, however, can be explained away by their teachers as lack of experience. As one teaching director said:

> The 2nd termers will say, 'I don't know how to say this line' rather than, 'I don't know why I come into this room'. They don't know how to see it yet, the layers underneath. The 2nd termers, as compared with the 5th termers, seem to ask the wrong sorts of questions.

As the students approach the midpoint of their training in the 4th term, their status will necessarily be ambiguous and the lack of legitimation granted their claims to self and role will be more painful. This is precisely the stage when student revolt, upheaval or disillusionment is recognised by students and staff alike. This will be dealt with more fully later.

In discussing the 2nd termers' acting training, I have stressed their relationship to the director. Relationships with co-actors are as, if not more, important but 2nd termers are hardly aware of each other's presence on stage. In one 2nd term production, the director told a student to stay in character when being spoken to as well as when speaking. Here, the student failed to complement the actions of his co-participant as he would in everyday life, for if the interaction were not defined as dramatic, he would at least appear to be listening. Another student had to be reminded that, 'theatre is for communication – don't forget the audience' – and that 'private moments must be made public'. In this case, the student was unaware of the additional requirements which a dramatic framework places on the interaction. The 2nd termers' mistakes,

then, were of opposing kinds; the first failed to act as he would
in real life and must also act in theatre, and the second failed to
add the specific dramatic requirements. It is not simply the case
that novice actors treat theatrical situations naturalistically;
their actions may take place on a third plane which is acceptable
neither in theatre nor in everyday life.

The 2nd termer is equally unfamiliar with theatrical conventions.
For example, in discussing costumes for a 2nd term production, the
director said that since several actors had to double in roles, it
would be better if all wore black leotards and tights. One student
asked, 'What about the people who don't double?', to which the
director replied that either everyone or no one should be in
special costume. Similarly, during a mime and improvisation class,
the students had to be told that a mixture of real and mimed props
would be jarring. And, there are conventional procedures of
rehearsal which they do not yet understand. To request a prompt
from the stage manager, one simply says 'line' as unobtrusively as
possible. In 2nd term rehearsals, such requests and the prompts
themselves were poorly coordinated, causing continual ruptures in
the flow of interaction.

The one role relationship in dramatic settings which actors must
come to terms with in order to succeed with all others (director,
co-actors and audience) is that between self and character. The
trainee actor must learn where identification of self with role is
called for and where separation of self from role is required.
Difficulty in separating self from role was evident in the 2nd
termers' reactions to playing characters which displayed what they
thought were objectionable qualities. One student said he didn't
want to be 'associated' with an arrogant character. Another was
clearly embarrassed by acting as though <u>she</u> was seductive. If the
students identified with their characters correctly, the director
would not have to say, 'Feel shy, don't just indicate shyness'.

Some of the notes (directions) given to 2nd termers by directors
illustrate the contradictory demands of identification and
separation. During one rehearsal, an actor was told to slow down
his delivery of the lines to show that the words were difficult for
the character to say. The actor had to deliver the lines from the
standpoint of his character and put his <u>own</u> reactions aside. In the
same rehearsal the director told this student that, 'You (the
character) must be warm – and you (the actor) <u>are</u> a warm person, I
don't know why it cuts off'. Here, the director wanted the actor's
own quality to inform the character's. Part of the 2nd termer's
problem here is that self-objectification is incomplete. Being
defined and defining oneself as a particular type enables one to
act on the basis of that definition.

Portraying one's character correctly is a matter of achieving the correct balance between self and role, or sustaining concentration. Concentration becomes possible when the self is used so uninhibitedly that one acts in character without subjecting the performance to self-conscious evaluation. When I asked students about the difference between rehearsal and performance acting, 2nd termers mentioned the relative safety or lack of finality in rehearsal compared to performance. Fourth and senior term students, on the other hand, said that, 'in performance, you no longer observe yourself'. Second term students have not reached the stage where their performance proceeds unhindered by self-observation. They are still trying to coordinate the various aspects of their training and have yet to experience the midpoint crisis which makes this possible.

The midpoint crisis

Judging from the students' programme as shown in Table 2.2, the transition from beginning to middle of the course seems fairly smooth and uneventful.

Table 2.2
4th Term Programme

Class	Hours Per Week	
	2nd Term	4th Term
Dance	-	1
Make-Up	-	1
Microphone Techniques	-	1
Mime	2*	-
Movement	7	7
Rehearsal	10	13.5
Singing	2	-
Speech	2	2
Stage Fights	1	2
Text	2*	-
Tumbling	-	1*
Voice	2	1* + 1
Voice and Movement	2	-

* = for less than full
10 weeks of term

Although several new technical classes are introduced in the 4th term - make-up, microphone techniques, and tumbling (fighting without swords or daggers) - the number of hours per week spent in class is not markedly different (about 26+ hours per week in the 2nd term compared to about 28.5+ hours per week in the 4th term) and the number of classes remains the same (nine in each term). Nevertheless, both students and teachers feel that there is 'so much work to do' in the 4th term. As a speech teacher explained:

In the 4th term, they don't really have time to concentrate on everything they'd like to, it's just one mad rush. And I think they sometimes get the feeling that they ought to have got somewhere by then and it results in the feeling of, 'I'm never going to get it completely right'. There is sometimes a slump. They all go through some torment at some time.

Another teacher's remarks indicate that the midpoint crisis, as I will call it, does not always occur precisely at the midpoint of the 4th term:

It's a well-known phenomenon, 3rd term blues; we try to get them round it, try and let them know it's likely to happen.

In their study of student nurses, Oleson and Whittaker discuss these depressions which were not only present in the nurses' training programme they studied, but which seemed to be 'also common to other institutions of professional learning' [16]. They state that:

Some hospital schools talk about 'the intermediate slump' as if it were part of the curriculum. Other schools talk about the 'senior slump'. Such institutionalized labelling provides a swift and ready-made diagnosis for a variety of observable ills and discontents. As such, it functions for both faculty and students and places within the range of acceptable normality what would otherwise give cause for more concern.[17]

But what causes this 'mad rush' and consequent 'slump' in the Drama School? I doubt that it is the increase in the number of evening rehearsals which are left to the discretion of the director and so do not appear in the official schedule. Nor do I think that a speech test in the 4th term could trigger a crisis. What is distinctive about the midpoint of the training programme is the unspoken debate between teachers and students over the right to define the relationship between self, body, personal worth and acting. I will set out below the argument implicit in the various statements made by students and teachers. Because the teachers are more inclined to articulate the process whereby 4th termers feel that their identities are jeopardised, I will use the teachers' assumptions to delineate the argument.

The students' first response in creating a character is to put their own habitual posture, gestures and vocalisations into it. But the actor's own nonverbal characteristics must not intrude upon or contradict the character's. It is easier to create the physical character by starting from a 'neutral body state' than it is to shift directly from one's own body use to that of an imaginary other. In order to 'communicate the right thing at the right time', in the words of one voice teacher, the actor must be aware and flexible; and:

> to find flexibility, you've first got to find neutrality - a benevolent neutrality - where the full personality is there, but, if you like, at rest, ready to work in any direction.

Although the desired change is characterised as a 'benevolent neutrality', the same teacher conceded that, 'the nature of the change that one is going to ask students to undertake is a radical change in the way they use their bodies'.

So, neutrality enables the person to take on the variety of bodily and vocal qualities that diverse characterisation necessitates. But what does neutrality mean, and how does one achieve it? In order to attain a neutral body state, one must be able to use the body as it was naturally meant to be used. Yet, what the teachers define as unnatural use of the body is not altogether clear from their statements. At times they seem to refer to signals which are inappropriately linked to the verbal elements of the communication - a contradiction of one channel by the other, or an idiosyncratic combination of the two. That is, the 'character' one normally conveys, one's non-neutral self, consists of various habitual uses of the body which communicate certain information precisely because of their unnaturalness. At other times, the teachers seem to imply that those uses put strain on other parts of the body. For example, a voice teacher demonstrated the way that a person might 'direct the windstream up his nose' which 'the body was not built to do'. Presumably, it is possible from the study of the body to determine which actions cause strain and are therefore unnatural. The School's physiotherapists and voice teachers certainly felt that the way that some students used their bodies in everyday life was inappropriate, wrong or unnatural.

In order to achieve a state of neutral and/or natural body use, students must accept that the way they habitually use their bodies is wrong (i.e., they have 'bad habits') and that this will hinder their acting. The first few terms of technical training 'acquaint' the students with their bodies, as they learn to objectify them. Towards the midpoint of the students' training, the teachers try to make them redefine this now familiar body use as unnatural and worthy of change. One voice teacher, speaking of the students' reaction, said:

To them, it's wrong, it can't be truthful. How can one express one's basic truth in something which is alien? That's the basic problem.

Or, in the words of a 2nd termer:

At the beginning, I was very confused; they were saying, 'do this' and I didn't know why. I mean, what's the matter with my own breathing?

A senior student, remembering her early training, said:

Whenever they told me that anything was wrong, I didn't want to hear about it - I thought, 'But that's me!'

From the student's perspective, the teacher's insistence that bad (body use) habits be changed is tantamount to devaluation of the real self that that body belongs to. Although, strictly speaking, the neutral body is situated in theatrical contexts [18], students do lose some of the physical characteristics which make them 'who they are' in everyday life. As one of the physiotherapists said:

When I first came, I used to measure them, and the differences are quite measurable. Measurements changed, the angle of the chin, measurements across the back; leg shape changes, buttock shape changes; sometimes they come in with flat feet and go out with slightly less flat feet.

Throughout this debate, the teachers dismiss the notion that their demands imply a denigration of the self. They concede that this notion is commonplace, but mistaken:

Most people interfere terribly with their voices and so you've got to find a way of liberating them from their interference. This means they're going to change the way they use themselves. Their whole mode of sensory appreciation is perverted, their instincts are wrong. Well, you start saying to someone, your instincts are wrong, and you're then into a very tricky area, because what you're really saying is - it seems to them - is that their personality isn't good enough. (emphasis added)

So many people will say to me at a party, 'Oh, do tell me what's wrong with my speech'. And if I did, they would really feel that I was mangling their personality ... We suddenly feel that we're under a microscope and we feel very inept. (emphasis added)

The teachers do not feel that they demand annihilation of the self - the self is in a neutral state, but it is there. It is not supposed to be conspicuously or obtrusively there. Furthermore, the neutrality which is worked for is a personally tailored one, as one voice teacher explained:

> We've got to get our terms of reference right: in the light of your body or your speech, or your voice - ultimately finding a neutral level, a neutral ground, where we can both work happily and not literally find ourselves with hangups. We like the students to go into a neutral vocalisation so that they're malleable after that.

The teachers seem to be saying that despite their attempts to neutralise the students' body use, their respect for the students as individuals must be taken on trust. The self is continually denied in practice while simultaneously taken as the starting point for change.

For the student, such change puts at risk the previously valued self. A conflict arises over whether to stay as one is or give in to the teachers' demands. The teachers have defined this change as necessary for effective acting and at this stage of the student's career, there is neither a public nor a circle of critics to contradict them. Moreover, one's immediate aim is to be a successful drama student, not actor; therefore these assessments are crucial.

The teacher cannot change the students against their will. For example, teaching Standard English to students with regional accents is impossible without their cooperation, as a speech teacher explained:

> They get into a quandary because they have to come to classes - There isn't usually a personal dislike, and they can see other people around them trying to do something, so they usually try in spite of themselves. But because they're resisting, they can't open up, and till they can, you're not really satisfied with what they're doing. Because you must start off with an open jaw, with an open sound - I tell them, 'If you hold back, you won't attain anything at all'.

If the resistance continues, the overriding aim which teacher and student share - that of producing a professional actor - can be used as a persuasive weapon:

> One doesn't resent resistance at first, unless it goes on and on - and so you say, 'Well, there are other people who may go for the job that you're after and they'll be asked to do this and they'll be able to do it and that's all there is to it - you've got to be practical'.

Resistance is finally overcome and the student gradually moves towards acceptance of the official perspective on self and acting. This is evident in the remarks of students at various points in their school career:

You forget all your bad habits ... drama school helps you to forget about them and teaches you the right ones - hopefully you become a better actor because you've forgotten your bad habits. At the end of the 2nd term, I sussed out what the whole thing was about, what they were trying to do with me, with my body, with my voice, whereas at the beginning, I didn't know why. (student just completing 2nd term)

When I came to drama school I needed to get rid of bad habits in my body. (4th termer)

I'd been warned by friends that ... they churn people out like sausages, and I think I was very frightened of losing my own identity there, so I went in with the attitude of not letting them succeed in changing me, which was totally wrong. Somewhere along the line I realised that they weren't trying to change me, they were only trying to help me, sift out the worst aspects of you and keep all the good aspects. They were trying to enrich your talent, not take it away. (senior student)

What factors are responsible for this change to the official perspective?

First, as I described earlier, the body is altered by exercise and physiotherapy. Similarly, continuous use of different accents gradually weakens one's original accent. The student is not, in these respects, the person he or she was.

Secondly, the student's very placement in the course means that one is supposed to be 'halfway there'. This supposed progress is signified and symbolised by a public performance at the end of term, included in the otherwise senior-dominated repertory season. The prospect of public display can increase fear and stress and thereby weaken resistance to change, as a teaching director described:

If you lose your acting ability because teachers criticise [the way you use your body], that doesn't mean you lose a skill, it means you lose faith in yourself, because acting is working with what you've got in you, your instrument. And if you're not trusting that, you can't act - you can't get up and be public if you're frightened or insecure about your own instrument. So until they're at one with themselves, they're frightened to get up there. And I'm saying never mind if there's still something wrong, you've got to go on and be public at the end of this term.

Thirdly, the weekly tutorial between student and teacher which continues until the 5th term weakens resistance to change by counteracting the feeling of personal disintegration. It could well be seen as an institutionalised antidote to other institutionally induced pressures. A teaching director explained its purpose:

> Tutorials are not necessarily designed for working on scenes; they can come and talk about personal problems if they want to, or not getting on with the part they're working on. Or, if they can't think of anything to do, you can often work on a part that's absolutely right for them, so they can come and have a little success!

The teacher can convey concern for the student in situations other than formal tutorials. This can alleviate fears of identity loss which may arise quite early in the course. When I asked a 4th termer if there had been any incident at the School which struck her as unusual, she said:

> One minute incident in the 1st term, in fencing class. My voice teacher walked in, didn't say a word, walked over to the cupboard, took out a sword, walked over to me, and we did some fencing together. He looked as if something really meaningful had passed between us, and put the sword back and left. We'd had a voice class the day before that had been sort of heavy ... He was saying, 'I care about you as a student, I'm on your side, I'm an individual, you're an individual' - the whole thing was so symbolic to me.

Finally, the increasing ability to act also contributes to change. The tasks of the previous terms, such as the teacher's acquaintance with 'Joe Bloggs as an individual', the students' ability to objectify their bodies and learn technical and acting skills, all proceed in a piecemeal fashion, and with good reason. Until awareness of self and technical ability have reached a moderately high level, they are of little use to the creation of dramatic characters. Until such time, the technical skills are only an adjunct to attempts at dramatic role playing. As a speech teacher said, the 3rd term consists in finding 'individual quality expressed in the voice', whereas the 4th term marks the stage when students concentrate on 'applying this individual quality to different characterisations'. The same process occurs in productions. As students are made aware of the body and learn to objectify it, they become more able to draw upon the resources of self in characterisation. At the same time, the created character can be distinguished from the self to make the rewards of training evident. In other words, the unspoken debate which emerges from technical training is affected by advances in acting ability; these advances reinforce the pressures towards neutralisation.

As the student becomes more skilled at acting, the general criticism given by directors in earlier terms ('Don't forget the audience') is replaced by more specific instructions. Once the ground rules are laid, the director can concentrate on polishing the performances. But the earlier form of criticism may be so basic that it appears less like criticism than the later specifics. Fourth termers continually mentioned their dislike of criticism and one described how the casting policy (as she perceived it) facilitated a negative rather than positive appraisal of the student's work:

> Someone comes along and says, 'Well, we know you can do that so we don't want you to do it' - And yet the girl playing it might make a balls of it and could never do it. I don't see the point of saying, 'That's to show you what you can't do or what you have to work on'.

A teaching director confirmed this emphasis on negative criticism:

> They audition and we say 'yes'; so they think, 'Christ, I've got something, there's some magic in me'. Then you get in here and they're not saying you're magic, they're saying, 'That's wrong, that's wrong, that's wrong'.

There is a reason for this negative approach. The dramatic character can be interpreted in a variety of ways, but the actor will 'contaminate' the characterisation with the intrusive elements of the self far more systematically. The very flexibility which is needed for dramatic role playing can only be achieved by continually excising the self from performance. Positive aspects of one's performance are the residue which continued negative criticism will leave exposed.

Whenever the self is excised, the student feels that it is being devalued. The reasons students give for wanting to become actors are, 'I think I have talent' or 'I think I have something to offer'. No one would dream of saying, 'I think I can un-be easily' or, I think I have something to detract - yet this is what they are asked to do. The student offers the photograph while the teacher demands the negative.

In order to act, the student must learn to separate from the character without suffering a loss of dignity. The objectification and neutralisation of the self make this possible, and the thrill of masterful performance is its own reward. The subjective changes

- 49 -

in personal identity and objective advances in acting ability reinforce each other. Together they propel the student towards the identity of the professional actor.

The process of change is facilitated by the symbolic rewards offered at each stage of the training programme in return for compliance with the teachers' requests. The entire programme is geared towards repertory-style performance in the last two (senior) terms, and as these are the only performances given before a paying audience (with the exception of two 4th term productions), they denote a quasi-professional status.

In the 1st term, students may serve as ushers on performance nights. Here, they are inside the theatre though not onstage. It is important to note that their involvement in the production does not consist of backstage work; a strict separation of stage management and acting roles is maintained throughout the training, thus reinforcing the notion of the special talent and status of even the novice. The ushering role provides the 1st termer with visibility ; although the strategy of attracting the notice of casting agents in places like Schwab's Drugstore may be a thing of the past, agents do attend senior productions (most probably to survey performances rather than ushers' appearances) and as such the ushering role is at least of symbolic significance.

Some 1st and 2nd termers are used as walk-ons in senior productions (this means that they have a role in the play as a physically present body but not a fully fledged character). It can only be assumed that such opportunities are awarded to those students who have established themselves as trustworthy in the teachers' eyes. As the students progress from 3rd to 5th term, they may be given actual dramatic roles in senior productions if there are insufficient numbers of seniors to play the parts in any one production.

Thus, certain incentives are given to students who adapt to the demands of the socialisation process, demands consisting of a reformulation of attitudes towards the self as well as the acquisition of objective technical skills. Although it can be assumed that students want the practical experience of performing in a quasi-professional capacity as early as possible, these pre-senior performance opportunities, especially in the absence of grades, are sought for other reasons - the same reasons which Roth observed in the case of hospital patients:

> How soon after admission (or after surgery or after some other reference point) is the patient allowed to go to the bathroom, to the day room to see movies ... When is he allowed to go out for walks? When can he get a pass every month? These

privileges are desired not only in themselves,   but for their symbolic value .[19]

Not least of all, senior productions have symbolic value for the seniors. Beyond the experience of putting on a play, and apart from signifying that they are nearing the end of their course, senior productions enable the students to see themselves performing in essentially the same roles as professional actors, contributing, through their work, to the financial stability of the theatre and performing under conditions of professionalism (in both the sense of company discipline and artistic standards) perhaps greater than that which will be required of them in the professional world. The last two terms lack the real-life problems of auditioning for parts and finding new ones when a production finishes, and this contributes to the students' feelings of confidence and competence in much the same way that Fox has documented in the case of the student doctor:

> the growing assurance of a third-year student does not result only from his greater knowledge and his conviction that what he is doing is important. It results also from the fact that in the third year he is relatively insulated from some of the diagnostic and therapeutic uncertainties he will encounter later.[20]

Thus, as advanced students rehearse their dramatic roles, they simultaneously rehearse their occupational role; as their dramatic characterisations become increasingly convincing to themselves and to others, their self definition as professional actors is similarly strengthened.

Towards a professional identity

The self-objectification process which I previously discussed benefits the rehearsal interaction which comprises more and more of the students' schedule as they progress through the course. Self-objectification permits the director to criticise the actor's characterisation without the actor interpreting this as personal criticism. The following extract from an interview with a senior student illustrates this:

Interviewer: Do you ever have trouble   understanding a
               director's directions?

Student: Sometimes.

Interviewer: Can you give me an example?

Student:	Sometimes they inhibit me by what they say - I take it personally. I remember once, a director telling me I was frozen inside - which of course made me freeze! I think he wanted me to find what was frozen inside and make me release it. But at the time I was very paranoid and it made me freeze.
Interviewer:	When did that happen?
Student:	In the 5th term.
Interviewer:	Do you think that kind of thing would happen now?
Student:	Now, I wouldn't - yes, I would take it personally, but I would know what to do about it. I would go off and say, 'What do you mean?'

Criticism which the initiate would interpret as a denigration of personal identity is defused by the advanced student who has learned the appropriate relationship of self to dramatic role. By achieving this balance, the student gains the confidence which is the hallmark of this stage of training. Self-objectification enables the students to evaluate their own performances as only the teachers could before. As two 4th termers said:

You see what people see - that's the consciousness I've acquired since I've been at [the School].

You become able to argue back whereas at first I thought they were in a position to tell me.

Capable of self-evaluation, the student becomes aware of wider areas of strength and weakness:

I feel much more settled now. I feel I know what I want out of [the training] and I'm getting what I want.

When I first came, it was entertaining rather than serious acting; but I now know what I like to see as regards serious acting, and I can accept myself doing that, and I know what kinds of theatre I like.

I'm more realistic now; you work out what your aims are and stick by them.

It's a bloody good training. They give you confidence. (What do you think it is that gives you confidence?) I don't know, just

by doing.   People will criticise you, but you're never ground
into the dust. I think they bring out your potential and that
helps you to   feel confidence. They make you   realise what you
can do.

The awareness of capabilities brings with it a degree of relativism
regarding those capabilities:

> (Has your view of yourself changed since you've come to drama
> school?) Yes, I think it's not as easy as I thought it would be
> to undo that spring which lets every performance unlock; but I
> think I'm much more self-contained and stronger than I thought
> as well. That's a negative and a positive.

> (What do you think is the difference between a 2nd,   4th and
> senior term student?) You get more confidence - just as long as
> that confidence doesn't make you forget that you're still a
> beginner.

When the student no longer sees the teacher as the sole source of
evaluation, the teacher is demystified. One 4th term student, for
example, noted that when she began her training, the teachers were
'gods' but then   'they're human beings and that's one thing you're
going to get round to learning'.   Whereas once the teachers had
seemed to be 'superhuman beings', one student said he then
discovered that   'it is only people who are trying to teach you'.
Both the teacher and the occupation are demystified. By learning to
evaluate their own work,   students achieve a firm grasp of the
occupational world which was once alien and exotic.

The increase in self-control manifests itself on the   level of
everyday interaction. As a voice teacher said:

> If a student actor, having left school, does nothing in his
> lifetime, going back to secretarial work or whatever, he is
> never going to be the same person. They have learned something
> which has given them a certain physical and vocal poise -
> authority - which will count in life.

Many of the students spoke of the need to 'get on' with their
co-workers in productions.   They cited this as the most essential
ingredient for success, saying little or nothing about the need for
shared interpretations of the text or other drama related concerns.
Only one of the students who emphasised this need for smooth social
relationships connected it directly with the business of acting
(saying that it wasn't possible to act with people one didn't like
or get on with). Other students mentioned the need for directors to
appear to have confidence in their actors whether or not they
actually did.   In these various ways,   the students indicated the

priority of correct staging of social performance over communication of genuine feelings.

It was clear from the interviews that students perceive only a fine line between consciously staging one's social performance and actually altering one's private feelings[21]. For example, one student remarked that there wasn't any one teacher whom he 'particularly loathed' and then said, 'I don't think you should let that happen'. Other students made similar comments about controlling their actual feelings towards fellow students. It may be that the practice of dramatic acting (the portrayal of diverse feelings by trade) makes possible the manipulation of actual feelings (or belief that one can do this). Directors, for example, often tell actors that while they may know what will happen to their characters by the end of the play, they must not prematurely reveal this knowledge to the audience through their performance. By holding the actor to the character's awareness at the present moment despite the actor's awareness of the future development of the plot, actual feelings may themselves become more manipulable [22].

Dramatic role-taking may increase the actor's role-taking accuracy in everyday life. The ability to base one's actions on an accurate appraisal of others' intentions, may lay one open to the charge of manipulation - of one's own and other's reactions. Taken one step further, it becomes clear that the actor not only possesses these abilities, but is also aware of possessing them. The following excerpt from an interview with a professional actor exemplifies this consciousness of empathic ability:

> The relationship of actors to actors that they like is a very different relationship than mates that go out drinking - because the actor actually understands the other actor's problem ... The friendship is always instant and generous - so I think there is a generosity there, a lot of the time very false. But there's the appearance of it, and that's acceptable to you, you like it - It lulls you and tranquilises you.

Similarly, another professional actor, when asked whether he thought that the experience of acting influenced his dealings with people in everyday life, replied:

> Yes. You become more adroit socially. Although you may be a shy person, you'll have acquired the technique to hide that shyness.

Both the skills and the awareness of them can be observed in incipient form in the actions and reflections of advanced drama students. The forced friendliness which they perceive as necessary for a successful production extends to the relationships they form with each other outside of rehearsal and performance. Although they frequently made statements like, 'I can't find anything in common with 90% of them', they equally felt that there was an artificial atmosphere of sociability. As one student said, 'Even if they're people you really don't know very well, you still have to pretend to have those kinds of relationships with them because you see them all the time'.

Since the students are together for as much as twelve hours per day, five days a week (or more), and because they perceive the need to remain amicable onstage and off, the pressures of constant dissimulation can mount up. The release of this pressure may find its outlet in dramatic form, as the following 4th termer's account illustrates:

When we were rehearsing Oedipus in the 3rd term, the director was a really heavy schoolmaster dictator - we'd walk into rehearsals scared. He passed around this mask, and we were supposed to feel the horror and make some sound. The mask came to me and I just started to get everything off my chest because I was so upset by this. And I just gave a huge sort of yell, agonised, which is what I wanted to do anyway, it was a good excuse. I put everything I'd got into this - and after that, when I'd done it, I suddenly burst into tears. It was very weird; I just wanted to scream to get rid of the tension, but I was a bit depressed at the time, so it all sort of came out, it was like releasing a bottle stopper. It's bad to keep things bottled up.

There is no simple formula which can tell a student when to display 'genuine' feelings, when to consciously stage an everyday performance, or when overacting or fooling around is permissible. A senior student remarked that 'theatrical types' amongst any group of new students are soon set straight; such blatant overacting is unacceptable. A 4th termer explained why:

They're never going to let you get up in the Common Room and make an exhibition of yourself; they're never going to be too much of an audience. They won't pander ... to you that much because each one in the room is also very ambitious, so there's the thing of watching what a guy's doing as well as enjoying it. Whereas at college, before, you could show off and be silly and they used to love it.

Thus, for the drama student, the delicate balance between being and acting is a crucial dimension of 'learning the ropes'[23] of the acting business.

Since the Drama School students were in the 2nd, 4th and 6th terms during the term in which I did my field work, and since the 6th termers' schedule consists almost wholly of rehearsal and performance, the career of the 'pure student' comes to a close with the account given here. My discussion of the growth of an occupational identity, however, can be said to trace the student's experience through to graduation, since it describes a process which only gradually develops. A lengthy excerpt from an interview with a senior student provides a comprehensive overview of the socialisation process I have described, illuminating the contrast between the younger student's expectations and the senior student's actual experience:

Interviewer: What about your first reactions to the training?

Student: It's a great novelty to begin with, but after a few weeks it began to wear off drastically - I became very skeptical and disillusioned by all the teachers that were setting themselves up to give judgements on people.

Interviewer: Was that in the 1st term?

Student: Yes, it got slowly worse.

Interviewer: What happened to that disillusionment, did it change?

Student: I think it was just a gradual process, and I think it had to do with me rather than [the School]. It's very difficult to know; I know a lot of people were very happy with the course. I just didn't believe some of the things I heard or saw.

Interviewer: Like what?

Student: I just began to feel that the teachers weren't working in your best interest - and I began to feel they weren't taking you for what you could do. They wanted you to be what they wanted you to be, not what you could be. And unless you kept your own belief going in yourself, didn't let yourself be ... I just found them all on big ego trips, like infallible beings. Since then, outside directors have been useful. It was like listening to someone, at times telling you universal things about acting rather than ...

Interviewer: Does that change as you progress?

Student: Well, they ignore you when you get to [senior term]! You become more discerning, more able to listen to what they say but have much more judgement. They can destroy you, they really do destroy you there - they do all they can - I don't think it's conscious, I kept on thinking it was, but I don't even know now - you have to keep in touch with your emotions, that's all.

Interviewer: So you don't know whether it's intentional, almost as a teaching device?

Student: To break down? Oh, yes, I think so - they have this shock treatment, when people say, 'You don't think people are going to come and see you with a speech pattern like that!' It may sound stupid, and you can laugh at it now, but I didn't at the time, I do now, because they did come, and they did listen to me.

Interviewer: Do you know of people who never recovered from the breaking down process or does it -

Student: I don't think they break everyone down because - no, most people do recover when they start acting again, although they lose something. Maybe you have to lose something to gain something ...

The occupational identity developed in drama school will, in the following case studies, be shown to be modified by professional experience. Participation in dramatic productions in itself alters personal and occupational identity as well as providing the actor with material with which to evaluate his or her career. In Mead's terms, the dual aspects of self - the acting 'I' and the reflecting 'me' - are mutually involved in the individual's activity and consciousness.

B. STAGING A PLAY

Introduction

From an examination of the ways in which the trainee becomes an
actor, we now turn to the work of the professional actor. The
following case study focuses on the actor in rehearsal rather than
in performance for, as we shall see, it is during the rehearsal
stage that actors develop their characters and create the reality
they will portray in performance.

As recently as last century, rehearsal lacked the importance it
generally has today; ensemble acting had yet to come of age and a
single dress rehearsal might be deemed sufficient to coordinate the
supporting roles with the lead's presentation. Today, however,
belief in the necessity of rehearsal is clear:

> the work done in rehearsal ... goes in a thousand different
> directions, [and] is always aimed at a definition, but if the
> definition could be formulated in advance, the work wouldn't be
> worth attempting.[24]

Of course, as I mentioned in the previous case study, the
definition of the production is sometimes formulated in advance by
the director who makes most of the artistic decisions for the cast.
The value of the present case study of a group I will call the
Theatre Company lies in its attention to a production in which
interpretive decisions were conceived by the director as a
collective effort.

The Theatre Company was formed to produce a new play (and, it was
hoped, others in future) by its producer/director whose full-time
job was that of floor manager for television drama productions.
Several other people provided financial backing for the production
and contributed their administrative, legal and designing skills.
Having formed the production company, they advertised for new
scripts and selected one which was a surrealistic musical about
life in a mental hospital. They hired a room above a centrally
located pub for rehearsals and a suburban theatre for the
performance week. The remainder of the production consisted of two
audition dates, two weeks of part rehearsal on various scenes, one
week of full rehearsal with the entire cast and one week of
performances.

The Theatre Company was one of many fringe companies, as distinct
from amateur, professional West End theatre, or regional repertory.
These are ongoing companies or one-shot productions which employ
professional (Equity Union) actors and sometimes non-union actors

as well, but which do not work on the basis of Equity contracts. Union contracts stipulate pay and working conditions, while the essence of fringe theatre is low budget production. The Theatre Company paid its actors expenses (less than 1/3 the Actor's Equity Union minimum) rather than a wage, which enabled the actors to claim unemployment benefits while at work on the Theatre Company production.

According to the 1975 Gulbenkian Foundation's report on drama training:

> Perhaps the most significant change of all has been the development during the last five or ten years of fringe theatre. Approximately 25% of working actors are now engaged in this area, operating largely outside the conventional framework of theatre buildings and taking their work directly to people who have previously had little interest in the established theatre.[25]

What attraction might fringe theatre hold for the professional actor? The most important reason for participating in a low budget production is that it enables actors to practice their craft when better paid employment is unavailable; with unemployment endemic to the profession [26], actors might not work for long periods if only well-paid jobs were accepted. As one of the older Theatre Company actors remarked:

> I used to want to be a star, but now I'd rather be an actor who's working and playing medium parts fairly solidly throughout the year.

Apart from the advantage of acting, fringe theatre enables actors to be seen by casting directors, thereby increasing their chances of being offered more lucrative and prestigious work. Apart from actually keeping actors from getting stale, the work can keep them from appearing to have gone stale by providing a recent job to list on the resume for the next audition. Finally, acting, for however meagre a wage, provides the necessary affirmation of an occupational identity which is not easily sustained in private.

As Goffman has noted:

> No doubt there are few positions in life that do not throw together some persons who are there by virtue of failure and other persons who are there by virtue of success[27]

in relation to their abilities, training and previous career histories. Fringe theatre is just such a setting. Actors on their way up can find themselves working with those whose previously successful careers have now waned, or those whose careers never quite got off the ground. For actors who are not ideologically committed to fringe theatre as an alternative to established theatre[28] (almost certainly the majority), fringe does represent this limbo between the definite statuses of unemployment and mainstream work.

The actors chosen for the Theatre Company's six central roles were in their late twenties to early thirties, with four to six years of professional experience since completing their training. Four of them had attended drama schools which are members of the Conference of Drama Schools (CDS) whose:

> importance lies in the fact that it represents the nucleus of established and reputable full-time vocational drama schools in this country.[29]

Membership in CDS is based on a government inspection of the school and evaluation of its size, equipment, syllabus and artistic standards. One of the other leading actors had trained in a part-time drama school in a Commonwealth country and the other had no formal training. Of the three out of four actors with minor roles whom I interviewed, two trained at CDS schools and one had had private training.

The employment record of the Company's lead actors varied from one who had worked nine or ten months of each of the six years since completing his training, to the one quoted below who had had long periods of unemployment:

Interviewer: In what terms do you view the development of your career?

Actor: Are you talking about the future, now, what I'm after? At the moment, it's moving sideways.

Interviewer: What is it that makes you say it's moving sideways? What would make it move up and down?

Actor: Well, I suppose it's moving down since I haven't got a job. To move up, it would mean getting decent jobs, decent money, a bit of television, just better than - Yeah, more money. I don't want to live on the breadline.

Such biographical data gives us clues to the actors' expectations of the Theatre Company production. Although most have trained in accredited academies and have had substantial professional experience, their employment records, as one would expect in this occupation, are variable. The 'staying power' of the professional actor has been found to be 'most severely tested' during the period of five to seven years after the completion of training[30] and since the Theatre Company actors fall within or near this range, they most probably hope that fringe work will provide the justification to persevere. The fringe setting also influences the actors' expectations of the script, for it is here that new plays are tested for dramatic viability. The actors will surely be optimistic about the production, but given the potential script problems, they cannot know whether their efforts will be worthwhile. Semi-professional theatre also influences the mutual expectations of director and cast; each may be loath to expect too much from the other. As the director said:

> Because they weren't being paid Equity rates, there was a degree of laxness and I found it difficult - I didn't scream at people who were late, partly because I didn't think I could.

The actors' expectations and ultimate assessments of the Theatre Company production were most clearly articulated in the interviews I conducted. The nature of rehearsal precludes, for the most part, discussion of these matters in the presence of co-workers. Therefore, my account of the Theatre Company's production will consist first of a summary of the rehearsal work taken from my observation notes. Secondly, I will develop a conceptual framework for the understanding of the interpretive work of rehearsal, drawing both on my observational and interview data. Finally, I will discuss the participants' assessments of their experience in the Theatre Company, relying heavily on their comments made in interview.

Diary of a production: three weeks of seventeen rehearsals

The director began the first rehearsal with a read-through of the play. He explained to the cast how the set, lighting and music within the play would carry through and reinforce the play's theme. He did not, however, provide the cast with an encapsulated statement of this theme for, as he told them, he hoped that the nuances of meaning in the play would be decided by the cast in the course of rehearsal and discussion. Some of the discussion following the read-through of the play concerned the experiences of the characters before they entered the mental hospital - i.e., prior to the action of the play itself.

The second and third rehearsals continued to consist of detailed discussion of the script and characters; it was not until the fourth rehearsal that the director and cast started to block the play on the floor of the rehearsal room. During this fourth rehearsal, one of the leading actors in the production who had been unable to attend rehearsals because of commitment to another, overlapping production, attended the Theatre Company's rehearsals for the first time. He challenged the conception of life in a mental hospital which the group had developed thus far, offering his own experience as an ex-mental patient as evidence. Some members of the cast countered his criticism with discussion of the theatrical requirements which they felt necessarily led the script and its production away from absolutely accurate depiction. The actors asked the director to explain several esoteric literary allusions in the script and questioned the prospective audience's understanding of these lines.

At the fifth meeting, the actors still rehearsed with scripts in hand; the director said he hoped they would soon know their lines well enough to work without them. The cast began to establish what they believed were appropriate characterisations of the mentally ill; they tried to create incongruities between voice, speech and movement in their characters. The director and actors alternated the rehearsal of scenes with discussion of new developments in their understanding of the play.

During the sixth rehearsal, the actors who were not directly involved in the particular scene being rehearsed began to act as an audience for the performers - listening attentively, laughing at jokes in the script. The performing actors started to improvise their own moves in relation to the scripted lines, and when this seemed to clarify or enrich the meaning of the play - or provoke a favourable response from the audience of actors - the director would tell the performers to 'keep that in'. Throughout the day, other members of the cast arrived to work on scheduled scene rehearsals. They were briefed on the changes which had occurred in the course of work earlier in the day.

The actors were still holding scripts at the seventh rehearsal and the director asked again that they learn their lines soon. Some of the improvised sequences which had been developed the day before failed to elicit the intense audience reaction. Discussion during this rehearsal once again focused on the relationship between a real-life mental hospital and their theatrical version of one.

By the ninth rehearsal, both problems in the script and potential problems in the staging of the production had emerged. After examining the progression of different characters' lines in great detail, the group decided that line cuts and scene changes might be required. The show's financial backers who attended this rehearsal told me that these newly acknowledged problems would be adequately handled by the actors 'because they're professionals'.

Although most of the actors were no longer holding scripts by the eleventh rehearsal, many had not yet learned their lines perfectly. Lines were still being cut or rewritten by the playwright who attended rehearsals from time to time; the basic meaning of lines was still being queried; and fundamental interpretations of scenes were still open to revision by the director and cast. Rehearsals still consisted of partial gatherings of some members of the cast for work on particular scenes, and several actors were still leaving rehearsals in order to fulfill their obligations to other productions. For the first time, the actors were given the actual props to rehearse with, including, for example, a hospital trolley which was borrowed from a nearby hospital. The group engaged in further discussion of the physical constraints of the actual theatre they would be performing in. They also talked about the ways in which the details of characterisation and performance which they had collectively decided on would influence the audience's understanding of the play.

Discussion at the twelfth rehearsal focused on the usual subject of problems of actual performance as well as, for the first time, the ultimate success of the production and the possibility of its transfer to a fully professional West End theatre. This coincided with the first full run-through of the play - from first scene to last - since the start of rehearsals.

In addition to the usual participants, the thirteenth rehearsal was attended by one of the theatre's lighting technicians, a reporter from a local radio station who had been called in for publicity, and the playwright. The actors continued to question the lines and, at times, the very structure of the play. One actor said he thought that the play might seem different at each performance because of the continual reinterpretation that the cast had, and still was, engaged in. The director told the actors not to worry about this. Further changes were made during this rehearsal in light of the director's realisation of the theatre's requirements.

The fourteenth rehearsal was devoted to refining the details of individual performances rather than to major changes in script interpretation or production decisions.

The fifteenth rehearsal took place on the day before opening night and was the last rehearsal to be held outside the actual theatre (i.e., in the room above the pub). The director explained that they would continue to rehearse the play in sections since the actual scene changes could not be adequately rehearsed without the real stage. The director was far more critical of the actors' performances than he had previously been.

The sixteenth rehearsal occurred on the morning of opening night. The cast discovered that the set was still being built and that they would have to rehearse around the builders. The producers again made comments about the 'professionalism' of the actors seeing them through these difficult conditions.

The final rehearsal was a dress rehearsal held several hours before the first performance. There were six performances in the course of a week, and a cast party following the final performance.

Rehearsals: defining the dramatic situation

As we saw in the case of the drama students, it is only by correctly assessing the kind of role assumed by the director that the actors can know whether their role will be largely that of faithful reproduction or creative interpretation. The director of the Theatre Company described the role he adopted:

> My opinion about a director's role is that he should encourage people to find their own meaning for the part rather than a more dictatorial approach. Therefore, any decisions which are made should come out of an actor responding to the character, within the framework of the play, and the encouragement is for him to do that in a logical, consistent way, a meaningful way ... If he goes completely astray, then you have to step in and say, 'Well, that's all very well, but don't you think you should consider this ...?'

A member of the cast described the Company's director in the following way:

> Mainly he was an orchestrator rather than a director. He modified things, rather than demand that they be done a certain way. You get all levels, from the tyrant who dictates every move to the guy who sits back and enjoys it, all of whom are valid in their own way.

Because of the stance taken by the Company's director, rehearsals consisted of interpretive discussion and the enactment of scenes. Once the actors realised that discussion was to play an important role (as early as the first rehearsal) norms arose governing the correct balance between discussion and rehearsal - although these norms were continually renegotiated. Discussion provided the actors with a medium other than dramatic performance for work satisfaction, status rewards and the expression of sentiments about the play and the cast. More will be said of this later.

The creation of a convincing character and the creation of a convincing dramatic reality are two sides of the same coin, for it is only through the words and actions of the characters that a dramatic reality can be said to exist (in much the same way that in everyday life the enactment of a social role implies the situation that gives rise to it)[31]. On the level of dramatic reality, this relationship between character and play is described by Tyrone Guthrie:

> A plausible performance is created by studying the role based on the factual evidence of the text - what the character reveals about himself, what others in the play reveal about him and by drawing deductions from actions of the character - by imagining situations deducible from the text.

> According to these prescriptions, a plausible performance cannot be created if the play itself lacks character development or exhibits logical inconsistencies which disallow the possibility of deducible situations.[32]

The participants in a production can thus be said to engage in theorising and hypothesis testing. The theories they construct are the general notions of what the play is about. On the basis of these theories about the play, they deduce hypotheses about the reasons for, or motives behind, the discrete units of behaviour in the play which are indicated by the scripted lines. The motives which they attribute to a character may have their reference in the character's past or future.

Goffman has noted that a person:

> makes a public claim that he is to be defined and treated as someone who possesses a particular value or property ... The limits to his claims, and hence the limits to his self, are primarily determined by the objective facts of his social life and secondarily determined by the degree to which a sympathetic interpretation of these facts can bend them in his favor.[33]

When the person in question is a fictitious one, existing in dramatic form only, the 'objective facts' inhere in the script and its logical possibilities, and the 'sympathetic interpretation' in the interpretations which are not only logically possible but also consensually validated. Looked at from the point of view of the play, rather than its characters, and again noting its correspondence to everyday life, we can say that the social actor's/dramatic actor's hypotheses about the nature of the social world/dramatic world must not only be logical but, in order to take on the aura of reality, must be shared by other members. Actors [34], then, test their hypotheses about their characters, using two

criteria and three modes of testing, as illustrated in Table 2.3
below:

Table 2.3
TYPES OF INTERPRETIVE HYPOTHESIS TESTING

Modes	Criteria	
	Logic	Consensual Validation
Privately, in thought	A	D
Interactively, in rehearsal performance	B	E
Interactively, in rehearsal discussion	C	F

The two criteria of logic and consensual validation are actually
employed simultaneously, but are separated here for purposes of
analysis.

Type A : This type of criterion and mode predominates in the early
phase of the production, particularly if there is a lapse of time
between the audition and the first rehearsal as was the case with
the Theatre Company. Once given the script, actors will begin to
formulate hypotheses about the motives which govern their
characters' behaviour. Asked how they 'go about developing a
character', the actors said:

> You think about his age, background, social and financial
> position. You look at everything about him that you may not
> even use at all. What he likes, what he doesn't like, why is he
> intense, who'd he say certain thing to.

> See what other characters say about your character, see what
> your character says to someone else, the tone and the attitude
> ...

The actors then test these hypotheses against the factual evidence
of the text. An hypothesis concerning the character's financial
position, for example, may be consistent with the textual evidence
and thus, insofar as the criterion of logic is concerned,
confirmed.

In their attempts to propose and test hypotheses which would fit
the data before them, actors work with certain assumptions about
the script. Some of these assumptions are derived from previous
experience of rehearsal work and are therefore not strictly
private. The first assumption they make is that the script is
meaningful. When they audition, they are given basic information
about the content and style of the play, especially if it is not
well known. For example, at the Theatre Company auditions, the

applicants were told that the action took place in a mental hospital. Although the lines which they read might not have meant much at the time, it was clearly the actors' expectation that, given the time and interpretive effort, the play's meaning would be revealed. Belief in the meaningfulness of the script highlights the implicit faith which the actors have in the producers and director, for they assume that they would not accept a meaningless or illogical script. The expectation on the part of the actor that the script is meaningful is most severely tested when he or she is faced with a script from which little or no meaning can be extracted, i.e., from which a context cannot be constructed which would give rise to the scripted statements and actions. It is when an actor faces this defeating conclusion that the underlying expectation of meaningfulness becomes so strikingly clear:

> The group discusses the fact that some of the parts of the play don't hang together. K. suggests that it could be because parts were rewritten and the rewrites might not fit perfectly with the original sections. (Observer's note)

This suggests a belief in the logicality of, at the very least, the original script.

Allied to this assumption that the script is meaningful is the notion that everything that happens in the script is intentional. Whether in the everyday life of real people or dramatic reality of characters, some of ego's expressions are intended to convey meaning to alter, while alter gleans additional information from other, unintentional expressions. However, when approached from the 'inside' (either by the actor interpreting the script or the audience watching the theatrical performance), the dramatic reality, since clearly artificial and purposefully created, is assumed to be intentional in all its detail.

An actor attempting to interpret a script assumes that each line either conveys meaning or contributes to an overall idea which is meaningful; one assumes that no line has been included arbitrarily. The same is true of details of staging:

> R. is seated with a group of actors on stage although she doesn't participate in their conversation in that scene. She asks the director if it might not be better to sit apart from them since her silent presence will be taken to mean something by the audience and will confuse them. (Observer's note)

In other words, the audience will take what is offered to it as intended, provided that it is included in a dramatic framework [35].

Although the script is taken to be meaningful and everything within it is taken to be intentional, a further assumption is that the full meaning of the play is only realised in its production. This belief - that the dramatic reality has a 'life of its own' beyond the script - delimits the role of playwright while extending that of actor and director[36]; as one actor remarked:

> You can't go to the playwright, because he may not understand what he's written, he's not necessarily right and it can be interpreted in other ways he possibly wasn't aware of when he wrote the piece. You don't automatically accept what the playwright says, because in dramatic terms it might not work, and in factual terms it can even sometimes be wrong.

No doubt the actor will continue to hypothesise in thought about the character and situation once rehearsal has begun and interpretation is accomplished in interaction with others. In fact, once the cast assembles to rehearse and discuss the play, the actor may have to revise or discard private hypotheses.

Type B : Although the assessment of a situation as logical or illogical requires private reflection (no matter how instantaneous), the source of such reflection may be interaction between actors as characters. One actor described the relationship between the privately thought and interactively performed (Types A and B) tests of interpretive hypotheses:

> There wasn't enough in the writing to give a clear indication as to what the relationships were. I think sometimes actors decided, 'there is obviously a relationship of some kind, it's not strongly written in' - and they developed it themselves. Sometimes I think there were very tenuous relationships developed - 'Ah, this is what determines this relationship, this is what governs our attitudes towards each other'. Quite often that would be built on very flimsy ground indeed. Suddenly they'd come to a scene where it didn't work to hold that attitude and they'd have to reassess all over again. I think that's the main fault of the writing. (emphasis added)

From this statement it is clear that the actor's private hypothesis is superseded by the interactive one, which is not surprising given the working assumptions about the limitations of scripted meaning.

What does it mean to come to a scene where it doesn't work to hold a previously established attitude (hypothesis)? In performance, this may mean that the role interpretation arrived at by one actor has made another actor's interpretation unviable. As Turner has said:

from the point of view of the role-making process an actor has
an infinite number of definitions of the boundaries between
roles which will serve equally well the logical requirements of
role-taking. But the placement of any one of these boundaries,
whether for a fleeting instant or a longer period, limits the
identification of other roles.[37]

Type C: Actors may also test the logic of their hypotheses in
group discussion, as one actor explained:

> I think the purpose of discussion is to enable us to seek a
> clarity about something, to seek what reasons and causes there
> are for things, what experiences the character may have
> undergone, or definitely has undergone, if it's scripted, and
> they usually have bearing on how he feels about things that
> happen in the play, or what he has to say in the play, or what
> other people have to say in the play.

This is akin to Type A testing except that instead of conducting
an internal dialogue in private thought, the process is
externalised and shared with other members of the group. The
products of Types A and B testing are used as material for Type C
testing; those interpretations formulated and tested in private and
then revised in the light of interaction between actors as
characters serve as the foundation upon which further hypotheses
are tested in discussion.

Types A, B and C hypothesis testing are concerned with the
elimination of those interpretations which, given the scripted
evidence, are illogical. This leaves a variety of possible logical
interpretations which could be superimposed upon (or found beneath)
the scripted lines. It is just such variety which makes the
reproduction of plays worthwhile, although, of course, plays vary
in their potential for diverse interpretation. But the important
point is that the group may be left with several logically possible
interpretations to choose from.

It should be remembered that in the case of the company led by a
director who makes most of the artistic decisions without
consulting the cast (but instead does so by observing them in
rehearsal), the choice of this interpretation is the director's.
However, in the case of a power sharing director like the Theatre
Company's, the members must agree on an interpretation in the sense
of both intellectually accepting it and dramatically conveying it.
Here, consensual validation is required if hypotheses are to be
confirmed.

Type D: In one sense, hypotheses tested privately in thought do
not require consensual validation because they are not shared. In

another sense, this kind of validation is ever present because of the nature of the self. To use Mead's terms, the 'I' creates the hypothesis (about the social or dramatic world) and the 'me' judges whether it is reasonable, given the actor's understanding of the social world and, therefore, the scripted lines. The validation of the hypothesis depends partly on the shared cultural meanings which constitute the actors' frame of reference.

Types E and F: These are best discussed jointly since they are used alternately by the group as it works towards an agreed definition.

Turner discusses two types of validation of a role:

(1) Internal validation lies in the successful anticipation of the behavior of relevant others within the range necessary for the enactment of one's own role.
(2) External validation ...is based upon ascertaining whether the behavior is judged to constitute a role by others whose judgments are felt to have some claim to correctness or legitimacy.[38]

Internal validation of one's dramatic role occurs through the interaction of rehearsal performance, and external validation through both rehearsal performance and discussion. Two issues are important here: first, the relationship between the actor's hypothesising (reality defining activity), dramatic status (as character) and social status (as actor); and secondly, the consequences for the individual actor of the group's failure to achieve consensus.

It is important to restate the kind of situation under discussion here. I am not concerned with dictatorial directors whose very status implies that they are the sole source of external validation of the actors' roles. Nor am I concerned with actors who are considered celebrities or stars and whose status in the present company is therefore defined by criteria external to it. Here, with a power sharing director and a cast of unknowns, status is established within and by the group.

The actor joins the production with a given dramatic role (this is not, of course, true of repertory theatre although even here one may be hired for a particular range of roles) and the importance of this dramatic role is usually fairly clear from a reading of the play. However, the social status which will be accorded the actor as actor in the company, as opposed to the dramatic status of actor as character in the play, cannot be totally determined before rehearsals start since it arises out of the interaction between members of the company. Nevertheless, the actor's dramatic status may exert a strong influence on social status as a discussion of the leading actor will make clear.

First, the actor who is given a major dramatic role has evidently convinced the casting director of his or her ability and suitability for the part. Since this may in itself be an indication of acting ability, the mere fact of getting a leading role confers status upon the actor before work on the part has even begun.

Secondly, since the play and its meaning exist through the words and actions of the characters, a leading role usually implies a relatively major portion of these, and with them the maximum opportunity to display one's talents. The attention accorded the lead is necessarily status enhancing.

Third, and most important, the lead's dramatic status enhances social status by providing the actor with an advantage in defining the dramatic situation. Turner has noted that by playing a recognisable role, one indicates the definition of the situation one subscribes to [39], and the lead is given the most material from which to construct a recognisable role. Obviously there are more characters fitting lines of action to the central character's and more actors accommodating their role interpretations to the lead's than vice versa. Simply by playing the lead, the actor's interpretation of the script prevails. Ultimately, all actors will require internal validation of their dramatic roles, indicating by their own performances that they have successfully anticipated each other's behaviour. It is simply that, in the rehearsal process leading towards validation, the central character leads and the others follow.

Any advantage in defining the dramatic reality is self-reinforcing. For example, through the portrayal of a leading role, the actor proposes a definition of the situation and communicates familiarity with the situation. With this clear grasp of the context which gives rise to the scripted lines, the actor is more capable of elaborating upon the scripted material through the improvisation of nonverbal detail. As I noted in the rehearsal summary, the improvised detail is often retained by the director who instructs the actor to 'keep that in' for future performance, as though it were scripted. What has naturally or spontaneously occurred is retained as fortuitous authenticity, although whether it will appear as spontaneous in subsequent performances is another matter! As the lead's actions are incorporated into the produced play, this actor's centrality is reinforced.

As the cast come to accept the lead's interpretation of the central role, they are thereby led to accept the conception of dramatic reality which underpins the interpretation. The lead thus becomes a source of external validation for the others' conceptions of their roles and the situation which gives rise to them [40].

The above is clearly an over-simplified sketch, implying that there is one clearly defined leading role and actor and a band of acquiescent others. On the contrary, a play is likely to consist of several well developed and important characters and casting contingencies are likely to produce leading actors of various abilities. Taken together, these two factors create considerable scope for a number of participants to strive for status and power rewards. As such, the preceding discussion of dramatic and social centrality describes the ideal to which the vying actors aspire. A challenge can be made either through the interaction of rehearsal performance (by playing the role that indicates the definition of the situation one subscribes to) or through the group discussion that often follows the rehearsal of a scene.

In such discussions, the participants make use of their familiarity with the everyday situation portrayed in the play, for the play derives its meaning for actors and audience alike from its relevance, no matter how remote, to everyday experience. However, dramatic reality is not a replication of everyday experience, but an interpretation of it; as one actor in the Company explained:

> You're not demonstrating what people in a mental hospital are really like; what you're doing is interpreting what the playwright thinks, or not even that - You're interpreting what he has written. He may not think that people in a mental hospital actually behave like that all the time. Then you have to find a way of making those characters real.

Although most actors made this distinction between everyday and dramatic reality in the course of their interviews, a good deal of time was spent in rehearsal discussing what would 'really happen' in the situation spelled out in the script [41]. In attempting to find out what would really happen, the actor may stand in one of several possible relations to the dramatic role which requires different forms of role-taking.

First, the actor may have experience of both roles of the pair. Where the roles in question are informal ones - fleeting roles - this is more likely to be true. For example, one may very possibly have experience of both the angry person and the person toward whom the anger is directed. When the roles are more formalised, actors are less likely to have experience of both roles. For example, they may have experienced the student, but not the teacher role, or the patient, but not the doctor role. Still, familiarity with the patient role may enable an actor to assume the role of doctor through everyday role-taking experience. On the other hand, actors may have experience of neither the role to be enacted nor its other-role:

> K. remarks that two disturbed people interacting with each other wouldn't be the same as one disturbed person interacting with a normal person - so how should the first be played? (Observer's note)

Where the actor lacks direct experience, reliance upon mass media portrayals will be greatest, just as we all rely upon second hand information for our knowledge of many aspects of the social world. But the mass media's inevitable stylisation of the unfamiliar (even in the case of documentary film, where the subject matter is selectively presented) influences the actor's conception of what would really happen in the direction of the stereotypic and possibly inaccurate.

The leading roles in the Theatre Company production presented this problem. For example, at one point, an actor remarked that since there was no indication from the script that her character was sexually inhibited, 'she must be inhibited in some other way'. This notion that some kind of inhibition is a necessary part of mental illness (regardless of whether this apparently widespread belief is correct or not) acted as a guide to the actor in the formulation of what she took to be a viable character. Similarly:

> K. and the director were discussing the motivation behind K.'s character's actions. The director said that, from the lines, everything seemed to be normal, and so to convey mental disturbance, something would have to be added to make them seem a little strange - some mannerisms, perhaps. (Observer's note)

In her description of an actor's performance as a grave digger, an actor indirectly outlined the commonsense expectations of someone in that occupation:

> Take V.'s part, for example: one could believe in him although the externals were wrong. A grave digger would look grotty, and V. never looked grotty. He would not have an RP [received pronunciation or standard English] accent, which V. did. The part was written as a very intellectual person which was a complete contradiction in terms. But he made a believable character out of it and that was his talent as an actor.

The actor chosen to play the role of doctor had himself been a patient in a mental hospital. He was therefore in a position to act as 'reality consultant' to the group and did correct some of the misconceptions voiced by the rest of the cast. However, because of his involvement in another show and its slight overlap with this one, he did not join rehearsals until the fourth day by which time detailed interpretive discussion was under way and formulations of 'what would really happen' had been made. Therefore, although the cast listened politely to his advice, they rarely incorporated it into the subsequent rehearsal of scenes.

It was clear, then, that the role of discussion was other than that of approximating the reality of the everyday world. One actor said:

> I think we talked a lot in the beginning - but this is the way actors work. If it's a straightforward thing, they'll still talk about it. With a lot of this discussion business, the actual answer arrived at is not so important as the confidence that arriving at such an answer gives the actors.

The confidence stems from the sense of community engendered by group discussion (the consequences of dissension will be dealt with shortly). Through talk, one participates in the life of the group. Through the acceptance of one's statements, one's acceptance as a member of the group is achieved and rejection of one's ideas expresses one's exclusion from the group.

One way to achieve low status in the group was to fail to participate in the discussion and/or to fail to construct a convincing character (the second being somewhat dependent on the first). An actor, H., who failed in both his and others' estimations, both dramatically and socially, speaks and is spoken about below:

> The director said my part consisted in my attitude offstage, but you cannot work that way with an audience. It has to go from you to them via action. Perhaps with a better written part you could do that, but it was impossible with this part. I just gave up. ... I searched that part from top to bottom and couldn't find anything to hang on to. I was just saying lines I didn't know the meaning of. (H.)

> His preference was always for what had been rehearsed which is boring, stifling. (Another actor, of H.)

> Discussion of interpretation of lines. K. says, 'Well, it's okay to have some lines we don't understand' (in reaction to H.'s continued questioning). H. says to the director, 'Just one more question' - and the others laugh. (Observer's note)

> The time spent in rehearsal discussing one sentence! You can go on forever, we were just bogged down. I was not the only one thinking like that. I don't mind a liberal amount of discussion, but to go on as we did about nothing! (H.)

- 74 -

H. sought clarification of his dramatic role through discussion but resented the discussion which occurred because it didn't meet these needs. Feeling lost, he (in the opinion of another actor) held on to whatever was tentatively decided, afraid to venture out into the unknown. An actor in this position does not <u>share</u> the definition of the situation created by the group, but only <u>complies</u> with it. Because one acquiesces rather than internalises, the secure base from which to improvise is lacking. Moreover, just as an advantage in defining reality is self-reinforcing, so is the disadvantage: H. remarked in the interview that he often failed to participate in discussion because he felt that the difficulty he had in developing a character gave him a relatively disvalued position in the group. The obverse of this was confirmed by one of the the highly valued members of the Company who said, 'I find I relate to someone who I admire for what he's giving in a show'.

What are the consequences for the individual actor of a failure to achieve consensus? Just as in the worlds of everyday life and scientific endeavour, individuals develop vested interests in their versions of reality, so in the case of dramatic hypothesising, the necessarily tentative formulations are held firmly by their creators. The director noted that:

> The selfishness of people always comes out. You try to support your own theory about the play. All the time, you're justifying your own situation; it's very natural. That works against a collective interpretation of the play. People have to be very secure to be that open.

People have to be 'that secure to be that open' because, despite the similarities between hypothesising in different levels of reality, it is perhaps more terrifying to be lost in a fictitious or dramatic world than in a real one. Zimmerman and Pollner, in their paper, 'The Everyday World as a Phenomenon', say:

> The attitude of everyday life sustains particular doubts, but never global doubts. Indeed, that the existence of the world is never brought into question is an essential requirement for any particular doubt.[42]

In the real world, should it become evident that members have failed to agree on the definition of a particular situation there is the remainder of shared reality to fall back on. One can strive towards acceptance of the others' definition or one can attempt to redirect the others' responses towards acceptance of one's own definition until some consensus is reached - or, failing to achieve consensus through either kind of adjustment, one may simply 'leave the field'.

In the case of dramatic reality, however, one's options are severely circumscribed by the events, time and place of the script. The dramatic 'self' cannot flee to a more congenial setting, for it is constructed out of the events of that very setting and no other [43]. The actor whose role enactment is not validated by others is not only lost, but trapped within the situation. As one actor explained:

> Actors get frightened - you get frightened if you're doing a part and you suddenly think, 'What am I doing?'. You're totally lost in what you're doing and you've got to go out on stage and you think you're going to get crucified because nobody else is going to understand you - and yet there is nothing you can do.

If, in a dramatic situation, one is left without a viable identity within the play, one immediately becomes - to oneself and to one's audience - actor rather than character. Dramatic theorists continually stress that the dramatic illusion cannot be sustained with audience awareness of the actor as actor. The slightest error can trigger a collapse from the dramatic to the everyday plane of reality. The error may be a technical one - the actor may forget or stumble over the lines or make a physical move which was clearly unintended. Or, either by failing to sustain total concentration on their roles and/or by holding discordant definitions of the dramatic situation, the actors may unwittingly destroy the dramatic illusion.

If one is revealed as actor when one purports to be character, one is clearly not a very good actor at all. Goffman describes this well:

> a person may be involuntarily deprived of a role under circumstances which reflect unfavourably on his capacity for it. The lost role may be one that he had already acquired or one that he had openly committed himself to preparing for. In either case the loss is more than a matter of ceasing to act in a given capacity; it is ultimate proof of an incapacity. And in many cases it is even more than this. The moment of failure often catches a person acting as one who feels that he is an appropriate sort of person for the role in question. Assumption becomes presumption, and failure becomes fraud. To loss of substance is thereby added loss of face.[44]

It could be argued that the possibility of humiliation is greater for dramatic actors since they have not only committed themselves to particular roles but have presumed to leap to a different level of reality. Yet, despite the potential for humiliation, the failure to achieve consensus must also be seen in a positive light. In my discussion of the negotiation of meaning in the course of training,

I referred to Stone's notion of meaning as lying midway between nonsense and boredom. Obviously, complete consensus would rob the actor of the challenge of creating a convincing character in the context of a collective performance. Thus, the anxiety which may accompany the fear of loss of identity on stage is offset by the thrill of being safely in character, described below by Hayman:

Every actor has experiences more or less like this with make-up and costume. Suddenly there is something about the figure in the mirror that you no longer recognize. It has acquired an independence from you. It has its own way of speaking and moving which you can no longer control quite in the way you did in all the previous rehearsals but you no longer need to. You feel safe. The character has acquired a backbone, strong but supple, and whatever variations get introduced subsequently, something basic has come right, which you can count on to go on giving you support.[45]

This relationship between the actor and the character as well as the relations between co-workers which influence it will be discussed in greater detail in the following section.

Assessing the work experience

If consensus and anomie are polar possibilities on the dramatic plane, then it is clear that actors may similarly agree or disagree in their assessment of the work experience on the everyday plane.

Many members of the Theatre Company mentioned problems in the script when evaluating the production in interview. Some felt that the problems they had had creating their roles stemmed from the fact that their characters were not fully developed in the script. Since, as I said in the beginning, the play had never been produced before, such problems could be expected. And, since the characters are unlikely to be uniformly undeveloped in the script, this can easily produce divergent assessments of the adequacy of the script.

The efficacy of discussion, as opposed to rehearsal performance, in making sense of the script was also judged differently by the actors. While one actor remarked that:

The best thing about the production was that decisions were made jointly -

and these decisions were often made through discussion - another actor felt that:

> There was a fundamental flaw in this production - there was a
> lot of talk in rehearsals.

Of course, had the script permitted discussion which settled
interpretive disputes adequately, a positive attitude toward such
talk might have been unanimous.

The disparate backgrounds of the participants in the Company
produced their equally varying evaluations of the competence of the
production staff. Those with experience in theatre felt that the
director, whose steady job was in television, should 'get someone
who knows about theatre procedure'. Another who had worked in
theatre, television and film remarked that without an experienced
stage manager, 'you can't concentrate on the job you are supposed
to be doing'. Yet another, with more experience in entertaining
than straight acting, said that, 'the fact that you're called to
rehearsal at certain times and have coffee, little things show that
someone has it organised'. The actors' differing expectations of
the production and the varying rewards which they ultimately
derived from it combined to form the conclusion of many that 'a
strong team spirit' was lacking and that the production was
something less than a resounding success ('It just didn't happen'
... 'I thought it would come out and all be and it didn't').

It is interesting to note that the actor does not accord the
audience the role of arbiter in aesthetic evaluation:

Interviewer: What do you think happened in this production,
                how did it develop from start to finish?

Actor: For me, I got worse. From the first night on it
                got steadily worse until it was splendidly bad.

Interviewer: Was this from your point of view alone?
                Supposing it had been the same audience all the
                way through, do you think it would have appeared
                worse and worse to them?

Actor: Oh, no, the audience, that's something else what
                they think!

Yet, it is the audience which bestows a dramatic definition upon
the actors' work; without the audience's implicit approval, their
work is mere play. Given that the actor's work is the audience's
leisure, the actor needs the audience but the audience can live
without the actor [46]. This inequity underlies the actors'
ambivalence towards their audience, expressed by members of the
Theatre Company:

An audience comes, basically, to be entertained - they don't
want to work too hard. The actor has the obligation to do what
the audience wants, not to indulge himself.

Most of the population of the world are pretty dumb; most
people going to the theatre are idiots.

As in any work situation, rewarding social relations may
compensate for dissatisfactions with the final product. How did
this potential reward fare in the Theatre Company? It will become
clear that this depends on the degree of mutual trust and
confidence that can be developed.

The 'paradox of dual consciousness'[47] inherent in the actor's
work has been widely discussed in the literature of drama and
refers to the requirement that the actor participate simultaneously
on everyday and dramatic levels of reality. The actor must 'knead
together emotion and detachment' [48], concentrating on the
dramatic in order to enact a role convincingly while also
monitoring one's own and others' performances with requisite
detachment. But, because participation in the dramatic reality is
the work, the actor 'cannot stand back and look at his work' [49].
If one tries to observe oneself, one ceases to be sufficiently
involved in the situation. To overcome this problem of the
inability to monitor one's own performance, the director functions
as an extension of the actor and this 'crudely and indirectly
permits the actor to see his own work as artists other than actors
see their own work' [50].

The director, then, is the actor's foothold in reality. As one
actor remarked when asked how acting was done, it involves 'reading
a play, setting up relationships with other characters and the
director'. The actors are referred to on the dramatic plane, as
characters, but the director occupies a position on the everyday
plane alone. The actor depends on the director to prevent a
discordance of definitions which could result in the actor's loss
of face. Ideally, what is good for the director is good for the
actor, since the successful production reflects well upon director
and cast. In practice, however, the contingencies making for the
inevitably imperfect production will become clear during the
rehearsal phase and the director will have to make choices which
may cast some actors in a less favourable light than others in the
performance itself. A great deal of effort is therefore expended
by the actor to ensure that he or she does not become one of the
few whose individual interests are sacrificed for the good of the
production. Throughout the interviews, the actors referred to this
need to maintain good relations with the director through the
avoidance of overt conflict:

If you've no faith in the director, take his advice and do what you want to do. I know it's naughty, but you have to save yourself.

Yet, the very fact that the actor can ultimately ignore the wishes of the director during performance creates a further problem - any other actor can suddenly deviate from the rehearsal directions and startle a co-worker with unexpected innovations. Fellow actors must also be dealt with as diplomatically as possible in order that perceived injuries are not avenged during public performance through the introduction of the unexpected. As a member of the Company explained:

> It becomes a question of being as polite and tolerant as possible, because it doesn't get you anywhere to argue, especially if you have to play with that person. With a facade of politeness, you can carry on doing what you have to. If the conflict surfaces, one person winds up trying to make it difficult on stage for the other. It's like two people carrying a big sheet of glass; one can't afford to have the other let him down.

In summary, conflict is avoided in order to maintain the illusion of mutual confidence so that suspicions do not arise which would lead actors to take precautions to 'save themselves', thereby disadvantaging other members of the cast. A cycle of trust or mistrust is set up, with its parallels in popular knowledge of actors' back scratching and bitchiness[51].

The form which deviance takes in rehearsals is related to the issue of trust and confidence. Norms prohibit the use of professional expertise in everyday level impression management; one's social performances are expected to be as sincere and undeliberate as any non-actor's would be. K., for example (the adjudged deviant of the Company), described the way in which he staged his non-dramatic behaviour during rehearsal in order to elicit particular responses from the other actors:

> One of the motives for my mini-explosion was frustration at my own self. Sometimes I wanted to play the fool in order to give the others confidence. ... If people had blown up, confronted me, then maybe we would have gotten somewhere. Maybe even with my explosion, I didn't give them enough to play off.

The repeated remarks of the other actors regarding their difficulty in working with K. highlight the discomfort inherent in the actor role. The opportunity for deception by co-workers attuned to nonverbal leakage and impression management by profession, coupled with a great need for mutual trust, engenders a situation in which the participants might not wish to be continually reminded of their potentially dangerous occupational skills through such evidently staged behaviour. Thus, K. was ostracised, as he, with his relentless self-consciousness, noted:

> I haven't mentioned relationships with other people in the cast, which is probably significant because it means I didn't have them

while the director remarked:

> K. could have been in a world of his own throughout that play, which actually makes him not a very good actor. Generally we, the group as a whole, had a very good working relationship.

Trust and confidence are somewhat dependent upon the establishment of relationships, the feeling that one is known by the other; but in order for relationships to develop, there must be continuity through time. Because of the nature of theatre, there is usually very intense interaction for a limited period of time (exceptions to this include the repertory company which remains together as a working unit over a series of productions and the long run which may go on for years). Once the production reaches the performance stage, actors are likely to arrive shortly before the performance and leave shortly afterwards; the longer the run, the more routine it becomes. Therefore, the bulk of non-dramatic interaction will occur, if at all, during the stage of rehearsal. How does the peculiar work of rehearsal influence the extent to which actors come to know each other?

Of importance here is the assumed correspondence between actors and their dramatic characters. This may play a part in their selection for roles, as one actor explained:

> Sometimes people get cast because the director sees part of that actor in the part itself, thinks the actor might be able to utilise that in making the part come alive, make it three dimensional.

During rehearsal, the actors' task is to become as familiar with their characters as possible; therefore, there may be some intentional choice of character related behaviours (where a distinction can be made between these and the actor's own). Actors spend a good part of each day acting in the role of their characters. Part of the playing around that occurs during rehearsal when the play is not actually being rehearsed consists in the handling of props that they use in the play so that they become more familiar with them and use them more naturally. Similarly, as a form of play, the actors often cross boundaries between dramatic and everyday realities by speaking their characters' lines to express relevant meanings on the everyday plane.

These examples point to the fact that the dramatic identity is the source through which the actors speak and through which they are known to each other in this environment, even when not acting in character in the rehearsal proper. Little is known about the actor except through the 'third dimension' which he or she adds to the character. When asked if he thought there was any correspondence between 'the actors and their characters', one actor noted:

> You see, the character is not distinct from the person who plays it; the character, as written, is only two dimensional, and the third dimension varies according to the person who plays it, and what that person gives to it is going to depend on what they have in them - so there must be something in common between themselves and the character.

Most of the actors interviewed took the question to be wholly answerable, going through the cast of characters and actors, describing the ways in which they corresponded to each other. The participants use the information available about the characters to flesh out their conceptions of the actors, just as what the actors can know about any particular character is in part determined by the person playing it. In this sense, there is an overlap or fluidity in the conceptions of actor and character, as indicated in the following actors' remarks:

> M. used her own crassness in her part; T. used his patronising nature.

> I found it very difficult to work with K. because of the person he is, not because I disliked him, simply because of the character he decided on, which was very much based on himself, and because of the kind of person I am.

The fact that rehearsal calls are based on social groupings on the dramatic plane (characters who interact in the drama become actors who interact in rehearsal) helps to reinforce the belief in actor/character correspondence. It enables actors to base their knowledge of their co-workers on the characters unless they actively seek out their company in non-rehearsal settings. With this exception, the end result of this process is that the actors never get to know each other very well. This proves functional for the actor's career, since the job market necessitates geographical mobility:

I used to feel rather sad when a show was over, the crowd you were working with would all disperse - you might well work with one another sometime in the future, in other cases you don't. If you've had an enjoyable time, quite often it's sad when a group breaks up. But now, it doesn't bother me at all; as soon as a job is over, the most important thing that comes to mind is, what's next?

Doing this play wasn't that painful. I'd just finished a play I'd enjoyed. I don't get terribly hung up about this anymore - it's only a couple of hours of your life every night for a week. That may sound very irresponsible, but it's realistic.

Despite the lack of close relationships, the teamwork required in order to successfully manoeuvre one's way through a performance can be a kind of interpersonal reward for the actor especially since, as I have tried to show, such teamwork cannot be taken for granted from the outset.

This study may have conveyed an impression of rehearsal as a work setting in which covert conflicts abound, social ties are weak, creative impulses may be thwarted ('for the good of the production'), and all this, perhaps, for very little money indeed. What does the actor get out of acting?

While the nature of rehearsal interaction may inhibit some kinds of interpersonal rewards, it does provide others not available elsewhere. A recurrent theme in the actor's assessment of the work experience is the discovery of character. When asked, 'what makes you feel that a rehearsal has gone well?', the actors replied:

If you've discovered something. It might be someone discovering something about the character, or a few people doing a nice scene together in a new or amusing way.

If I've felt at the end of the day that I know something more about the play, the character I happen to be playing, the function of the character in the play, then it's been a good day. Some days are kind of bad days in which you come out feeling more confused than you did that morning. In lots of ways, the rehearsal is far more exciting than doing the show itself, because it's a period of discovery - discovering what the play is about, discovering what the characters in the play are about, discovering things that weren't apparent. Extending yourself a bit, trying things out.

If something has happened. When you've been working on something and the time has gone so quickly because you have been so involved, and you have got something solid out of what you've been doing - you've built up something.

When actors say that they have 'discovered' something, or something
has 'happened',they express those moments when an understanding of
or penetration to the core of the character is achieved. These are
the glimpses which lead to the thrill of being safely in character.
Discovery and creation, which are the rewards of an actor's work,
entail the subjective experience of a transposition from role to
self. The actor starts out with scripted lines which sketch the
role of the character in the play, and from here embarks on the
arduous journey in search of the sense of inward unity [52]. One
actor described this achievement in the following way:

> If you've worked on your character enough, you shouldn't be
> limited to one way to respond to anything; you should have so
> much knowledge of the person that there are certainly things it
> wouldn't do, but there certainly isn't one way to do it.

The sense of unity is the stage of development reached when the
actor feels safe enough but not completely safe:

Interviewer: Do you ever have difficulty understanding a
                director's directions?

Actor: Yes, when he gives you an attitude and you can't
                justify it; you think, why am I doing it this
                way?

Interviewer: So then every addition changes the whole of the
                character as you've already constructed it?

Actor: Well, there isn't really a whole. A whole to me
                is something I can see - and there is no whole
                in people any more than in characters. You just
                find another aspect of the character.

Interviewer: So it is possible to work that way without
                feeling disjointed?

Actor: Yes, but it can leave you feeling uncomfortable.

There is no whole in other people - only words and gestures to
which we impute meaning, purpose, continuity. But our own words and
gestures stem from what Tiryakian calls the 'really me' [53]. We
may perform discrete actions and reflect upon their relevance to
this sense of self; the whole and the bits, the self and its
expression through role behaviour, stand in dialectical relation to
each other. For the actor, the character is like 'other people'
until, through a succession of discoveries, it approximates the
knowledge we have of only ourselves. It is in this second order
self-knowledge that actors achieve the intimacy which is otherwise

- 84 -

lacking in their work situation. I will return to this issue of real and dramatic identities in Chapter 4.

Part of the thrill of performance resides in the inevitable risk which accompanies the assumption of a strange role; without really being the person one pretends to be, one can never fully dismiss the possibility of a slip-up. Unless one truly possesses the core, one may err on the periphery of self-presentation. Discovery, creation, concealment and exposure can only take place through social interaction. Actors speak of something 'happening' - of 'sparks' and 'good friction' in rehearsal. Only by continually testing the effectiveness of performance, in rehearsal and ultimately on stage, can individuals affirm their identities as characters, and thus as actors.

C. WORKING FOR TELEVISION

Introduction

Little is known about the television actor [54]. While the literature of dramatic theory and acting technique usually concern theatre acting, popular literature focuses on film-based stardom. Television - the 'bastard medium', as one actor described it - is largely ignored, even though it offers the most well-paid steady employment for the majority.

This case study reports the experience of actors in a commercial television drama production which I will call the TV Group. Given the nature of TV drama, it provides a useful contrast on a number of counts to the preceding study of the Theatre Company. First, while the organisation of fringe theatre is usually informal and lacking in a strict division of labour, TV's more formal organisation defines the duties of its numerous personnel. Secondly, whereas the occupational standing of fringe theatre's participants is often unresolved and ambiguous, participation in television is itself indicative of placement in the established middle range sector of the profession. Thirdly, the unproven script of fringe theatre which necessitates extensive interpretive work contrasts with the often simplistic script of TV drama which the actors find unproblematic. Finally, these differences in organisation, status and material produce a situation in television in which well-paid actors work short hours and find their work relatively routine and undemanding, while in fringe theatre a high level of commitment is expected of actors who work long hours for little pay. Moreover, the technology of the TV medium <u>creates</u> the characteristic features of this setting. For this reason, I will examine the impact of the organisational and technical constraints of TV on the work experience and occupational identity of the actor. In doing so, I will show that the actor's evaluation of TV work is strongly related to the values adopted by the actor in the course of training.

The play which the TV Group produced was a serialised adaptation of a novel in six half hour episodes. Two such episodes constituted one production unit which meant that they were rehearsed and recorded together. (In order to use time and personnel most efficiently, outdoor scenes from various episodes were often filmed in the same day.) I observed the first production unit which spanned a period of four weeks. It was apparent from the production schedule that the following two units would be executed in much the same manner as the first, and since TV drama does not engender the typically theatrical 'opening night' <u>or</u> final performance atmosphere, my concentration on the first production unit did not seem disadvantageous. Since TV drama is radically different from theatre production, a description of the stages which the TV Group's production underwent is necessary. This description will reveal the very different roles in production of TV and theatre actors, a matter which will be discussed in greater detail later.

Stages of TV drama production

Television drama may take the form of a single play, usually 1/2 to 1-1/2 hours in length, a serial - a play divided into episodes, usually with one episode broadcast each week in the same time slot - or a series - a collection of dramas which are unrelated except for the main characters and situations or settings. Regardless of form, production follows the same pattern.

Much of the work which goes into the production occurs before the actors are ever summoned to the rehearsal room; this is the stage known as preplanning. Over twenty-five years ago, Ann Todd remarked that:

> In America they get by with a short rehearsal period because pre-planning is all-important and their organisation is immensely efficient and thorough [55].

Nowadays, preplanning is as much a part of British TV production as it is of the American. The preplanning is usually initiated about six months before the actors start work on the play. The producer - the person responsible for coordinating and overseeing the aesthetic, administrative and technical details of production - may suggest scripts to the drama department or the drama department may offer scripts. Despite the complex organisation of a TV company, there are in this respect loose role boundaries and the informal pooling of ideas and suggestions.

The case under study began with plans for a series of thrillers, each of which would itself be in serial form. The script was commissioned after deciding on the novel to be adapted and discussions were held between the producer, writer and script editors. The producer began with knowledge of the time slot that the play would fill on the air; as one of the script editors remarked, because of the early viewing time (7.30 p.m.), they sought a thriller which would be 'psychological' rather than 'violent'. Such overall planning decisions affect both the choice of the script and its subsequent editing.

The preplanning stage includes not only script related activities, but also the scheduling of the production. The studio and required technicians must be scheduled - even the food van must be booked for outdoor filming. The actors must also be cast. Casting is ordinarily a collaboration between one of the company's casting directors assigned to the production, the producer, director and writer. The latter three must agree on the final choices, thereby creating a unified concept which will underlie the production.

The organisation rationalises its casting procedures by hiring actors who are clearly of a particular type, whether by virtue of physical characteristics or past experience of playing particular kinds of roles. This reduces the margin of error in a situation in which the interdependence of personnel and activities discourages delays and unanticipated problems. Typecasting is more important in TV than in theatre because the character cannot be established over time (i.e., repeated performance) and must be evident from the outset, given the shorter rehearsal period and single taped 'performance'. From the standpoint of the actor, typecasting can reduce the 'discovery' rewards of acting which the Theatre Company actors talked about. One actor in the TV Group, for example, who had been cast as a police officer in single plays, series and serials, was said by a colleague to be a deeply dissatisfied victim of typecasting. Another actor in the TV Group, commenting on the reasons for his being selected, said:

> [I was chosen] because this director had worked with me before; before, I played a well brought up young man, nice boy, intelligent, but a bit stupid, like this character - but a smaller part, less written. Therefore, I guess, this director suggested me for this part - same character, but extended.

Casting is only one example of the institutionalisation of the most rational practices which have probably evolved, in the short history of television, from early trial and error procedures. In staffing a TV company, prestige and financial backing make possible the selection of personnel with combined organisational and aesthetic skills required for TV drama production. The same resources also permit the selection of actors who can work within a complex organisational framework. They must be pleasant, unobtrusive and extremely reliable in order to mesh easily with the overall production plans which have been so precisely ordered.

Once the preplanning was completed, the actors were called for a read-through of the entire six-episode script. Because of the clarity of the script (the result of a fairly uncomplicated story and skilful writing), the read-through proceeded without interruption. In fact, to an observer the atmosphere was that of a big board meeting; business was attended to, communication pared down to the essentials.

The first rehearsal began with amendments to the script being given to the actors by the stage manager. The floor of the rehearsal room had been marked out with coloured tape denoting different rooms of the studio set, pieces of furniture, doorways, etc. The director and actors blocked the first few scenes and did a sketchy rehearsal of the scenes with scripts in hand.

With a rehearsal period of less than two weeks, the Group made rapid progress. By the third rehearsal, the actors had learned most of their lines and were requesting and being given more specific directions by the director. This close relationship between actors and director is only possible in the middle phase of production when the number of organisational and technical staff is limited.

The 'writer's run' was held on the fourth day of rehearsal. Following the uninterrupted performance of the first two episodes, the writer discussed his reactions to the production thus far with the director and actors. After several more days of rehearsal, outside filming and weekend breaks, the producer attended a run and gave the Group her reactions and suggestions. Swift describes the producer's run from the standpoint of the actor:

> You've had two weeks' rehearsal for an hour's play. Towards the end of the second week the rehearsal room will be visited by the producer and his staff and a representative selection of technicians who are working on the show. They will know the script and will no doubt have had meetings with the director, agreeing on what can or can't be done. But this is the first time they've seen the piece in action. Atmosphere in the rehearsal room grows more tense that day. This is your first audience (and will be your last) ...[56]

The last rehearsal before the actual taping was used as a technicians' run; cameramen[57] took notes from the director concerning the way the scenes were to be shot and became familiar with the actors in the flesh and their movements throughout the sets.

All of the previous work was merely preparation for the two days of taping at the TV studio where the bulk of the play – the indoor scenes – was taped. The outside filming was used largely to connect the indoor scenes. In the studio, the activity was divided between those on the 'floor' – including the actors, cameramen, and floor manager – and those in the 'gallery' – including the producer, director, writer, production assistants, vision mixer and sound technicians. Those in the gallery watched the activity on the floor on the monitors. These show the shots captured by the two or three cameramen as well as the shot, already noted in the cameramen's scripts, chosen by the director for the final version. The director may choose to communicate directly with the actors from the floor during the rehearsals preceding the taping. However, once taping begins, the director views the action from the gallery, communicating notes to the actors via the floor manager who receives these through earphones and either repeats or diplomatically rephrases them to the actors.

In this last phase of production which will directly include the actors, one is struck by their subordination to the production personnel and by their relative passivity compared to actors in the theatre. The TV actors place themselves in the appropriate positions within the sets, but it is the technicians who are most physically active and who create the appearance of movement by filming the actors from different angles for varying lengths of time. The vast number and variety of personnel involved in the entire production process have been listed by TV drama producer, Irene Shubik [58]. They range from video, tele-cine, grams and boom operators (and their assistants) to carpenters, special effects people, costume supervisors and film editors.

The predominance of organisational and technical personnel is even more evident from an examination of the ratio of such personnel to actors in the various settings connected with the production of a single play. For example, at the TV Group's read-through, the ratio of production personnel to actors was 19:7; at the technical run which took place in the rehearsal room, 11:4, and in the outside filming required for the production, 42:4. Although I did not take a similar count for the studio taping, a fair estimate would be nearest to that which prevailed in the outdoor filming. In fact, Shubik estimates that:

> A total count of the number of those concerned with one seventy-five minute "Play for Today" studio production in 1973 would probably have reached at least seventy, behind the cameras alone - i.e., excluding the actors [59].

One gains a similar impression of the subordinate status of the actor from reading the script. Three kinds of script are necessary for TV production: the rehearsal script for actors, the filming script for outdoor camera and sound technicians and the taping script for studio technicians. In a fifty page filming script, there was only one direction ('See what the actors want to do here') which allowed the actors to improvise on the scripted action.

The final phase of production entailed the editing of the film and tape. Since this did not involve the actors, I did not observe the editing process. Yet, even here, the mere knowledge of future editing must reinforce the actors' sense of subordination for, as they are told in an early guide to radio production:

Be prepared to have your part decimated by line cuts to fit the
play to broadcast time [60].

The impact of TV organisation and technology on the actor

It has been difficult to postpone discussion of the organisation
and technology of television while describing the phases of a TV
production. However, I want to examine these influences more
closely in this section.

While the organisation of TV drama, from the standpoint of its
creators, makes possible the rationalisation of labour, it also
serves to inhibit the actor's job satisfaction. Etzioni discusses
this problem more generally in his book, Modern Organizations :

> The problem of modern organizations is ... how to construct
> human groupings that are as rational as possible, and at the
> same time produce a minimum of undesirable side effects and a
> maximum of satisfaction [61].

Later, he elaborates on the origins of this problem:

> According to Marx, the modern factory hand is alienated from
> his work since he owns neither the means of production nor the
> product of his labor. Specialization has fragmented production
> so that each worker's labor has become repetitious, monotonous,
> and lacks opportunity for creativity and self-expression. The
> worker has little conception of the whole work process or of
> his contribution to it; his work is meaningless. He has little
> control over the time at which his work starts or over the pace
> at which it is carried out. To this Marxian analysis, Weber
> added that this basic estrangement exists not only between the
> worker and the means of production, but also between the
> soldier and the means of warfare, the scientist and the means
> of inquiry, etc. This is not just a legal question of ownership
> ... but rather that with ownership goes the right to control,
> and that those that provide the means also define their use;
> thus the worker, soldier and researcher - and by implication
> all employees of organizations - are frustrated, unhappy since
> they cannot determine what use their efforts will be put to
> since they do not own the instrument necessary to carry out
> independently the work that needs to be done [62].

In the case of TV actors, however, the issue is complicated. They
must work in an organisational framework where they are essential
(more profoundly than most organisational employees) to the
creation of the product, but are only a part of the total process
of production. Furthermore, they are, in part, the instruments

'necessary to carry out the work that has to be done' - and are so, more independently, than other TV workers. In one sense actors exercise total control over this instrument of production - the body - but in accommodating to the organisational and technical demands of production, they surrender that control to various personnel involved in the recording of their work for mass consumption. Whereas in theatre, actors carry through a performance from beginning to end, following the sequence as scripted and without disjunctions in action, in television they submit their performance to the fragmenting requirements of the organisation's method of production. As Swift remarks, the actor:

> has to be able to switch himself on and off like a tap, or else contain his feelings and thoughts (his 'character') within him - through tea-breaks, technical difficulties, the general paraphernalia that is Television.[63]

The organisation finds itself in a similarly difficult situation. These temporary employees who are central to the production - the actors - have to be 'kept happy' so that they perform well. Yet, because of their impermanence in the total organisation, their needs are not as salient as those of the permanent staff. As far as possible, then, the actors' work routine is subordinated to the needs of these other employees whose interests are guaranteed by union rulings [64].

The actor is thus in the paradoxical position of being the person around whose work everyone else's is organised, but who is a relatively unimportant figure in the organisation itself. The artistic/practical division makes this anomaly an even greater one and is evident in the strain between actors and technicians and even actors and extras. Before discussing the social relations of TV drama production, however, I want to continue my examination of the technical constraints on acting for television, for the technology of television necessitates the organisational arrangements discussed above.

Technical requirements of modern TV drama production

Naturalism: Earlier I noted that typecasting contributes to the smooth running of the organisation. In addition, typecasting is the outcome of the naturalistic requirements of the medium itself. With a visual focus on the actor which is so much closer than that achieved on stage, the actor is forced into a kind of naturalistic typecasting which limits the range of roles to physical type. In this sense, naturalism contributes to the routine quality which television has for the actor.

One actor in the TV Group noted that casting directors differ in the range of roles they deem suitable for a particular actor. Since several casting directors are employed by each company and a number of companies offer work to each actor, the actor may have some scope for varied characterisation. Ironically, success in a popular role may limit the actor's choice of roles; because of mass exposure and the intimacy of the TV image, the association between the actor and the character may be ineradicable. Thus, it is to the actor's benefit to 'maintain a low profile' - not to be, as one actor put it, 'in anything too stamping'. In other words, the best insurance of future employment is adherence to an easily identifiable type and a rather neutral rendition of roles.

The requirement of naturalism affects the actor in yet another way. Because of the close focus on the actor, minute expressions will be clearly revealed and boredom or staleness in the performance will be more apparent. In order to keep the performance fresh, rehearsals are shortened as the day of taping nears. Consequently, the actor is gradually disengaged from the work group at just the point where, in theatre, participation would increase. This is, incidentally, good preparation for the passive role the actor must adopt during the final recording.

Discontinuous performance and out of sequence acting:
Discontinuous performance is the absence of a full run through the play without interruption. In out of sequence acting not only are the performances interrupted, but often they are not rehearsed or taped in chronological sequence. These practices are not required by TV drama production, but rather result from the way in which TV production has developed over several decades.

In the 1950's, TV plays were often filmed before live audiences and so resembled theatre plays which were being filmed for transmission over television. Cameramen had to quickly follow the actors from one set to the next and try not to get their cables crossed as they moved in time with the actual dramatic changes. Since the number of sets and costume changes were necessarily limited, the demands upon the script writers were great, as they were required to take the limited technical facilities and ordinary dramatic requirements into account.

The problems of continuous live filming were, at the same time, its challenges (the first being the view from the fifties and the second the present perspective on that period) [65]. Nevertheless, video recording and sophisticated film editing were welcomed once developed. The writer's job became easier because actors' movements no longer had to be engineered through a live set. Since this was now accomplished through editing - the director's responsibility - this role was augmented.

Television drama became less like theatre and more like film, both technically and experientially. Autonomy and responsibility for the final product changed accordingly. If, in theatre, the actor is the ultimate decision maker by virtue of stepping onto the stage before a live audience, then in TV and film the director or producer or editor exercises control over the final product. They select from the actor's performance those takes which accord with their conception of the production rather than, as in theatre, surrendering the conception to the actors on the night of performance.

These processes associated with the technical requirements of production were evident in the TV Group. Here, outside filming was done before the read-through at the TV studio took place. This meant that the actors acted scenes whose relevance to the story as a whole may have been unclear. And, in order to use technicians' time efficiently, outdoor scenes from production units 2 and 3 were filmed during the scheduled filming dates for unit 1. Even the read-through itself, which was fairly continuous, could not be a wholly continuous movement throughout the story because the filmed sequences without dialogue were necessarily absent.

Technical concerns are largely suspended during the rehearsal stage but inevitably intrude from time to time. For example, during one rehearsal, the director told an actor that his nonverbal reaction to the previous line had to be immediate; a second later he would be off camera.

The organisation of the transmission of the play into six episodes adds to the temporal difficulties of which the actor must be aware. As I mentioned earlier, each two of the six episodes formed one production unit for rehearsal and taping purposes. Several times in the course of rehearsal, actors made remarks which indicated that they could not remember where the first episode ended and the second began. This introduced ambiguities in their acting, as the following exchange indicates:

The actor says to the director, 'Should I be going into that again?' (an explanation within the script of part of the plot.) The actor says this has been described 'over there' (in another part of the set, in a different scene). The director says, 'Yes, but that was last week'. In other words, they are rehearsing two episodes together which will be shown a week apart, and the audience has to be reminded of this part of the plot in the second episode. (Observer's note)

The practices employed during the taping stage also produced discontinuity. Whereas some TV companies divide taping days into two parts, one for rehearsal of the play and the other for taping, here a scene by scene rehearse/record sequence was used. The predominance of technical concerns in the taping phase is further illustrated by the fact that much of the rehearsal in the rehearse/record sequence used in taping is mainly for the benefit of the technicians; any problems the actors may have are assumed to have been resolved in the rehearsal room.

The technical requirements affect the actors in other ways. For example, in the opinion of numerous onlookers (including the producer), only the relatively long, continuous and uninterrupted scenes seemed to have dramatic impact. Not surprisingly, the actors said that they found these scenes the most challenging and rewarding. An even finer illustration of the effect which filming has on acting is contained in the following conversation I overheard on one of the two days of taping:

Actor: What happens at that point, do you have the cameras on me?

Director: No.

Actor: Then I don't have to motivate that shot, I just have to appear in that spot when the cameras get me.

Finally, it must be remembered that the 'one performance only' nature of TV drama reduces the actor's potential for unpredictability and surprise (both central to the notion of what makes for a 'great actor') [66]. One can only rise above predictability through a number of performances or overcome boredom by subjecting oneself to the threat of it. (Likewise, how can one demonstrate the occupational values of dedication and reliability - 'the show must go on' - without a full house that awaits one's entrance?)

The importance of the live audience to the actor's satisfaction is generally agreed upon and evident in such statements as, 'it would be almost a miracle for an actor to impose himself on the public in a single hour and a half's performance never to be seen again ' [67]. Swift tells that actor that:

Most actors enjoy the relaxation that 'non-live' performance brings. ... But we are performers, in the instant performing market. We mustn't forget that we're doing our job because we want to expose ourselves. If we stop wanting to do that - or are not prepared to do it, we must question our professional motives.[68]

The social relations of a TV drama production

If we examine the social relations of a TV drama production, we can clearly see the pervasiveness of technical influences on the actor's work experience. It seems appropriate to begin with discussion of the relations between actors and production personnel.

<u>Actors and technicians:</u>   This relationship will vary with the actor's interest in the technical aspects of production. Although the data did not allow for firm conclusions on this point, it seemed that those actors who described themselves as 'mainly theatre actors' tended to dissociate themselves from the technical concerns of the production. One such actor comments:

> Some people are very close to the cameramen, those who have worked a lot and know the cameramen well; I don't. I don't even know which camera is on me half the time. There are actors who know exactly which camera is on them, but I prefer not to know at that moment; so, if I'm in half profile, that's just too bad.

On the other hand, had the actors identified themselves as 'mainly TV actors' (and none of those interviewed did), interest in the technical aspects of production might sustain them through periods of boredom at work. Even 'mainly theatre' actors might have an interest in the actor/technician relationship, arising out of the need to familiarise themselves with the requirements of acting in this medium. For example, a member of the TV Group remembered that:

> When I didn't have the experience with cameras, the cameraman was so helpful, so I would never think of them as part of the machinery, but as other actors, if you like, really.

This same actor who had, by the time this production took place, acquired TV acting experience spoke again of the benefits to be derived from treating technicians as something other than 'parts of the machinery':

> I will expend a lot of energy smiling at someone. If someone's made a particularly lovely prop, I'll find the prop man and tell him so; and then, maybe, if I do want something else, he'll understand what I mean.

When asked about their relationships with technicians, the actors noted the distance between the two groups and attributed this to the brevity of the entire production. They explained how the varieties of TV drama - the single play, series, and serial - influence the nature of this relationship (in the same way as would an actor's repeated employment by the same TV company). If, for example, the actors are regulars in a series, technicians emerge from the technical environment in which they are extensions of complicated machinery and are seen as individuals with whom some working relationship can be developed.

If the production of TV drama requires a combination of organisational, technical and aesthetic skills, one can see how the various production personnel require different combinations of these. Production assistants, for example, require a high degree of organisational skill although the skill is employed in a technical/aesthetic setting. The actor's skills are predominantly aesthetic. The technicians, however, are the backbone of the production, for their expertise makes transmission of the aesthetic product possible. If, as I said in the previous case study, an audience makes the actor's work more than mere play, then in TV the technician is the essential intermediary in the defining process. Moreover, the technician's role determines the actor's non-autonomous role in TV as opposed to theatre. Because of the technician's high stakes in the organisation and relatively low stakes in the aesthetics of the production, it is not surprising that the TV Group cast felt that the technicians were very much 'job oriented' and, consequently, 'union oriented':

> I thought they were good ... Their energy was there, they weren't all over the place, wondering what time is tea break.

> You get to know them after a while, and with film crews, you get to know them quite well if you're on location, away from London, you get quite matey. Television crews, not so much so ... I don't think they're awfully interested in anything other than the job itself, the angle of the camera or the microphone.

Actors see technicians as the people least likely to 'bend a little' for the good of the the production and they resent this, for it highlights the technicians' dominance in this work setting. This was confirmed by a member of the TV cast when, in his interview, he discussed a cameraman involved in the outdoor filming:

> The cameraman we had before was good; the one we had on Monday night, I didn't like. He didn't do anything nasty or anything, but he was not - I was there to fit into his camera, he wasn't there to photograph what I was doing, and there is a distinction. And I'm not surprised that it was out of focus and we're going to have to do it again. In fact, I'm almost pleased.

Finally a word about directors and technicians is in order. Because neither the actor's nor the director's knowledge of the technical side of production is likely to equal that of the technicians, the director, too, is somewhat at their mercy, particularly during the outdoor filming. Whereas in studio videotaping, the taped product is visible on the monitors and the director can demand a retake if dissatisfied, he or she must rely on the cameraman's judgement of filmed sequences since they cannot be seen until the film is developed. In this case, if the director is unfamiliar with the cameraman's past work, the latter's appearance of expertise must suffice. During a break on the first night of outdoor filming, the director and production manager discussed this problem, admitting that the cameraman's display of competence was, for them, a psychological necessity [69]. Ultimately, the director has more control over the technicians than do the actors; the director can supervise the editing of tape and film, but the actors can only hope that these others have shown them to their advantage.

The actors and director: Some characteristics of directing style prevail regardless of dramatic medium while others vary accordingly. One of the TV actors offered her views on this:

Directors are as different as anyone in any profession. You have someone like this director, or someone who's got every last detail down, and you do that, or else. Or you'll have one who will improvise to get the characters out. There's the director who will leave it all to the actor because he trusts his personality. There's the director who knows you have that talent to be somebody else, so he will go on and on at you to find that other side of you that is like the person he's trying to find. ... I think that the same director, in theatre and television, would be different; I am different in theatre and television. For example, this director in theatre would probably talk a lot more over lunch; it's a longer process and the finished product is something he won't be around to see and control, so he probably wants to say more before the first night, as it were ... Whereas in television he can ... correct it at the last minute – maybe use a bit from one scene and a bit from another. And in television, if it goes wrong on the first take, it can be done again; whereas in theatre, every night is live before an audience.

The TV Group had in common with many TV productions a simple, relatively undemanding script and a cast of experienced actors. The experienced actor works efficiently with co-actors and director in a kind of shorthand representing shared meanings. Through the repeated interaction of actors and directors, actors learn to take the role of the director towards their own actions:

The actor stops to say that her co-actor should pour his own
drink earlier so that her later line, 'All right, I'll have a
sherry', makes more sense.

During rehearsal, the actor comments on his own performance,
saying that the scene feels 'a bit vague and fuzzy'. He
suggests that in the next few explanatory lines, the main
message should already have been conveyed. It feels
uncomfortable because it isn't linked with the appropriate
action and motivation.

In discussing some of his lines with the director after doing a
scene, the actor says, 'I think that's a throwaway'. This is a
shorthand expression by means of which the participants discuss
the underlying intent of the lines or their motivational
status. (Observer's notes)

The director and actors can take many procedures and points of
interpretation for granted, run through scenes without much
interruption and maintain smooth work relations - because of the
absence of characteristically theatrical problems. The very fact
that performance mistakes can be obliterated and rectified
contributes to the relative absence of tension in TV drama [70].

All of the actors interviewed in the TV Group noted the easy and
relaxed atmosphere which they attributed to the director's working
style. He allowed them to make minor decisions themselves and
interrupted as a way of clarifying rather than dominating the
action at hand. One would expect that, given the requirements of
naturalism and the tendency to typecast actors, the actor would
often know best what his or her character would do at any point. In
addition, the actors' familiarity with this type of work enabled
them to work with the director as a collaborating team. Unlike the
semiprofessional situation of fringe theatre described earlier,
professional TV freed the director from the task of showing or
teaching the actors how to do something, in addition to telling
them what he wanted done.

The distinctive thing about the actor/director relationship in TV
is the continual influence of technical considerations. The theatre
director views the production from the standpoint of the audience;
the TV director (in rehearsal) does not 'see' the performance that
the viewer receives unless he or she limits perception to that
partial view afforded by the TV camera. The theatre actor, though
involved in the acting of the dramatic role, can take the role of
the spectator who witnesses the play in its full visual scope.
Since the transmitted view of the TV drama depends on the
director's choice of shots, the TV actor loses the opportunity to
imaginatively reconstruct the visual image of the action received

- 99 -

by the other, the viewer. In an almost literal sense, the actor and director lack what Schutz calls 'a reciprocity of perspectives' [71].

Related to this lack of reciprocity of perspectives is the fact that the actor performing on the floor before the cameras cannot always know whether the director requests a retake for technical or aesthetic reasons. This introduces the possibility of disingenuous communication between actor and director, as I learned during the taping:

> The director feels that this take was okay except for the actor's mistake (which has clearly upset the actor). The director, communicating with the floor manager via the earphones, tells him to tell the actor that they were quite happy to have the chance to do that scene again for technical reasons, despite the mistake. An American TV director who is sitting in today, watching the taping from the gallery, tells me that they always tell the actors that the retakes are for technical reasons and the actors always know it isn't true. (Observer's note)

Like the director and cameraman, the TV actor may be satisfied by the director's display of approval. One of the actors remarked:

> With this particular thing we're doing now, we have had heavy notes coming down from the box on the day of recording and this doesn't help, because any heavy acting notes should have been gotten out of the way during rehearsals. All one should be concerned with is getting it spontaneous. If you've suddenly got new interpretations coming down from the box, it can be very throwing to people's confidence. The ideal is to be very relaxed so that you believe that everyone thinks that what you're doing is lovely. (emphasis added)

Even if the reasons for wanting a retake are really technical, the decision may be made to forgo the possibility of a better take because of the effect it would have on the actors (an inferior dramatic performance). Here, there is a trade-off between the aesthetic and technical aspects of production. Similarly, retakes for technical reasons may have to be accommodated to the acting needs of the actors:

> Towards the end of the third take, the atmosphere becomes very tense. They have to redo the take for technical reasons from point B but in fact do it from point A because the director says the actors could not, dramatically, slide into point B without its antecedent scene. (Observer's note)

Technical concerns are not always foremost in the mind of the TV director whose job, in the early stages of rehearsal, is very much like the theatre director's in that interpretation of the play must precede the details of staging. As the production progresses, however, the TV director becomes more engrossed in technical details and less involved with the actors. As one actor said:

> The television director serves his cameras well. A good director will keep you fairly unaware of his technical problems, but he has to serve someone else - and once we get into the studio, the actor is forgotten, really.

The director shared this view:

> Once we get into the studio, your main attention - you're watching the performance, but not wholly watching the performance. You're looking at angles and lighting, so you have to assume that you've got the performance right before then, before you get near the studio.

During the two days of taping, the director tried to counteract the inevitable estrangement from the actors by minimising reliance on the floor manager. He spent the studio rehearsal time on the floor with the actors rather than in the gallery 'in order to keep the personal contact going'.

Clearly, the director and actors expect that, as they are working in a technical medium, these extra-dramatic concerns will intrude upon rehearsal; the director may tell the actors what he or she wants to see when the camera 'goes up'. Even in rehearsal, the actor's reaction to this intrusion of the technical may vary:

> In rehearsal, if I see a director move to check a shot, it can have one of two effects: if I think I'm acting very well and I see him think, 'It's not going to fit over there', I think, he's not really looking at my acting, and I get angry. If I couldn't be bothered that afternoon, I think, oh, that's okay, he's not looking anyway. I think the best directors, you don't notice when they're checking those things. This cameraman stopped me in the middle of a scene saying, 'You can't do that because I won't see this' - and I was actually working.

It is even more likely that the actor's reaction to the director's involvement with technical matters will vary from rehearsal to taping - the nearest thing to performance in television. The actor may not only expect to be subordinated to technical concerns, but may wish to be. Taping makes actors nervous, just as any performance would. One actor compared the situation in TV where the director attends to the actor's performance during taping with that in theatre where the director stands in the wings giving criticism between scenes.

Finally, the type of dramatic production (single play, series or serial) influences the social relations between director and actors. The series will have its regulars - those actors playing central roles around which each episode is constructed - and its guest artists who make single appearances in particular episodes. Not only will this create a separation within the group of actors involved in any one production but, as one actor explained, it will make for differing allegiances of these regulars and guest actors to the members of the production team. Since the director is likely to change from episode to episode, the regulars' allegiance is to the producer of the entire series; since the guest artists are usually cast by the visiting director, their loyalties will be to this person. The implication is that occasions arise when producer/director disagreements occur and support from the cast varies accordingly.

<u>Actors and co-actors:</u> If social relations in theatre are tenuous, they are even more so in television. This medium of drama production ensures, for one thing, the brevity of relationships. Six episodes were rehearsed, filmed and taped in the space of six weeks. More importantly, the Group met for only a fraction of the working hours characteristic of theatre. They rarely worked more than five hours a day, never worked weekends and, if the previous day's schedule was arduous - for example, included outdoor filming - they skipped the following weekday as well. Efficient planning enabled the director to dismiss some actors before the end of a rehearsal day which meant that rehearsals often consisted of short scenes between two or three members of the cast.

If TV provides the actors with a work schedule similar to those in other occupations, it clearly allows them more time than theatre actors have for outside interests and personal relationships. This was confirmed by a conversation with one member of the cast; referring to another actor's aloofness, he noted that while at one time he might have tried to 'draw that sort of person out of her shell', his present family and financial commitments precluded such involvement.

In TV, then, actors can manage to do their jobs without involving themselves, either very deeply with the production:

> C.: I like the production. I'm enjoying it. That's about all. It's a nice part; basically, that's why you do anything. I like the story

or with the other actors:

M.: So far I've only worked with C. whom I like very much, we get on well. No, that's all I can say, we get on very well, there's no problem.

That the intensity of relationships is dictated by the nature of the medium is revealed in C.'s description of the work relations:

In television, they nearly always tend to be pleasant. You don't get crises where people's unpleasantness comes out. It's very smooth. We come in and we go home. Therefore, it tends to be easy and pleasant; there's no reason for anything else to happen. Therefore, it can happen that you don't get to know people very well, and nobody wants to know you very well, and this happens by accident; you get to know them if you give each other lifts home. So you don't have to face up to any problems in your own personality.

The easygoing relations between TV actors is partly a result of their status security. The financial resources of established TV companies enable them to select from the pool of working actors. Those who find employment here have fairly stable career histories and are in the mainstream, rather than on the periphery of, their occupation. In the semiprofessional theatre case described earlier, status concerns were rife. The interpretive discussion which at times dominated rehearsal interaction may have met the status needs of the individuals while inhibiting the progress of the production. The TV Group's actors, by virtue of continued employment in theatre and TV (most of them were regularly employed and several were already committed to future engagements through the next six to twelve months) have 'arrived' and are able to get on with the work at hand.

The theatre actor's control over the final product and the TV actor's corresponding lack of control engender different relations between actors in each setting. In theatre, actors must invest time and energy in maintaining the appearance of cooperation and friendliness - otherwise, one actor may sabotage another's performance on stage. For example, one actor's unconcealed hostility during rehearsal may lead another to upstage him or her in performance. This means that one actor 'steals' another's focus by engaging the audience's attention during a scene in which it has been decided in rehearsal that the second would dominate. Upstaging is less of a problem in TV since editing influences the relative importance of the actors. This decreased interdependence of actors weakens the social bonds between them (whether authentic or apparent).

The actor's position in the TV production company does not allow for unpleasant or disruptive behaviour. Knowing that any delays caused by individualistic and/or unreasonable behaviour entail extraordinary expense and knowing that such behaviour will endanger one's chances of future employment, successful TV actors present themselves as paragons of cooperation.

One member of the TV Group said that, although he had never worked with the members of this cast before, they all 'knew' each other - probably by seeing each other's work on television. This passive knowledge which TV actors have of one another parallels the passive performance which the medium demands of them. In fact, it is difficult to separate the lack of interpersonal interaction on the everyday plane from the lack of characterisation opportunities on the dramatic plane, for the two are somewhat interdependent.

Characterisation and the TV actor

I have already shown how the technical requirements of TV drama production inhibit the opportunity for characterisation. Characterisation entails assuming strange roles, acting from the standpoint of people unlike oneself rather than 'playing oneself'. What remains to be established is that the actors themselves perceive this as one of the drawbacks of working for TV.

First we must examine the expectations and values they adopt in drama school. Drama school training is strongly associated with a theatrical tradition, which is hardly surprising given the long history of theatre as an English institution and the relatively short history of acting for mass media made possible by modern technology. Moreover, historical factors have produced a situation in which light drama and popular entertainment have come to be associated with limited characterisation, while high culture for elite audiences has presented opportunities for intensive characterisation [72]. Since TV is the major contemporary medium for popular drama (whose intrinsic technical nature inhibits characterisation), drama schools provide their students with the skills and values appropriate to higher status (theatre) work.

The very organisation of drama training is at odds with the experience of TV acting. The intensive process of becoming an actor requires a small-scale personalised setting which clearly contrasts with the complex organisation required for TV drama. Whereas the scale of drama school is such that it is likely to offer experience in radio work - it is not that difficult to set up a small recording studio - only one of the recognised drama schools offers continuous television experience. Other schools (including the Drama School) arrange with TV companies for infrequent student training sessions. The Drama School students expressed a desire for more experience of filmed acting [73].

Limited financial resources are not the only reason why drama schools fail to provide more training for TV work. One of the TV actors felt that the rationale for this lack of opportunity was, 'if you're good enough to get into drama school, you're good enough to learn or do the naturalistic acting required for television on your own'. Thus, the inferior status accorded TV acting may in itself prohibit the solution of practical problems which impede exposure to TV.

The impact of early training was highlighted by the comments of one of the adolescent extras in the TV production. These young people who were already professional actors appeared in some of the outdoor sequences and were hired to be themselves (as extras often are); teenagers with Northern accents were needed for the scenes and several were brought down to London from Manchester. While waiting for cameras to be set up, one of them told the writer of the script that he would only go to drama school if he became unable to find this kind of work. The important point is that here was the case of an 'actor' socialised into a totally modern occupational identity of naturalistic acting for mass media, expecting to carry out required <u>actions</u> without being required to undertake much characterisation work, or <u>acting</u>.

The drama school's stress on theatre acting was evident in the self-conceptions of the professional actors I interviewed, They thought of themselves as 'mainly theatre' actors, thereby rationalising their present participation in TV. Such rationalisation was perhaps apparent in the comments of one TV actor who attributed increasing boredom to increasing age:

> I enjoy pretending to be somebody else, and therefore I like parts which draw something out of me which I haven't used before. The longer you go on in the job, the more you build up - become carbuncled with things you've done before. ... When you're young ... you don't know what you are, and it's nice to feel for things and put yourself behind different disguises. ... But in time, the more parts you play, the more you find the things that are you. ... What is exciting is when you play a part which is unlike anything you've ever done before and you start to find something new which you hadn't discovered before. But this gets less and less as you get older; inevitably you fall into certain patterns.

Another actor made this more explicit by saying that he tended to feel guilty when not working in theatre, while another fully described the difference, for him, between theatre and TV work:

> On television, you have to control everything and you have to have everything really real, which means that at times you

literally are not acting, you're being. At times you're putting everything into the subjugation of yourself. You're putting the part in that, you can't be big on television. If you're on the stage and you rant and roar, there's a satisfaction in that, you get rid of a lot of things, but you can't do that on television - it's too real.   You couldn't shout and scream because nobody would really believe that you behave like that. Television has a reality but doesn't have a reality. On stage, you're not real, but you're allowed to indulge in more real - In television, you compress everything inside yourself, you're never allowed to get rid of something. And then, the ultimate judge of what you've done is other people, mainly critics. You never get a chance to repeat the performance, they like it, you do it, that's it, it's finished.

During both rehearsal and recording, the actors made sardonic, role-distancing remarks when they remembered that I was observing them, saying, 'What does this tell you about acting? This isn't acting !' They seemed to feel that this was a kind of work that actors did, but which was not acting.

The director of the American Academy of Dramatic Arts gave an opinion of TV drama which could well have been voiced by the director of a British drama school:

An actor does a full season of repertory in his final year ... which means Strindberg, Ibsen, O'Neill, perhaps Moliere or Shakespeare, as well as some modern plays - then he goes out into the commercial market, where he's lucky if he gets cast as an extra on Kojak .[74]

We need not characterise all mass media drama as being of lesser quality than the drama produced at school and a limited professional sector; we need only recognise that this is generally the case, and as such will usually characterise the actor's evaluation of such participation.   Shils, voicing this moderate view, writes that:

The argument against which I am contending implies that certain genres are incapable of offering an occasion for important achievement;   entry   into   them is   the   equivalent   of self-condemnation to ruin. The very fact that, here and there in the mass media, on television and in the films, work of superior quality comes forth seems to be evidence that genuine talent is not inevitably squandered once it leaves the traditional media of refined culture to work in the mass media, which tend on the whole to present mediocre and brutal culture. (emphasis added)[75]

- 106 -

In the same way that Shils argues for a relativistic view of mass media, I do not wish to imply that all theatre is more conducive to the traditional rewards associated with acting. In fact, Taylor and Williams note that theatre actors, who constitute 'an isolated overworked and underpaid group '[76] justify their work with belief in the 'magic of theatre' [77]:

> These artists needed the darkness and the auditorium to establish that they were actors. [The theater is] a dramatic form whose intrinsic superiority they maintain over television or films, because neither of those forms have the 'excitement or magic of the living theatre'.[78]

Taylor and Williams' findings are mentioned here only to demonstrate that the TV actor, although neither overworked nor underpaid, yet suffering other career related indignities, lacks even the justification of the magic of theatre! In other words, the unfulfilled theatre actor has the consolation of carrying on the venerable tradition of the impoverished roving player; the unfulfilled TV actor forfeits this comforting image upon entering the brightly lit, soundproof, machine-dominated setting of the TV studio.

As Stuart Hood says in A Survey of Television, 'The majority of viewers turn to television for entertainment, distraction, and escape' [79]. It is to be expected that the kind of drama offered (and so potential characterisation rewards) will be influenced by these audience requirements. Although, from time to time (and on British TV much more frequently than on American TV), drama of either classical or serious modern writers is presented, the bulk of drama transmitted tends to be that of the popular variety - situation comedies, police/detective stories, adventure, hospital drama, etc. It is just such material which provides the magnitude of work opportunities for actors unknown before the advent of television [80].

Hood, in reference to the TV series, notes that:

> The most common and favourite type of narrative is one with continuing characters to whom the viewer becomes attached, with whom he is familiar, from whom he knows he can expect certain types of action and reaction.[81]

While this is best achieved through a TV series, in which the same characters come into the viewer's home daily or weekly, the same effect can be achieved through the single play which presents typical and relatively unproblematic situations for the viewer's reception. Thus the actor may find that he or she is cast in similar roles over time because the motivations behind characters in popular drama are limited in variety and the actor 'looks' most like a particular kind of common character. The problem of typecasting, referred to earlier, is mentioned here as one of the ways in which the quality of drama filters down to the subjective experience of the actor.

Some of the features of social relations between TV workers which I discussed earlier in terms of organisation and technology are also affected by the quality of drama or characterisation potential typical of TV. For example, we saw in the previous case study that script interpretation is often the impetus to interaction in rehearsals. If, however, the meaning of the script is fairly clear (in the TV study, because of the identifiable genre of the thriller), then this will affect the tone of the relations in two ways. First, there will be a smoothness of relations because personal interpretations of the dramatic reality are uncalled for, and secondly (or as a result of this), the experience may be one which fails to involve or stimulate the members of the production. They may interact less closely on the everyday plane because there is more that can be implemented automatically [82]. One actor in the TV Group illustrated this relationship between script and social relations by saying:

> I don't think close relationships will be made on this, because it's not the kind of demanding thing where people need to know each other well in order to do it.

The experience of acting - or directing - may become routine because of the kind of drama undertaken. A study of a TV serial showed that in TV drama:

> Safe material is preferred to untried categories of writing. Improvisation is out of the question...And set routines are allowed to replace creative experimentation.[83]

The TV Group director confirmed this view:

> [The work relations have] been very smooth. Mind you, it's not a highly complicated production; a lot of scenes are quite simple - domestic scenes, police officer scenes - It doesn't involve a lot of action or difficult technical shots, weird lighting or enormously flamboyant acting. It's kind of tight and there's not an awful lot of subtlety in the characters, for the most part, which is where you're liable to spend a lot of rehearsal time, if there are a lot of psychological things going on which could be interpreted in a dozen different ways. The interpretation, in this case, is what's written on the page; you speak the words and that's the situation, for the most part. Occasionally you can give it a bit deeper texture than that, but a lot of it is plain.

And a TV Group actor echoed the director:

> I'm determined to make it a challenge; television isn't for me,
> a challenge, because the parts, usually, unless you're the
> lead, only show one aspect of a character. You've got to know
> the other aspects but you are not usually given an opportunity
> to explore, so you're not absolutely concentrating.
>
> In this production, it's because it's a plot - he wants to get
> interesting people, but the writer is leaving it up to [the
> actors] to be themselves. It's a story, which is everything.
> Everything that's rewritten is to make the story clearer,
> neater. There isn't much room to manoeuvre. If I wanted to
> create a problem, which I do very much [in one particular
> scene], of a lot of different things happening ... that might
> make the director impatient with the actual story ... That's
> why there are [what some actors call] 'television people', who
> come on and present a very clear story, that you can say, 'Ah,
> yes' - like reading a thriller, and not a very good thriller,
> where there aren't - the story is all.

The actors' negative evaluation of TV work was also apparent in
their attitudes to another group of TV workers - the extras. The
way in which actors express disdain for extras illuminates the
troublesome aspects of the TV actor's role. For example, when
actors disapprovingly say that the extra is 'in it for the money'
and 'works all the time', they are faced with the truth that they,
too, have succumbed to the lure of TV's financial rewards. To say
that the extra has 'jobs on the side' is to say that the extra is
not <u>committed</u> to acting, just as the TV actor, compared to the
theatre actor, is not. If the roles of extra and actor were really
distinct, the following occurrence would have been unlikely:

> One of the actors told me that during the outdoor filming the
> other night, the bystanders asked the actors for their
> autographs; <u>then</u> asked who they were; and (with an even greater
> tone of disgust), he said, they <u>also</u> asked the extras for <u>their</u>
> autographs! (Observer's note)

Swift notes that 'A lot of television acting is behaving'[84] and
this is even more true of the outdoor link scenes where extras are
used. The supposed difference between actors and extras is that
actors assume the roles of characters different from themselves
while extras are there to permit the filming of bodies which would
be present were the dramatic situation real. Where the <u>acting</u>
becomes behaving, this distinction between the actor's and extra's
roles breaks down, resulting in the antipathy evident in the
actor's attitude towards the extra.

The actor is distinguished from other personnel in the various scripts and notices connected with the production as the artiste. The walk-on or extra is described in these pages as the crowd artiste. If, as one actor explained, the tension between the actor and extra results from the actor's feeling that, 'there but for the grace of God go I', then the ambiguous meaning of this word artiste illustrates the difficulty in separating the relatively important from the unimportant, the artistic from the non-artistic personnel within the production.

It may be useful at this point to mention another (although more amorphous) group which also highlights aspects of the actor's role - that is the group known as bystanders, the populace, or even 'real people'. These people who mistake the extra for the actor in their quest for autographs of the famous must be controlled to avoid interference with the workings of the production:

The producer mentions to me that bystanders can be 'intrusive'.

One of the actors, in talking about the outdoor filming done last night, says that the bystanders become more 'unruly' by night because they're hidden by the darkness. (Observer's notes)

The first 'take' may be fine or you may have to do umpteen. It isn't only actors who are fallible. Aeroplanes materialise on the word Action ... The light may change during a shot; the local populace might infiltrate (local populace have scant regard for the business of filming).[85]

The bystanders must be managed although the production team, in fact, infiltrates their natural environment. The bystanders constitute a live audience, but without the voluntarism which characterises the theatre audience. The latter's purposeful presence bestows dramatic value on the actor's performance. The bystanders are to the actor, in terms of the control required to minimise their unpredictable actions, as the actor is to the production, complete with organisational and technical trappings. Put differently, the passivity required of the bystanders in their own environment parallels the subordination of the actor to the demands of TV where he or she is supposedly an actively performing focus of attention.

The relationship of the bystander to the actor is not unrelated to the lack of characterisation available in TV drama. An audience becomes important when the illusion of another life is conveyed. In fact, the actor may not bother to create the illusion unless an audience is present:

During today's writer's run, with various production staff present, the actor actually wrote the words on the piece of paper in his scene for the first time, instead of feigning writing as he has done in the past. (Observer's note)

In television, the actors do not always act to each other; rather, they display what could be called 'coordinated autism' [86]. Each actor portrays an easily identifiable and distilled character, executing the role rather than generating it through interaction. This was evident on those occasions when the stage manager stood in for an absent actor to enable another to rehearse the part; the actor's rendition of the role did not vary in the least with the substitution of a different partner. The performance and audience are mutually influencing, as one actor explained:

The satisfaction of having done a really good scene is good, because you've done it well, but television doesn't give you the time, and more often than not, the scope of going to the extreme in performance. Now, on stage, if you go to the extreme in performance, unlike television, you get the immediate audience appreciation, always gratefully received.

This brings me to the more general discussion of satisfactions - or reward trade-offs - of television work.

Reward trade-offs

Few work situations provide all potential rewards; complete satisfaction is the privilege of the famous and powerful. The spontaneity, immediacy and intimacy of live theatre - particularly when the show is touring or based in the provinces, away from most actors' London base - is rarely equalled in television [87]. Yet, for the middle range actor, most theatre offers little financial return. TV is more lucrative and within the medium the series is the most lucrative of all. However, Swift notes that:

Long-running TV series pose problems ... What happens is that the actor sinks into his character; it may become his doppelganger. You are either happy with a fixed identity (the public knows exactly who you are) and regular work and marvellous pay, or you're not. ... In some ways the more famous you are (as your character) the harder it might be to get new work. Still, you've lived a bit, ridden high, made a million friends and admirers. You're an actor, aren't you? What did you expect?[88]

The TV series is viewed not only as a danger to future employment through association of the actor with character, but more

- 111 -

fundamentally, as destructive of the talent which is the best insurance of future employment. As Rod Steiger said:

> The fatigue of doing a television series is enough to destroy any talent an actor might have. I asked Charles Chaplin whether he could do a good television series. He said, 'God couldn't do thirty-six good shows'.[89]

Of course, actors are taught to value characterisation <u>and</u> financial rewards - therein lies the problem. The spectre of unemployment is never far from the actor's mind. Not only is it prevalent in the occupation, but it presents special difficulties to the person who cannot practice a craft alone while 'between jobs'.

The actor who opts for the financial rewards available in TV grapples with the ambivalence in occupational identity induced by the inescapable inclusion, obvious even through its denial, of the idea of a <u>calling</u> attached to the work;

> There comes a point when you have to realise the fact that you're just doing a job. I've never treated it as a vocation, like a priest; it's something I do quite easily, reasonably well, and I get paid for it.

Yet, this actor went on to divulge that his loftier expectations and aspirations had been discarded along the way:

> I think I was under the misapprehension when I went into the business that I would receive a sort of satisfaction in doing something which has never been a privilege of mine to have.

Swift warns the young actor:

> No matter how talented you are television tames you. The power of a Peter O'Toole or an Olivier is not contained by the small screen. It may not be to your discredit if television eludes you. But it will be to the detriment of your earning power! Most actors come to terms with television - if they're given the chance.[90]

The organisation of work throughout the various media produces, for the majority, an incompatibility between the creative and monetary rewards of the occupation. In its favour, the choice of financial rewards enables actors to act more often than they would otherwise do, albeit in diluted form. Additionally, the popular acclaim made possible by TV's mass audience is as much a part of the mystique of acting as is the assuming of strange roles. Nevertheless, the irreconcilability of the two rewards engenders a kind of disillusionment which one might not at first associate with an occupation noted for its escape from the plane of the routine and mundane.

NOTES:

[1] Michael Shurtleff, quoted in W. Goldman, The Season, p.213.

[2] All quotes which are not footnoted have been taken from my interview data.

[3] Broadhead refers to 'individuation' in discussing the process whereby 'individuals presentationally organize their multiple identities in such a way that self and others are struck with the phenomenological sense of a distinct person rather than a single categorical identity' ('Individuation in Facework: Theoretical Implications from a Study of Facework in Medical School Admissions', p. 51). Drama school applicants have the difficult task of individuating themselves in performance - through the character - at the audition.

[4] The auditioners refer obliquely to what is often called 'presence' or 'stage presence.' For a discussion of presence in everyday life, see A. Travers, 'Ritual Power in Interaction.'

[5] This also shows that students are aware of the importance of impression management at auditions. Haas and Shaffir ('Taking on the Role of Doctor: A Dramaturgical Analysis of Professionalization') analyse the dramaturgical aspects of doctors' professional socialisation, comparing their medical school applications to auditions, selection interviews to callbacks, and so on. The selection for drama school, however, is more than dramaturgical in a metaphorical sense; professional life will continue to consist of real auditions and callbacks.

[6] See E. Goffman, The Presentation of Self in Everyday Life, p. 114; the back region is the place "where the suppressed facts make an appearance".

[7] The drama student, in direct interaction with his or her teachers, learns the relationship between nonverbal behaviour and 'character'. It is interesting to compare these teachings with social psychological literature on the same topic (for example, M. Knapp, Essentials of Nonverbal Communication) which comprises the teaching material for trainee academic psychologists in a contrastingly abstract way.

[8] See G. Mead, Mind, Self and Society, p. 69.

[9] A. Strauss, Mirrors and Masks, p. 45.

[10] See E. Goffman, Encounters, p.108.

[11] T. Sarbin and N. Adler, 'Self-Reconstitution Processes: A Preliminary Report'.

[12] Layder contrasts the 'personal' method of direction, which allows actors to develop their own characterisation with the 'positional' type of authority which directors may exert, shaping the characterisations on their own. Structure, Interaction and Social Theory pp. 134-5.

[13] Actors must develop their characterisations in interaction with each other if they are to 'develop[] the import of the work' (I. Mangham and M. Overington, 'Performance and Rehearsal: Social Order and Organisational Life', p.210). However, it is clear that they may be required to make their contribution to the work, if not to the import of the work, without doing so.

[14] G. Stone, 'Appearance and the Self', pp. 88-9

[15] See I. Mangham and M. Overington, 'Performance and Rehearsal: Social Order and Organizational Life', p.210.

[16] V. Oleson and E. Whittaker, The Silent Dialogue, p. 253.

[17] Ibid.

[18] I am grateful to Paul Rock for this point.

[19] J. Roth, Timetables, p. 4.

[20] R. Fox, 'Training for Uncertainty', p. 225.

[21] Hochschild uses the term 'emotion work' to describe the 'act of trying to change in degree or quality an emotion or feeling' in, 'Emotion Work, Feeling Rules, and Social Structure', p. 561.

[22] M. Natanson uses the term condensation to refer to the process of 'seeing the full range of an event in a perceptual unit, and then setting aside what is known in favor of the immediate givenness of that unit.' Phenomenology, Role and Reason. p. 148.

[23] See B. Geer, et al., 'Learning the Ropes: Situational Learning in Four Occupational Training Programmes'.

[24] Peter Brook, quoted in R. Hayman, Playback, p. 42.

[25] C. Gulbenkian Foundation, U.K. and Commonwealth Branch, 'Going on Stage', p. 11.

[26] 'A survey of employment and earnings of Equity members was carried out by the Union in 1971. This survey showed that 40% of the sample had been unemployed for a median period of 13 weeks and that 32% had done temporary work, ranging widely from grave-digging to modelling. However, this survey was conducted by means of self-completion questionnaires addressed to the entire membership of Equity (23,000), of which 4,809 were returned. The sample was therefore self-selecting and not fully representative.' Ibid., p. 16.

[27] E. Goffman, 'On Cooling the Mark Out: Some Aspects of Adaptation to Failure', p. 463.

[28] Although part of the ideology of fringe theatre consists in the idea that greater artistic freedom exists under conditions where commercial success is not a salient factor, the hope of those working in fringe theatre (as indicated by the participants interviewed in this, as well as other cases) - that the production will 'transfer' to the West End - makes commitment to the freedom to experiment, for its own sake, questionable.

[29] C. Gulbenkian Foundation, 'Going on Stage', p. 27.

[30] Ibid., p. 18.

[31] See M. Overington and I. Mangham, 'The Theatrical Perspective in Organizational Analysis', p. 178.

[32] T. Guthrie, Tyrone Guthrie on Acting, p. 18.

[33] E. Goffman, 'On Cooling the Mark Out', p. 461.

[34] It will become clear that the director also participates in this activity.

[35] In a Kentucky nightclub fire in 1977, the bellboy who interrupted the stage act with news of a fire in another part of the club and warning to leave, was taken to be part of the comedy act being performed; he was ignored and many deaths resulted.

[36] 'It is more than likely, however, that except for the most determined of directors, the playwright's choices will have reduced the scope for wayward interpretation and realization

in performance'. I. Mangham and M. Overington, 'Performance and Rehearsal; Social Order and Organizational Life', p. 209.

[37] R. Turner, 'Role-Taking: Process vs. Conformity', p. 22.

[38] Ibid., pp. 29-30.

[39] See ibid.

[40] In the case of the central dramatic role, it is clear that status goes hand in hand with power. There is one case in the theatre company where high status is accorded to someone precisely because of the attitude he or she takes to a powerless position: the actor who combines a minor dramatic role (with its ostensibly low self-rewards) with a high degree of cooperation and commitment to the production.

[41] With this quasi-concern for the authenticity of their dramatisation, some obvious knowledge appeared to be forfeited - for example, when the cast discussed the scene in which the hospital inmates rehearse a play. The discussion at this point centred on "what would really happen at a rehearsal", although the actors themselves were at that very moment engaged in one!

[42] D. Zimmerman and M. Pollner, 'The Everyday World as a Phenomenon', p. 84.

[43] This is qualified in the case of improvisation, although even here, the requirements of shared meaning place constraints upon the activity. An analysis of improvisation, which is used in actors' training, as a rehearsal aid, and sometimes as the material of performance itself, is unfortunately beyond the scope of this study.

[44] E. Goffman, 'On Cooling the Mark Out", p. 454.

[45] R. Hayman, Techniques of Acting, p. 35.

[46] See H. Becker, Outsiders, p. 82 re characteristics of service occupations.

[47] W. Archer, quoted in R. Hayman, Techniques of Acting, p. 24.

[48] Ibid.

[49] T. Shank, The Art of Dramatic Art, p. 77.

[50] Ibid.

[51] Layder attributes actors' emphasis on trust to the 'tension between the isolating individuation produced by the organization of the occupation and the need for collaborative involvement in specific work situations.' Structure, Interaction and Social Theory, p. 121.

[52] See G. Allport, Becoming.

[53] E. Tiryakian, 'The Existential Self and the Person', p. 77.

[54] For example, C. Taylor's, Making a Television Play is about the writing of television plays; I. Shubik's Play for Today deals with the production of TV drama; P. Elliott's, The Making of a Television Series deals with a documentary series; M. Cantor and S. Pingree's, The Soap Opera, M. Cassata and T. Skill's, Life on Daytime Television, and D. Hobson's, Crossroads, concern the soap opera as a dramatic form.

[55] ABC Television Ltd., Armchair Theatre, pp. 43-44.

[56] C. Swift, The Job of Acting, p. 79.

[57] This is the term used by males and females.

[58] See I. Shubik, Play for Today, pp. 44-7.

[59] Ibid., p. 44.

[60] W. Kingson and R. Cowgill, Radio Drama Acting and Production, p. 13.

[61] A. Etzioni, Modern Organizations, p. 2.

[62] Ibid., p. 42.

[63] C. Swift, The Job of Acting, p. 78.

[64] For example: television production requires a person responsible for 'continuity' - a person who ensures that, despite the discontinuous method of production and sequencing of action, the final product reconstructs an apparently continuous sequence of action. The usual example given is that of the lit cigarette: if a shot of an actor smoking a cigarette is used, and the camera then switches to another actor or scene, the cigarette must be shown to have burned to the point one would expect if the action were continuous, when the camera returns to the first actor. In the TV Group, there was no separate position in the organisation of continuity person. Therefore, the production assistants performed this task. However, because they were not paid separately for this,

they could not be held responsible, officially, for any mistakes in continuity. A continuity mistake could make an actor look ridiculous and thereby destroy the performance's credibility; yet, the risk was taken because of the work arrangements with the permanent employees of the organisation.

[65] This may account for Swift's view in his 1984 book The Job of Acting that 'those who did live shows rightly think themselves warriors of a different sort from today's softies' (p. 83).

[66] See J. Gielgud, Distinguished Company, p. 88 and R. Hayman, Playback, p. 88.

[67] T. Worsley, Television, p. 211.

[68] C. Swift, The Job of Acting, p. 84.

[69] In a similar vein, Layder writes of actors that 'trust must be made socially visible.' Structure, Interaction and Social Theory, p. 121.

[70] I am indebted to Paul Rock for this point.

[71] A. Schutz, Phenomenology and the Social World, p. 61.

[72] See C. Williams, Theatres and Audiences.

[73] Similarly, the Gulbenkian Foundation reported: "We do not see any case for standardising existing courses at drama schools, but we believe that there should be more opportunities for drama students to work in the television, radio or film studio situation during their training. We believe that major employers such as television have a responsibility to contribute to the training process." 'Going on Stage', p.75.

[74] George Cuttingham, quoted in S. Fife, 'No Place to be Somebody - Acting Schools: Only the Strong Survive', p. 39.

[75] E. Shils, 'The High Culture of the Age', pp. 328-9.

[76] L. Taylor and K. Williams, 'The Actor and His World', p. 189.

[77] Ibid.

[78] Ibid.

[79] S. Hood, A Survey of Television, p. 133.

[80] For example, an examination of the Radio Times, TV Times and The Times indicated that 61 theatrical productions ran in

London during one week in April, 1978, as compared with 39 British-produced TV dramas screened on all three channels in the London region for a similar period. This may appear to contradict my contention; however, (1) TV provides work opportunities for a greater number of actors since the engagements are of shorter duration. The absence of constraints of the physical stage and the frequent use of natural settings makes for a greater number of work opportunities on any one TV production as compared with theatre; and (2) actors employed in a TV production tend to receive a higher rate of pay than they would for comparable roles in theatre, as well as receiving 'repeat fees' when programmes are shown again (without having to do any further work). I am indebted to David Downes for these ideas.

[81] S. Hood, A Survey of Television, pp. 134-5.

[82] See C. Swift, The Job of Acting, p. 73.

[83] M. Lauritzen, Jane Austen's "Emma" on Television, p. 31.

[84] C. Swift, The Job of Acting, p. 76.

[85] Ibid., p. 89.

[86] I am indebted to Paul Rock for this idea.

[87] However, I do not wish to suggest that all theatre work is satisfying! See L. Taylor and K. Williams, 'The Actor and His World'.

[88] C. Swift, The Job of Acting, pp. 85-6.

[89] F. Baker (ed.), Movie People, p. 109.

[90] C. Swift, The Job of Acting, p. 77.

3 The socialisation of the actor

The learning of any role entails a process of socialisation; the individual comes to adopt those skills and values which indicate appropriate role performance to significant others. This transformation of identity is sometimes fostered by a formal training programme and always depends on the influence exerted by interaction on self-conception. Dramatic actors usually begin their careers in a formal training programme and go on to participate in various semiprofessional and professional activities which effectively continue this socialisation process. Whether or not their professional engagements are prestigious, rewarding and career enhancing - in their estimation and others' - they will come to see themselves as professionals of a certain standing (failed, aspiring, middle range or highly successful). Those who remain committed to their occupational role despite the absence of expected rewards demonstrate the triumph of socialisation over circumstances.

In this chapter, I want to place the data of the preceding case studies within the broader conceptual framework of studies in socialisation.

The literature on adult socialisation rarely addresses general issues [1], tending instead to examine the problem of socialisation into particular occupations. The relevance of these studies to the case of the dramatic actor is questionable, since the socialisation of actors, I would argue, has more in common with the extreme socialisation of, for example, religious converts than with the ordinary secondary socialisation of, for example, nurses.

A specific programme of socialisation can be considered to fall somewhere along a continuum from minimal to maximal alteration of self-identity. At the minimal end, objective job related skills will be required, while at the maximal end the occupational skills will largely consist of interpersonal or otherwise self-involving skills.

An example of an occupation at the minimal end of the continuum would be the bank clerk, well described by Natanson in his essay, 'Anonymity and Recognition':

the self may be bracketed off from the role-taking so that the agent is out of touch with the person. Action then becomes automatic: the bank clerk greets his depositor, takes his deposit, goes through the movements of counting, stamping, arranging, clipping, banding, etc., and dismisses the customer with a receipt-thank you. The next one in line gets similar treatment, and so do all the rest. Routine role activity of this variety may be relieved by a variety of factors, but the ultimate extension of such role-playing is the stasis of consciousness [2].

Given the requirements of the job itself, the bank clerk's socialisation may consist of no more than several weeks' basic training about facts and procedures (although informal socialisation into the role will obviously be a gradual process).

The nurse's job occupies a position further along the continuum toward the maximal self-involvement pole. Though consisting of objective skills, the job also requires interpersonal involvement and a reorganisation of typical self-other relations including a restructuring of norms of commitment to strangers. Still further along the continuum one would find the actor. A comparison between the socialisation of nurses and actors will demonstrate the inadequacy of such occupational studies to an understanding of the actor. While acting and nursing are obviously worlds apart, the comparison is instructive if only to highlight the differences.

In their study of nurses' training, Oleson and Whittaker state that the 'single most prominent theme' of nurses' socialisation is that of 'emergent self awareness' [3]. This is fostered not only by the natural, interactional stuff of training but also by group dynamics classes which serve as a stimulus to 'enforced self examination' [4]. It is worth noting that no parallel of explicit 'introspective instruction' existed for the trainee actors I studied. In fact, they were not even encouraged to develop an objective identification with the occupation through a programme of reading and discussion about techniques of acting or the history of theatre [5]. Given the differences in course content and consequent activities of the nurse and the actor, it is clear that the actor does not need enforced self-examination as does the nurse. As one Drama School student said:

> It's like living in a mirror ... all the time, people giving you information, information, information about yourself, not about your external being but about me, inside, cut up, in the different parts you might play.

The process of acting brings actors closer to themselves than any deliberate instruction might do. Contained in the ideology of the occupation is the notion that 'thinking too much' can prevent the actor from responding spontaneously and convincingly in the dramatic situation. For the actor, self-awareness is achieved experientially, not cognitively.

The advanced student nurse, according to Oleson and Whittaker, takes 'identity risks' in order to become 'more' of a nurse:

> the wish or need to place oneself in new identity predicaments is partly a product of successful integration in socialization. Levels of integration already acquired in assuming the identity of a nurse appear to generate a wish to expand these boundaries of identity still further and become even more of a nurse.[6]

If actors take risks and continually invite 'identity predicaments', they do so because this is the very stuff of the job, and therefore qualitatively different from the nurses' risk-taking. Nurses may strive to deepen their identification with the same role, but the actor cannot become more of an actor by increasing involvement with the same identity; one can only become more of an actor by taking on diverse dramatic identities [7]. The model of the nurse's subjective socialisation task, as in most other occupations, is a convergent one in which the trainee focuses in on the occupational role; the actor's is a divergent one in which attention is continually diffracted to various roles, albeit on a dramatic level.

This difference between the actor and nurse roles is also evident in the nature of student-teacher relationships in the two programmes. In nursing, teachers'

> evaluations appear to be based on the ideological premise that a student's errors of identity and performance must be pointed out to her, but in such a manner that she is not subjected to undue psychological stress[8]

- 122 -

whereas in drama school, incisive evaluations of self and performance are considered justified. This reflects the differential status of identity in the two occupations: it is merely an aspect of the nursing role, but the fundamental core of the acting role [9].

Although newcomers to various occupations undergo 'doctrinal conversion'[10] - exchanging lay views for professional ones - in the case of the actor, the lay view is particularly entrenched. Via its consumption of mass media drama which sometimes includes dramatisations of actors and acting, the public is bombarded by typifications of the occupation, acquiring a false familiarity with it. The intending actor, as a member of the public, is susceptible to these images and must exchange them for the professional view in drama school. Such exchanges may vary in intensity, as McHugh notes in his definition of radical change:

> Radical change will be treated as the substitution of one set of value orientations for another. Here we make the usual distinction between specific norms of low generality and overarching values of high generality.[11]

Most studies in occupational socialisation provide inadequate models for the understanding of dramatic actors because the former are instances of ordinary secondary socialisation while the latter is a case of radical resocialisation. The study of the Drama School described the ways in which initiates came to abandon their most fundamental values regarding the relationship between self, body and others. Therefore, in order to place the socialisation of the actor within its proper conceptual context, we must examine non-occupational studies of adult socialisation.

Conversion is a term which is used to describe the radical resocialisation undergone by some religious adherents, brainwashed prisoners of war and clients of various schools and systems of psychotherapy. Sarbin and Adler[12] traced the similarities between these different kinds of conversion; it will be clear to the reader that their findings are largely applicable to the case of the dramatic actor. For example, they found that:

> The need for the active induction of stress, of directed organismic involvement, is a central factor in all the systems we have reviewed. ... Such acts as staring, closing the eyes, praying, speaking in tongues, repeating sentences monotonously, singing, chanting, dancing, jumping, regulating the breath, and other methods are used in the various systems to limit the convert's span of attention and enhance his concentration on the objects, goals and means of conversion.[13]

This parallels some of the techniques employed in the training of actors. The conversion of 'the self as a social identity'[14] is common to each form of conversion regardless of ideological or behavioural goals:

> The individual not only changes overt behaviour to meet role expectations and demands, but in the process his conception of self becomes modified.[15]

This process generally consists of three stages:

> (1) a physical and/or psychological assault; a developing confusion about self and other beliefs ... (2) surrender and despair (becoming a non-person), and (3) a working through, active mastery, reeducation or adaptation process ... We have found the forms of the process to be constant, though the metaphors vary to meet the needs and values of groups or individuals.[16]

Drama students were shown to pass through these stages. Training began with extreme and usually unfamiliar physical exertion followed by the midpoint crisis which students referred to as the teachers' attempt to 'break them down'. Finally, in the advanced terms, they achieved the active mastery of their craft and conception of themselves as actors.

Conversion is often accomplished in a setting which Goffman has called the 'total institution' [17]. He writes:

> The central feature of total institutions can be described as a breakdown of the barriers ordinarily separating these three spheres of life [work, play and sleep]. First, all aspects of life are conducted in the same place and under the same single authority. Second, each phase of the member's daily activity is carried on in the immediate company of a large number of others, all of whom are treated alike and required to do the same thing together. Third, all phases of the day's activities are tightly scheduled, with one activity leading at a prearranged time into the next, and the whole sequence of activities being imposed from above through a system of explicit formal rulings and by a body of officials.[18]

Can we legitimately describe the drama school as an institution which controls all spheres of the trainee's life? Although the student does not sleep at the drama school, the intensive programme of training often excludes social contact with non-students to a greater extent than is found in other training programmes. The student is likely to be physically present at the school from morning to night, attending classes, rehearsing and performing.

Leisure time will be spent in the company of other students and one is very likely to share accommodation with members of the same group. It is rare for a drama student to live at home with family while attending drama school, the most obvious reason for this being that the students selected are often from distant localities. The isolation of the student from familiar influences lends an intensity to the training experience. Similarly, whatever reasons may be offered for the reluctance to admit older students to the training programme (for example, the greater 'trainability' of the young), it is clear that their more extensive outside experience and current external social networks might exert a 'contaminating' influence on the other trainees; their very presence could legitimate alternative social worlds and introduce relativism into the absolutism of the socialisation process. The selected drama student tends to be fairly young, from the provinces, rooming with other drama students, and thereby subject only to the influences of the socialising agents. Thus, while the metaphor of the total institution may be stretched slightly in the specific sense of physical setting, the social relationships and time allocations engendered by the programme make it a useful tool.

Conversion is always conversion to something - and for the actor, it is a way of being in the world characterised by objectification: objectification of the self and body in training, objectification of personality on the dramatic level of character construction, and ultimately objectification of other real persons by the actor in the real world. In everyday life, we tend to perceive ourselves or others as objects only when interaction fails to run smoothly. We momentarily suspend our usual, unreflective stance in order to analyse the qualities and motives of self and others in somewhat impersonal terms. Such objectification does not ordinarily pervade our relationship to the external world. The case of the actor is distinctive in that, from training through to professional life, one's experiences have this objectifying quality in diverse and reinforcing ways. For the actor, objectification is the rule rather than the exception.

OBJECTIFICATION OF THE BODY

Objects are human constructs[19] and are not defined or reacted to in the same way by all people. The body, for example, is a different object for the fashion model, the black in a white society, the manual labourer and the sportsperson. The different qualities of attractiveness, colour, strength and skill both emerge from and help to form our particular relations to the social world. In this sense, the body exists as a different object for the actor before, during and after training. Changes in body use or awareness simultaneously produce changes in self-concept, as Manning and Fabrega note:

Minimal requirements for a social analysis of the body are an appreciation of the following factors: ... the self is the means by which bodily states ... alter the self-concept; ... perceived connectedness of self and body, of being and doing, are problematic; alterations in their relationships can affect social conduct ...[20]

Drama students learn to view their bodies as objects which can be manipulated to produce different effects; they acquire skills of flexibility, applications of the body to different ends (characterisation), and, while doing so, learn to perceive the body differently. A voice teacher at the Drama School described the way this aspect of body use, which is usually taken for granted, becomes an object of awareness and reflection within the training programme:

Each person has his own tape, all the time they're here, and they keep this one tape throughout their history so they can refer back to the way they started and see that at least they're getting better, or whether they think their personality is really disappearing under our treatment or whether it's blossoming.

Drama students learn to direct their own actions with a control which the non-actor would find strange (unless one were model, athlete, or the like) and students may have difficulty effecting this passage from one status (non-actor) to the other (actor). Once achieved, however, this new relation of body to self makes more real and immediate the world of theatre which requires it; as Berger writes:

The same process of socialization generates the self and internalizes the world to which this self belongs.[21]

What does this world of theatre require? Most importantly, the actor must learn to take on dramatic roles. Tiryakian's comments on the consequences of objectification of the body for the self give us a clue to its efficacy for later characterisation work:

To view the body as an object is to introduce a scissure in the primary, incarnate ontological unity of the self. It leads to what Laing has aptly termed the 'schizoid' state, which is a crucial separation of psyche from body at the level of subjective experience.[22]

Without wishing to imply that acting either reflects or induces any form of mental illness, I should note that this parallel is drawn explicitly and implicitly throughout the literature of both theatre and psychology. More important for my purposes here is the fact

that this 'separation of psyche from body' is necessary because the
actor's job is to assume strange roles with a degree of
identification not required of practitioners of other occupations.
By perceiving the body as an object alienated from the self, the
actor is able to alter its use in the service of dramatic
characterisations. The various relations of self to character will
be discussed more fully later. At present I wish to explore the
varieties of objectification in the actor's experience.

OBJECTIFICATION OF OTHERS

One may not only objectify one's body, but also other people; these
others may be real people or characters:

> Objectification also involves interpreting others as if their
> activities were determined by single attributes. Thus, to
> account for the total activity of someone by saying this stems
> from his "bourgeois background" or his "anal-compulsive"
> character is to objectify that being.[23]

The above quotation highlights one of the ways in which
objectification occurs in everyday life. This brand of character
analysis is also resorted to when actors discuss the meaning of a
play and motives for characters' actions. It can be transposed to
the everyday world in such a way that the actor comes to view real
people as similarly 'condensed' in their attributes or motives. The
actor's familiarity with a number of social worlds, attained
through attention to dramatic scripts, objectifies these worlds and
their inhabitants, as one member of the TV Group described:

> You deal with different topics every day, which has to broaden
> you in some way - sometimes they broaden you but they don't
> give you any knowledge - it's very vague. You go into all sorts
> of topics, abortion or homeless families, but it's a surface
> level kind of knowledge.

This vague attention to diverse social worlds can effectively blur
the distinction between real and dramatic experience to the point
where one actor commented that his brother, who at different points
in his life had been a military man, clergyman and insurance
salesman, 'could have done all that by being an actor'.

Objectification of others may be fostered by the drama school
experience. First, training at an early age facilitates radical
resocialisation [24]; it may also further the objectification
process itself. One actor, recalling her drama school days, spoke
of a student who had been in the merchant navy before coming to
drama school. This particular student disagreed with some of the

teachings offered because, according to the interviewee, 'They'd say at drama school, "people behave in a certain way", and he knew it wasn't like that'. Thus, early training can implant an objectified worldview in the aspiring actor, facilitating the process of objectification at its many levels.

Secondly, drama school engenders such a high degree of physical and interactional closeness that the students develop a more subtle means of constructing privacy and maintaining distance. A 2nd termer said:

> Here, the way the situation works, you don't particularly need close friends, because everyone's so friendly

while a 4th termer, immersed in the midpoint crisis, made a similar comment while significantly omitting to mention lack of need:

> It's funny, you don't really get too close to many people - you're friendly.

This distance from fellow workers, learned in drama school, is functional for later occupational life in which the freelance nature of the occupation will make for ever changing work groups. In George C. Scott's words:

> You meet a number of interesting, sad people in this business. There's a tinge of melancholy about the whole damn thing. People come together, they're very close, very intimate for a specified period of time. Then they all drift away.[25]

OBJECTIFICATION OF SELF

Given the reciprocal nature of interaction, we can see that the objectification of one's body for the purpose of acting and the consequent overlap of objectification of real and dramatic persons can lead to an objectification of the self. One's own self comes to be viewed as an object capable of manipulation and direction for various ends. The organisation of the occupation may require this alienated stance towards the self [26]; the individual actor charts an unsteady course through an occupational world characterised by chance, uncertainty, and a low level of structure. In day to day interactions with actors, directors and agents, the actor becomes a public relations figure on his or her own behalf and must always be concerned to appear in a favourable light. The actor must employ a perspective of self as object when considering the relative career potential of employment options and more informal interpersonal encounters (for example, attending a fellow actor's opening night performance on the offchance of a fortuitous introduction to an influential casting agent) [27].

Self-objectification is evident in the trainee's renunciation of familiar markers of identity. One of the most important losses is the loss of one's name [28]; in some total institutional contexts (such as prison or the military) the name is replaced by a number. What is the significance of name loss in the case of the actor? The drama student's 'name' is an ever changing one, consisting of a character name for the duration of any production; this assumption of strange names continues throughout professional life. The student on the verge of professional life who finds that the actors' union already contains an actor of the same name must choose another (real) name [29]. Finally, it is interesting to view the quest for fame as a means of recapturing the significance of one's own (as opposed to character) name. This is implied in many phrases which signify the achievement of fame in various fields: 'making a name for oneself', 'becoming a name', 'becoming a household word'. Ironically, if the actor achieves this status, it may be through an inescapable association with a memorable performance as a particular character (dramatic name). Failure to disengage one's own name from this character's in the public mind can make the achievement of fame a Pyrrhic victory.

The loss of importance of one's own name and the various objectifying experiences which are the actor's all contribute to the self-conscious adoption of a fluid identity. When asked to do so in interviews, actors were reluctant (or unable) to describe themselves in specific terms. One actor, when asked at the close of an interview, whether he had anything further to say, remarked:

No, I think if you want to know about me, I like to think, you have to look at what I do in my work, really - I'm not a chatterer.

If, as Tiryakian asserts:

subjectivity is ... manifested in one's words: I am what I say [and] the existential self as an integral whole of body and psyche also manifests itself in nonverbal gestures[30]

then the effect of dramatic performance on the actor's sense of self is clear. Actors spend a good deal of their time authenticating the existence of dramatic others, or at least seek to through consistent employment. Although, as I will show, the unstable structure of the occupation tends to contribute to a heightened awareness of occupational self, acting may produce a diminished capacity to verbally elaborate upon one's own self-conception.

Of course, given the actor's impression management skills, a vague self-concept may not be a consequence of dramatic performance, but rather a consciously presented defence against the public's insatiable curiosity or a consciously chosen means of sustaining the public's interest. Jack Nicholson has been quoted as saying:

> every single article, interview, is always trying to be definitive and I've talked to a lot of people and managed to keep from being definitive. I think people are - and actors should be - hard to pin down.[31]

Jack Nicholson is an example of an actor who, without formal training, has acquired the appropriate professional persona. Such deviations from the normal socialisation process will be discussed below.

DEVIATIONS FROM THE NORMAL SOCIALISATION PROCESS

Given that professional qualifications are not required for participation in the occupation, it is clear that some professional actors never undergo the formal socialisation process described here. Unfortunately, the data collected for this study do not permit description of the variations in occupational identity which one might posit for this group since all but two of the actors interviewed were trained in accredited academies. However, the transformation of self continually referred to here is intended in a dynamic sense. As a consequence of the actions performed by the person, one continually revises one's self-concept which then manifests itself in a redirected choice of actions. The untrained actor, performing many of the same activities as the trained one, can be expected to undergo a good deal of the same self-impinging experience.

When I use the concept of self to describe drama school socialisation, I do not have in mind a vessel which is emptied of a familiar liquid and replaced by another 'new self' substance, but rather a process comprising the continual flow of experience, interpretation and action carried out by a conscious agent. Thus the drama school experience is crucial to the formation of actors' occupational identities insofar as graduates subjectively interpret their training as a meaningful accomplishment. It may seem to them to be a soul-searing battle in which they have emerged victorious over their teachers; alternatively, they may feel that the completion of the course has proved their perseverance and so their worthiness of professional status. The symbolic significance of the training may be more beneficial than the objective experience acquired. Eric Bentley's remarks about Stanislavskian technical exercises could as easily be true of training in general:

For what has happened is that theatre people have been invoking
scientific terminology for the sake of its authoritative sound
on the assumption that anything with a scientific name must
have a scientific basis. Once we see through this fallacy, we
realize that 'exercises' given to actors may not actually do
the work they are supposed to do.   But this is not to say that
they have no value. By way of an analogy, take prayer. There
may not be a God sitting Up There listening to it, but that is
not to say that the person praying feels no better for it.[32]

Thus, it is not surprising that many of the students interviewed
valued above all the confidence that training had given them. A
professional actor,   Cheryl Kennedy, similarly noted that 'as a
result of missing that training, I lack experience and confidence'
[33].

While some actors never receive formal training, others start a
course but fail to complete it.   In studying any particular
socialisation programme, it is useful to examine the student
mortality rate as an indicator of failure on the part of the
socialising agents or, conversely, failure of the trainees to adapt
to the programme's demands.   One surveyor of British drama schools
writes:

If you get into drama school (roughly one in 10 applications is
successful),   and succeed in getting a grant, then you'll
probably stay the course. Only two schools deliberately take on
more students than they expect to see through;   [one] whose
present final year contains half the people who originally
started, and [another] who once asked as many as half of their
second year to leave at the same time - but they point out that
all but three got jobs afterwards.[34]

What accounts for the low drop out rate in most drama schools?
It might be the auditioners' perspicacious selection of only those
students 'strong enough' to withstand the training, though if this
were the major factor we could reasonably expect a greater degree
of error than occurs. The trainee's experience during training is
more likely to influence the low drop out rate than is any presumed
omniscience on the part of the teachers. Radical resocialisation in
a near total institutional setting and the belief that acting
requires dedication (extreme commitment) probably combine to
influence the student's evaluation of possible choices of action
(to stay or not to stay).

Dornbusch, referring to military socialisation, writes that:
Every cadet who voluntarily resigns is a threat to the morale
of the cadet corps, since he has rejected the values of the
Academy.[35]

- 131 -

In the span of four entering classes in the Drama School (about 80 students), one left the programme for personal reasons and two left to take up professional work [36]. The case of these two is interesting, in that the early leaver who takes up professional work is not viewed as rejecting the values of the institution. Were the students to leave before the turning point of conversion, their departure would probably be defined as an inability to cope with the training programme. If the departure occurs after this point, it is viewed as a mark of the institution's success.

Hearn, et al., commenting on the mortality rate in the socialisation of American drama students, say:

> The faculty agree that the typically high freshman mortality rate is inevitable ... There is no formal policy of rejection; the students are simply allowed to drop their theatre courses.[37]

Contrasting this with the case of British drama schools it becomes evident that the modes of selection and retention of students in Britain and America appear to reflect the more general divergence in educational systems characterised by Turner's 'norms of sponsored and contest mobility' [38]. The British system of sponsored mobility represents the case where one is given the privilege of training; the American training for theatre follows the contest model in which easy entry to the system is countered by difficulty in reaching completion. The American trainees, by virtue of insufficient motivation, encouragement and/or talent, gradually slip away or are 'weeded out' as the authors explain:

> In play production students learn the "dirty work" of the profession. They are made to perform various cleaning jobs. It is essential to staging a production but it is also a mechanism for weeding out the less talented or motivated who must do "dirty work" while others are on stage.[39]

The strict separation of acting from stage management courses at the Drama School is what we would expect in the case of sponsored trainees. The case of the two drama schools which admit a larger intake than they expect to graduate does not contradict the assertion that the British system follows the sponsored mobility model, since the weeding out of students is conducted by those in authority. However, one may view these two schools as representing a mixture of sponsored and contest models; the contest ethic applies until a specified point, after which the second wave of selection takes place and the remaining trainees are treated as a sponsored elite.

Also responsible for the differences in the training systems is the differential value accorded the institution of theatre in the two societies. Manning and Hearn describe the situation in America:

> Americans view acting with ambivalence, uncertainty surrounds the evaluation of performance and competence, the theatre is notably subject to fashions and fads in actors and actresses (linked to current "hot" production modes), and commercialism dominates theatre operations.[40]

The authors later conclude that the:

> training context in microcasm (sic) reproduces some of the problems inherent in the artistic career in a capitalistic society .[41]

The awareness in Britain of its theatre as an internationally acclaimed cultural asset (and thus both a source of national pride and income) partly accounts for the fact that in some ways the training system conforms more to Manning and Hearn's ideal type of traditional professions than that of the arts [42]. Most notably, the closed entry criteria, low dropout rate and high cost of training (given the low British student/staff ratio) which are cited as characteristic of professions approximates the British training situation.

In America, Manning and Hearn note:

> Sponsorship is an important feature of the internal training situation ... but it works very weakly from the collegiate programmes to the larger occupational sphere.[43]

As I have already noted, sponsorship plays an important part in the British system; the Drama School often acted as an informal placement agency with the principal liaising between casting directors and senior students or graduates. In addition, the practice of hiring outside (professional) directors to direct senior productions provided potential work contacts for students and widened the pool of sponsors. That a system of sponsorship operated was clear from the principal's remark that, although not supported by national statistics on actors' employment, almost all the students from his institution would find their first jobs within three to six months of completing the course. In other words, the informal and formal advantages of training in a prestigious institution produced an elite cohort of graduates who would escape the dismal fate of the national pool of chronically unemployed actors.

CAREER AND COMMITMENT

Earlier I argued that the student's interpretation of the training may outweigh any objective value it has. In a similar way, the professional's subjective assessment of the jobs acquired rather than their 'objective relevance' may influence the actor's career.

This view is supported by Stebbins' writings on the <u>subjective career</u> and I begin with his definition of the various components of career:

> subjective career is the individual's view of certain career-related occurrences in his life. It is distinguished from two other components of the general idea of career: career as a series of stages (career line or career pattern) and career as progress of an individual through these stages from the observer's standpoint ("individual-objective career").[44]

Stebbins finds the concept of subjective career:

> instructive whenever one can find a consensually recognized course of movement through a series of stages with relatively clear beginning and end points...[45]

Clearly, in the case of careers pursued within organisations or that of the lone professional who possesses formal qualifications and recognised membership in a professional community, the notion of subjective career can be seen against the backdrop of a more objective one. Equally obvious is the fact that in the case of the dramatic actor - a <u>non</u>-professional freelancer - this objective career line is almost wholly lacking. There is a course of action which an actor can take in the hope that it will constitute a gradual and orderly development; this path consists of formal training, the professional apprenticeship of regional repertory, followed by a return to London in which a combination of fringe theatre and small TV or professional theatre roles leads to more important professional roles and a fairly steady influx of such roles, if not fame and fortune. Yet, the <u>actual</u> paths travelled by those who do reach the top demonstrate that none of these activities is a necessary or sufficient condition of success; these particular individuals' career paths may deviate so markedly from this pattern that it is a pattern in only the weakest sense [46].

Thus, where the practitioner of an occupation which contains an objective component may, according to Stebbins, have the subjective career activated by the experience of 'falling behind one's reference group' [47], the actor is continually subject to bouts of 'retrospection and prospection'[48] as a sense of career movement is achieved by evaluating the importance of various jobs to:

his own goals, abilities, biography, and self-conception - in short, to his own personality.[49]

Stebbins writes that:

> the concept of subjective career is frequently an essential element in the social psychological explanation of role conflict reduction ... Role conflict is defined by Gross et al. ... as "any situation in which the incumbent of a focal position perceives that he is confronted with incompatible expectations". Such conflict may be seen by the person as existing within a single social identity or between two or more of his identities.[50]

Unless the dramatic actor achieves fame (by which I mean the power to choose jobs as opposed to being chosen for them) [51], this role conflict will be experienced even if one is regularly employed. Conflict stems from the difficulty for all but the famous of realising simultaneously the occupational values of financial success and artistic excellence. The same conflict has been observed in jazz musicians and Hollywood studio musicians [52].

An actor may achieve recognition and the power to build a career through the selection of roles which indicate to significant others and to the public that one is a particular 'kind' of actor - but one may lose that power by slipping back into anonymity through the reinforcing effects of an unsuccessful engagement. Similarly, an actor who appears in a production which ostensibly guarantees career advancement by providing temporary objective standing, can find that the problems of securing the occupation's rewards accompany the closing of that show:

> Miss Lopez [of the original cast of A Chorus Line] has also tried television. "It's sort of like Broadway," she said. "If you do it enough, you'll probably land a good show." Last year she did a pilot film that didn't sell. This summer she is doing another pilot film. "I still love the theater," she said, "but you can't make any money in it. If you have a hit on television, then you get the security and freedom to do things like theater".[53]

In a career in which objective standing can be viewed as either nonexistent or subject to extreme fluctuation, both subjective components of career and dramaturgical aspects are activated [54]. The actor must continue to appear to be an actor, especially in the face of frequent spells of unemployment; the unlikelihood of continuous activity within the occupation means that confirmation to self and others of that identity must be sought elsewhere. Thus, while it may be true for all social actors that:

- 135 -

no matter how compelling one's biography may be, it is always reconstructed in a situation where its relevance must be established[55]

it is clearly moreso for the dramatic actor. One of the responsibilities of an informal network of colleagues is to validate the worth of these retrospective and prospective biographies, often with the aid of very little evidence. Unemployed actors need their associates to bolster their occupational identities just as they need them to support their dramatic identities on stage.

The occupational identity of the actor cannot be sustained on the efforts of a sympathetic group of equally needy friends; actors are responsible for presenting themselves favourably to those with the power to give them work. Given the characteristic uncertainty of the occupation - the reliance on chance or absence of clearly defined steps to be taken towards the goal - and given that the very substance of the work is self-presentation, non-dramatic impression management is given extraordinary weight in making sense of career outcomes. This is clear from the following quotes which stress the importance of confidence and of arrogance (which apparently refers to claims to occupational identity in the face of poor odds):

> Good teachers (at the pre-Drama School stage) do very little for their pupils except open their eyes to the possibility of what the word self-expression means. They will try to instil self-confidence (that king-pin of the actor's life) ...[56]

> I don't know whether I have the energy I had then, but I hope I've still got that confidence, arrogance and cheek. They're wonderful qualities for an actress.[57]

> If an actor really works at his craft, really does his homework and thinks of himself as something special and that nobody can do it better, with those kinds of attitudes and a kind of personal arrogance, he will be pulled out of the barrel. Whatever it is that I radiate, it seems to be appealing to somebody.[58]

> And this is all explained with enthusiasm, conviction, and charm so you can't help but say at one point: "You're a cocky bugger, aren't you Albert?"
> "Of course," he says, not gravely but not without consideration, "but correctly arrogant".[59]

Self-presentation is also important in work settings. Actors must indicate the proper degree of enthusiasm; they must express commitment to the production without displaying a desperation for work. They must indicate that they possess the calm, professional attitude which denotes the insider's stance. As a journalist observed of the actors in a major television serial:

> At the beginning I had half expected to witness shows of some sort of temperament, even scenes. By now I realised how professional the entire unit was. They were doing their job, turning up on time, knowing their lines and behaving fairly ordinarily. They held conversations at lunchtime and didn't talk in anecdotes.[60]

The actors involved in the much publicised and prestigious serial referred to above (The Glittering Prizes) have achieved a degree of power insofar as they manage to secure the financial rewards which television offers while combining these with artistic challenge - a relative rarity in TV. Thus, their lunchtime conversations may not have focused on legitimating their participation as did those of the actors in the fringe and TV productions I observed. Throughout their careers, actors must coordinate their subjective conceptions of self with participation in the working world, and these influence each other in an endless series of modifications of self-concept and consideration of work options. It is by no means only the star who rejects certain offers of work in an attempt to sustain a particular occupational identity [61]; rather, it is only the star who can do so without incurring major loss. Fringe and TV drama usually lack financial and characterisation rewards, respectively, and lend themselves to collective appraisal of the consequences of this work for career and identity. The continuing socialisation of the professional actor is conducted during these lunchtime conversations, and:

> Because the solutions the group reaches have, for the individual being socialized, the character of "what everyone knows to be true," he tends to accept them.[62]

In fringe theatre, this can take the form of a collective appreciation of the freedom of fringe from the constraints of large scale professional productions (union rulings may both protect and constrain); in TV, the relative merits of mass exposure and generous financial reward are offered up for group endorsement as the reasons which 'everybody knows' counterbalance the lack of artistic merit and individual satisfaction of character construction. Yet, the fact that these conversations are so frequent and emotionally charged points to the distress involved in the role conflict which accompanies such activity. The fact that actors subject themselves to this discomfort is itself a mark of their commitment to the occupation.

Young actors leave drama school with little indication of the final ranking they will achieve in the professional world, and despite the difficulties involved in fixing an objective ranking for any acting career [63], we can nevertheless distinguish three broad occupational tracks: (1) those actors who hardly ever find work (while still considering themselves to be actors 'waiting for a break'); (2) those who are fairly steadily employed though unknown as 'name' actors to the public; and (3) the group of well known actors or stars who work not only continuously, but selectively [64]. The uncertain status of the beginning professional can effectively continue for the first five or ten years of one's career; as one actor in the Theatre Company with six years of professional experience remarked:

> If I knew where I was going, I think I'd get there. The
> debilitating factor is not knowing. At the moment, I'm simply
> affected by fate.

The experience of TV work and more prestigious theatrical engagements enabled a young member of the TV cast to formulate his feelings of uncertainty more coherently:

> I guess my ambitions are, when I'm being ambitious, to be a
> great actor, a famous actor, a rich actor – but then the next
> day, I don't want to be an actor at all. In some ways, acting
> supplies everything and in some ways it supplies nothing ... I
> think it's me - I think, maybe I won't become a great actor, or
> a rich or successful actor – Can I be an actor who's just -
> working? Probably I'd find out I could. I think that has
> something to do with age; the burning that comes from youth
> eventually levels out.

Here we are given an indication that the actor constructs a subjective placement against the backdrop of these broad occupational tracks or rankings. It is such a ranking which enabled a middle aged actor in the TV cast to place himself at the 'middling level' of the occupation.

The peculiarities of the occupation lead actors to fall prey to commitment despite the unfavourable odds of success. The notions of innate talent and dedication required of artists (who may struggle against an 'unsympathetic' and 'ignorant' public), combined with the uncertain relevance of any one job for one's overall career, can foster this commitment which enables the individual to:

> engage in a variety of disparate acts [and still see] them as
> essentially consistent; from his point of view they serve him
> in pursuit of the same goal.[65]

Commitment can also lead one to participate in activities which are not intrinsically satisfying. A 28 year old member of the Theatre Company said:

> When you start, you do it for the fun. When you're doing it all the time, there's not that much novelty, you're not just doing it for the fun, you've got work to do.

Whereas the younger actor realises that one has 'work to do', the comments of an older actor (aged 40) indicate that one's career can become a social object towards which one's actions are oriented:

> I am beginning to think in terms of furthering my career - I'm beginning to not only think, is this going to be a nice job?, but, will it further my career? One does tend to think this way when you get to my age.

Commitment to an occupation means that the individual views that work as the means of realising other life plans, as another TV actor explained:

> For people in their forties, [acting] isn't as much fun because the first flush of enthusiasm has worn off, and certain financial obligations have to be met.

Thus, the pressures toward commitment are cumulative. Initially, participation in discrete activities is symbolised in career terms and one continues because this is one's career; the personal investment in a career usually means that any alternative career plans are neglected, increasing the importance of success in (and so commitment to) the chosen one; and, one's occupation tends to become the linchpin for other life plans, such that career, financial and family obligations form an interlocking web of commitment.

In the case of the actor, commitment not only ensures continued activity within the occupation; it also justifies the non-activity of long stretches of unemployment. Commitment enables the person to view these periods as the normal void between an actor's jobs rather than as a sign that one's career is becoming a thing of the past. Commitment has been expressed in interviews with several actors in more or less the same terms as the one who told me:

> I thought I would give myself a certain time and if I hadn't made it, I would give up. But now I know I won't give it up.

NOTES:

[1] See W. Sewell, 'Some Recent Developments in Socialization Theory and Research', p. 578; and J. Mortimer and R. Simmons, 'Adult Socialization', p. 421.

[2] M. Natanson, Phenomenology, Role and Reason, p. 166.

[3] V. Oleson and E. Whittaker, The Silent Dialogue, p. 282.

[4] Ibid., p. 285.

[5] This was true during the term in which I did my field work - but possibly different during past or future terms.

[6] V. Oleson and E. Whittaker, The Silent Dialogue, p. 275.

[7] See P. Manning and H. Hearn, 'Acting: Selves, Careers and the Social Organization of the Occupation', pp. 18-19.

[8] V. Oleson and E. Whittaker, The Silent Dialogue, p.275.

[9] See P. Manning and H. Hearn, 'Acting', p. 13.

[10] F. Davis, "Professional Socialization as Subjective Experience: The Process of Doctrinal Conversion Among Student Nurses".

[11] P. McHugh, 'Social Disintegration as a Requisite of Resocialization', p.356.

[12] See T. Sarbin and N. Adler, 'Self-Reconstitution Processes'.

[13] Ibid., pp. 608, 612.

[14] Ibid., p. 610.

[15] Ibid.

[16] Ibid., pp. 614-15.

[17] E. Goffman, 'On the Characteristics of Total Institutions: The Inmate World'.

[18] Ibid., p. 17.

[19] See K. Plummer, Sexual Stigma, p. 11.

[20] P. Manning and H. Fabrega, Jr., 'The Experience of Self and Body: Health and Illness in the Chiapas Highlands', pp. 256-7.

[21] P. Berger, Invitation to Sociology, p. 112.

[22] E. Tiryakian, 'The Existential Self and the Person', p. 79.

[23] Ibid., p. 78.

[24] See J. Allison, 'Religious Conversion: Regression and Progression in Adolescent Experience', p. 23.

[25] G. Perry, 'The Hindenberg Rises Again', p. 41.

[26] See D. Layder, 'Social Interaction and Occupational Organization: The Case of Acting'.

[27] While Layder sees the agent as somewhat protecting the actor from objectification, he also says that actors are subjected to continual evaluation in informal and formal settings. Structure, Interaction and Social Theory, p. 124.

[28] See E. Goffman, 'On the Characteristics of Total Institutions', p. 26.

[29] See A. Weigert, Sociology of Everyday Life, pp. 159-60; and D. Drury and J. McCarthy, 'The Social Psychology of Name Change: Reflections on a Serendipitous Discovery', for an exchange perspective on name change.

[30] E. Tiryakian, 'The Existential Self and the Person', pp. 80, 81.

[31] D. Pirie and C. Petit, 'One Flew Over the Cukoo's Nest', p. 15.

[32] E. Bentley, 'Emotional Memory', pp. 277-8.

[33] T. Sutcliffe, interview with Cheryl Kennedy.

[34] J. Hiley, '"Super! We'll Be in Touch!"', p. 14.

[35] S. Dornbusch, 'The Military Academy as an Assimilating Institution', p. 321.

[36] As far as could be gathered through informal contact with the students after the formal period of field work had ended, this was so.

[37] H. Hearn, et al., 'Identity and Institutional Imperatives: The Socialization of the Student Actress', p. 55.

[38] R. Turner, 'Sponsored and Contest Mobility and the School

System'.

[39] H. Hearn, et al., 'Identity and Institutional Imperatives', p. 55.

[40] P. Manning and H. Hearn, 'Acting', p. 6.

[41] Ibid., p. 7.

[42] Ibid., p. 8 Table II.

[43] Ibid., p. 11.

[44] R. Stebbins, 'The Subjective Career as a Basis for Reducing Role Conflict' p. 388.

[45] R. Stebbins, 'Career: The Subjective Approach', p. 43.

[46] See D. Layder, 'Notes on Variations in Middle Class Careers', pp. 167-8.

[47] R. Stebbins, 'Career', p. 36.

[48] Ibid.

[49] Ibid., p. 38.

[50] R. Stebbins, 'The Subjective Career as a Basis for Reducing Role Conflict', pp. 384, 385; N. Gross, quoted in R. Stebbins, ibid., p. 385.

[51] Layder estimates that only 5% of all actors 'can pick and choose work offers and be professionally engaged on a continual basis.' 'Sources and Levels of Commitment in Actors' Careers', pp. 148-9.

[52] See H. Becker, Outsiders, pp. 82-3 and R. Faulkner, Hollywood Studio Musicians, pp. 116ff.

[53] Priscilla Lopez, quoted in B. Carragher, 'Does a Smash Hit Guarantee a Performer's Future?', pp. 1, 18.

[54] See D. Layder, 'Notes on Variations in Middle Class Careers', p. 168.

[55] C. Edgley and R. Turner, 'Masks and Social Relations', p. 8.

[56] C. Swift, The Job of Acting, p 4.

[57] Deborah Norton, quoted in N. Mills, 'Children's Tears', p. 11.

[58] Paul Rudd, quoted in J. Klemesrud, 'Paul Rudd - Every Inch a King', p. 1.

[59] Albert Finney, in interview with S. Fay, p. 5.

[60] J. Bernard, 'A Little Bit of Drama', p. 31.

[61] I am indebted to Derek Layder for this point.

[62] H. Becker, 'Personal Change in Adult Life', p. 47.

[63] D. Layder, 'Notes on Variations in Middle Class Careers', p. 166.

[64] Layder characterises the groups as 'the mass, the outer circle, and the elite.' 'Sources and Levels of Commitment in Actors' Careers', p. 149.

[65] H.Becker, 'Personal Change in Adult Life', pp. 49-50.

4 Acting, life and theatre

This chapter examines some erroneous assumptions made by writers about the relationship between actors and their characters and then moves on to a consideration of the dramaturgical analogy between everyday life and theatre. I shall examine first the commonly held view that actors lose (or find) themselves in their characters and secondly the alternative assumption that they maintain distance from their characters in order to deliberately monitor their performances. It is this second view which is at the root of the dramaturgical analogy according to which life is compared to theatre because everyday actors exercise conscious control over the impressions they make on others, as actors purportedly do vis-a-vis their audiences. If, however, the relationship between actors and characters is not necessarily a choice between these two extremes but is instead more complex and varied, then the dramaturgical analogy itself must be qualified or refined to remain useful. Towards this end I will raise several questions suggested by my research concerning the differences between life and theatre.

THE ACTOR: IN SEARCH OF A SELF?

Henry and Sims' paper entitled, 'Actors' Search for a Self'[1] concerns the identity of the dramatic actor and uses Erikson's notion of the stages of man[2] as its conceptual framework. They begin:

with the assumption that one prominent characteristic of the
professional actor is his failure to develop the identity of
which Erikson speaks. We also hypothesized that one of the
things that sustains the creative life of the actor is his hope
that the repeated portrayal of the lives of others will provide
for him that very identity, the absence of which motivates him
in this search.[3]

The authors felt that these original hypotheses were conclusively
supported by the data they collected. They constructed a semantic
differential identity scale 'composed of 56 pairs of words or
phrases designed to elicit responses relevant to the issue of
identity' [4]. They established the validity of this scale by
means of comparison to an independent measure of identity. Henry
and Sims administered the test to a general population of 'some 500
men and women in substantially different occupations - nurses,
executives, civil servants, schoolteachers, housewives'[5] and, in
comparing these results with those gained by administering the test
to their sample of thirty-two professional actors, they found the
actors to be generally 'more identity diffuse'. They also
conducted lengthy interviews with this sample of professional
actors.

The researchers also requested an unspecified number of actors in
training to describe themselves as honestly as possible, as the
varied occupational sample and professional actors had been asked
to do. They then compared this first set of results of the
trainees to a second set obtained when they asked the same
respondents to describe themselves as they would feel when
rehearsal for a role was going particularly well. The researchers
found that the respondents demonstrated a more cohesive identity
when imagining themselves doing well at work; they write:

> This is not unexpected, perhaps, since anyone might do this
> when things are ideally imagined as going well. And indeed a
> group of junior executives of similar age does the same.
> However, actors change more, and the difference between the
> amount of their change and that of the executives is
> significant.[6]

They then administered the test to the professional cast of a
play, once on the second day of rehearsal and again after three
weeks of rehearsal on the same play. For Henry and Sims:

> Conclusions to be drawn from these two tests are inescapable;
> not only do actors believe that they will possess coherent
> identities under conditions of intense identification with
> their roles, they also bear out their opinions in practice. The
> closer they come to total identification with a role utterly

alien to their habitual, "real" one, the more identity they
seem to possess.[7]

Actually, the authors give no evidence of the 'distance' between
the respondents' characters and the respondents' self-identities;
nor do they mention the problem one would have trying to establish
values for these two nebulous variables. Nevertheless, they
confidently conclude that:

> The real function of [the actor's] work is indeed internal,
> residing in the sense of personal identity it provides.[8]

I do not find Henry and Sims' conclusions ' inescapable', and the
following discussion will demonstrate the shortcomings of their
research.

First, because the authors are misguided by their own theoretical
assumptions, they forfeit the insight which might have been gained
from the junior executives' results. They misinterpret the
statistically significant differences between the two samples as a
theoretically significant confirmation of their hypotheses. I find
nothing strange in the evidence that actors feel a greater personal
stake in the outcome of their endeavours than do junior executives
(or civil servants, nurses, schoolteachers or housewives); I would
expect the actors' evidence to mirror that of other artistic
practitioners or indeed anyone whose work entails a high degree of
personal involvement. This idea finds support in Layder's
statement that:

> the intrinsic nature of performing dramatic roles means that it
> is possible to have levels of involvement in the work
> activity... that are far beyond those possible in more
> conventional occupations.[9]

Moreover, I would expect the study of self-involving occupations to
show that actors do not find their identity in their characters;
rather, their occupational identity is an exceedingly important
part of their identity. Actors might still score higher than these
other self-involved groups because of the precarious nature of
dramatic identities (characters), not because the identity of
'actor' is essentially more precarious. The importance of work to
the worker is brought out in the authors' concluding remarks,
though they confuse the issue by linking it to the concealing
effect which dramatic acting has on the self:

> The interviews with experienced actors more than amply
> documented their own conviction of the vital importance to them
> personally of acting - an importance far outweighing that which
> anyone else might be expected to attach to his means of

livelihood. The words of two famous actors, in interviews in the New Yorker in 1961, testify to the intensity of the need to act:

Ingrid Bergman: "I hate to make an entrance. It is difficult for me to get up on a dance floor, because I feel everybody is watching. But if I played somebody else walking into a restaurant or getting up on a dance floor, I could do it. I couldn't be blamed. It wouldn't be me."

Henry Fonda: "Acting is putting on a mask. The worst torture that can happen to me is not having a mask to get in back of."[10]

Furthermore, Henry and Sims confuse an identity instrument which 'measure[s] quantitative differences'[11] with a theoretical finding of 'more identity' [12]. Their fallacy of misplaced concreteness rests on a static conception of identity, for they view the actor as an empty (or diffuse) vessel which awaits filling by dramatic roles. Allport warns against conceiving of self as a static and 'mysterious central agency'[13] which either directs activity or, according to Henry and Sims, fails to in the case of the actor. The authors would do well to consult Mead for a more dynamic concept of self:

It is a social process of influencing others in a social act and then taking the attitude of the others aroused by the stimulus, and then reacting in turn to this response, which constitutes a self.[14]

Their failure to see that dramatic as well as real selves arise out of interaction enables Henry and Sims to say that:

[The actor] is living someone else's life; he is enacting a role that he did not invent ... [His occupation] demand[s] the portrayal of identities of other people ... who are invented by still different people, the playwright and the director.[15]

In other words, they overestimate the directive power of the scripted aspect of the characterisation and underestimate the scope of responsibility required of the actor in defining the dramatic situation and the characters contained therein.

Henry and Sims imply that characters constitute ever changing identities for the actor, thus failing to realise that socialisation into the occupational role of actor provides its own stable identity. This coherent self-identity is nurtured by colleagues in times of unemployment, when there are no dramatic roles to fill that purportedly empty vessel, more so than is the case for other kinds of workers. Henry and Sims concede the markedly interactional nature of the actor's work but overlook the equally marked importance of informal networks for the maintenance of identity when they state that:

> His rehearsals bring him into a situation where interaction is possibly more crucial than in any other ... And yet this interaction is only periodic – actors presumably learn their parts by themselves [!], and they spend time between roles in an environment where there is no external organization for them whatsoever.[16]

The shortcomings of Henry and Sims' work can be traced to the features of identity diffusion which they ascribe to actors[17] but which in fact emerge from an inaccurate, stereotypic, lay image of the occupation. These features include: (1) Lack of intimacy: Although this may be true insofar as interpersonal relationships are objectified, one of the things the authors have in mind is 'tenseness in interpersonal relations' [18]. With the actor's skill for self-presentation in everyday as well as dramatic interaction, it is difficult to agree with them on this point. (2) Time diffusion: 'The inability to maintain perspective and expectancy; a distrust of waiting, hoping, planning, of one's relationship to the future; a disregard for time as a dimension of organizing one's life' [19]. On this score, Little and Cantor say:

> In a strange way, the search for work imposes more order and discipline in an actor's life than the mythology of the theater world would lead one to believe. Nina Vance, the founder and director of Houston's famous Alley Theatre, once suggested that tracing the footsteps of an actor making his rounds week in week out would reveal a recurring pattern: so many hours spent at lessons, so many at auditions; certain times for seeing agents; certain times for visiting the casting offices; certain days for seeing people in the theater, and others for checking with friends in film and television.[20]

The fact that one's occupational future is more uncertain than others' does not necessarily lead to a distrust of the future; actors exhibit an extraordinary degree of faith in the future. This is indicative of commitment to the occupation and the identity it provides, albeit in the face of a seemingly contradicting present [21]. (3) Diffusion of industry: 'A disruption of the sense of workmanship which manifests itself in an incapacity for concentration and an inability to complete tasks or in an excessive preoccupation with one-sided activities' [22]. It is well known that:

The actor must work out his role and create a dramatic
illusion. He is compelled to concentrate and always have his
wits about him ...[23]

Furthermore, an appreciation of the collective nature of the
enterprise usually ensures that the actors complete their tasks in
the sense of fulfilling performance obligations. In addition,
acting is hardly a 'one-sided activity', either insofar as dramatic
character construction or the staging of a theatrical production
(given the attention to character, other actors, audience, cues,
props) is concerned. (4) Identity consciousness: Among other
things, the authors have in mind an 'ashamed recognition of one's
incomplete, inadequate identity' [24]. This contention is at odds
with my findings of consciousness of fluid identity as a positive
value in the occupational culture [25]. (5) Choice of a negative
identity: 'a hostile and snobbish rejection of those roles that
society offers as proper and desirable and the contrary vengeful
choice to become, as Erikson put it, "nobody or somebody bad" [26].
This again originates in a lay image of the actor as deviant which
is not borne out by the evidence [27]. Henry and Sims are
understandably misled since, as I have argued, the trainee actor
undergoes conversion and, according to Travisano, 'the ideal
typical conversion can be thought of as the embracing of a negative
identity' [28]. Both Henry and Sims and Travisano acknowledge
indebtedness to Erikson[29] for this idea. Henry and Sims appear to
be taken in by the sort of propaganda given by a professional actor
to the novice, a view which is disconfirmed by the actual practices
of the working world:

We take lightly what others take gravely ... It is difficult
to take the material world seriously and more difficult to take
serious people seriously. The roof may fall in, the heart stop
beating. Live. Express. Excite. Be excited. Give. Be jolly. Be
daring.

It is said that long-range thinking is a sign of man's highest
intellectual potential: foresight, planning, the ability to
wait for reward. Acting induces the opposite: living for the
moment.[30]

The rest of this book contains practical suggestions for carving
out a successful career as shrewdly, deliberately, and cautiously
as possible. In the face of such apparently mundane strategics in
an occupation which requires living in the moment (responding
truthfully to the dramatic reality), not for it, the author's words
may be soothing. Nevertheless, actors who heed this advice will
find themselves unemployable: the professional, formally organised
production of drama (whether in theatre, TV or film) is literally a
serious business, and neither the novice nor Henry and Sims should

accept so gullibly the stereotype of actors as a viable description of their modus operandi.

Finally, Henry and Sims have a moralistic bias against what they term identity diffusion which blinds them to the positive rewards of acting - namely, the thrill of risking claims to a proffered dramatic identity. Putting forward an uncommon and perceptive viewpoint, Pepitone writes:

> A consideration relevant to experimentation with self-identity is that existential personality theorists have probably exaggerated the negative character of the 'human condition'. The fact is that weakened self-identity is not always a phenomenologically unpleasant condition and certainly not a condition from which the individual invariably strives to escape.[31]

The actor acts in order to experience the thrill of risking dramatic identities rather than as a means of fulfilling any search for one's own. Commenting generally on the elusiveness of dramatic performance, Alan Howard, a member of the Royal Shakespeare Company, has said:

> A genuine acting performance is a very odd thing. It's a kind of sacrifice, in an odd sense, that's happening in front of you. It fascinates me that it's dead as soon as it's done, yet while it's being done it's the most living thing that probably is happening there. It's intended. It's been organised and structured so that a number of people should be in a place at a given time and a number of other people will fulfil that contract of trust. As each second goes by it's absolutely lost. We know that happens in our lives, but it's amazing to organise an occasion for it.[32]

Howard's remarks support Pepitone's claim that the falling away of identity or the dissolution of the situation within which it exists can be a rewarding experience. The thrill of participating in such an occasion comes from successfully convincing oneself and others of the credibility of one's character; the actor is not thrilled to have 'found' an identity, but thrilled to have met the claims to one. Thrill is also associated with harmony or the total involvement of worker with task - a sensation equally characteristic of such disparate activities as truck driving and acting [33].

Henry and Sims, by combining an image of the actor as essentially irrational (mad, deviant, identity-diffuse, defiant) with a rationalistic evaluation of the effects of this 'identity diffusion' (an inability to cope as others do in the working world), manage to convey a distorted picture of the relations between identity and dramatic acting.

BEING 'ON' VERSUS BEING 'NATURAL'

In a paper entitled, 'Life as Theatre: Some Notes on the Dramaturgic Approach to Social Reality' [34], Messinger et al. adopt an opposing but equally erroneous view to that of Henry and Sims. They begin with a general description of the difference between being 'on' and being 'natural':

> under some circumstances in everyday life the actor becomes, is, or is made aware of an actual or potential discrepancy between his "real" and his "projected" selves, between his "self" and his "character" ... insofar as he consciously orients himself to narrow, sustain, or widen this discrepancy and thereby achieves a sense of "playing a role" or "managing a character", he is "on" in the sense intended here ... It is at these other times, however, when the actor is not "on", that we shall refer to his perspective as "natural". At these other times persons tell us that their conduct appears to them as "spontaneous". [35]

Actors are assumed to shift between natural and on stances as are various others who may manage false identities before their publics, such as poolroom hustlers[36] and homosexuals [37]. Messinger et al. choose to explore the ways that such alternation provides special difficulties for mental patients. Their dilemma stems from the fact that they must stage their social performance for others (especially doctors) in order to demonstrate the normality which guarantees release from the mental institution. At the same time, however:

> the mental patient is not satisfied to appear "normal", he strives to be normal. Paradoxically, this means, in part, that he wants to "appear normal" to himself . Striving to "appear normal" for others - "putting on a show of normality" - interferes with this objective.[38]

This dilemma, according to the authors, is not experienced by the dramatic actor, whose:

> task, as usually defined, is to employ whatever means will facilitate the "coming alive" of the character for the audience. This leaves the actor free, or relatively so, to select an attitude toward the character he plays. He may, for example, conceive that getting "inside" the character will aid the accomplishment of his task; he may conceive that this is

not necessary, taking a "classical" stance rather than a "method" one. So long as he convinces the audience that the character he portrays is a plausible one, his obligations are fulfilled. It is presumably only "method" actors, however, who succeed in experiencing the characters they are projecting as their selves, however temporarily.[39]

The modern actor is afflicted by the mental patient's dilemma to a greater extent than the authors realise. An actor must stage a dramatic performance in such a way that it appears natural to the audience. Yet one's own awareness of its fictitiousness can impede the crucial aim of making it seem natural. As one actor I interviewed commented, regarding another's performance, 'she tried so hard that it became false'. Therefore, one strives to appear natural to oneself. Clearly, one does not strive to be or become the character, but one requires a kind of spontaneous reaction to the actions of others on the dramatic plane if one is to appear, to oneself and to others, to be authentic. What I have in mind is a leap to the realm of the 'as if' which enables the reactions themselves to be, in some sense, real [40]. Two actors in the Theatre Company described this sensation:

The greatest reward is when, if you're pretending to be somebody and someone else is pretending to be somebody, and you do it together and it's believable, that's like two electric wires sparking off, because you know you're both kidding and believing it.

It's when you are pretending so well that you believe and they believe what you're saying.

Shifting into this 'as if' dimension can actually influence bodily functions, as when 'a person can feel his ears becoming red and his face becoming flushed when he imagines a former embarrassment' [41]. I had the memorable experience of this uncanny sensation while participating in non-professional drama classes. At the point in a scene where the character was to experience embarrassment (when the ceiling fell in during a dinner party at which she was hostess), I felt this facial glow of embarrassment, decidedly not as actor, but as character. When we realise that this momentary physical reaction which can accompany belief in the dramatic moment simultaneously influences the beliefs and physical reactions of fellow actors, we begin to truly comprehend the remarks of the actors quoted above.

This type of authenticity is achieved by aligning the 'as if' dimension as closely as possible with oneself. If one does role-take vis-a-vis one's own character, it is in a moment of reflexive thought during rehearsal. Once performance begins, the role-taking is conducted from the standpoint of one's own character in relation to alter characters; the character has become 'one's own'. One is sufficiently in character to relate to other actors as characters; and, paradoxically, both are sufficiently in character to relate to each other as people rather than as remote fictional constructions:

> You must speak as one actor/person to the other actor/person; you must never speak as one character to another character. If you don't get through to the person playing the part, forget it - because your eyes are your eyes, and that's what we're going to work on.[42]

> My ambition? To keep on doing quality work. To keep on operating on some kind of emotional level, not mechanical. When you don't bring some kind of element of yourself to a part, you're in trouble. Always operate with yourself, even if it's masked. Alec Guiness - he's still somewhat in touch with himself when he plays all those characters. If it's not you, you'll put me to sleep, I'll tell you. If you try to emulate imagined emotions, you can't do it. If you're here and the character's there, you're in trouble.[43]

A sense of the unity of the character's personality or nature enables the actor to act from the standpoint of that character - to achieve a sense of being in character which lends authenticity to one's own, and through interaction, to others' characters. Through the repetition, refinement and development of the role, the actor discovers new facets of the character. Any clarification of the dramatic situation in which the character exists is at the same time a clarification of the fine points of that character's 'nature'. Obviously, the character's nature is only presumed, in the same sense that, as I shall later discuss, presumed biographical pasts and futures inform the scripted present.

Given the shared cultural meanings which underlie dramatic communication and the actor's need to believe in the drama, Messinger et al.'s assertion that the actor's obligation is fulfilled if the audience alone is convinced is true in only the weakest sense. The same is true of their statement about the actor's freedom to 'select an attitude toward the character he plays' [44]. They allude to what is sometimes called the difference between working 'from the inside out' or 'from the outside in'. Some actors find that they can best develop a character by concentrating on its emotional life, with the appropriate outward appearance of such a character flowing from that; others develop what they take to be the appropriate gestures, mannerisms and appearance of the character and from this the authenticity of the inner life of the character emerges. In either case, maximal involvement with role can be achieved, assuming that this is the actor's goal which, as I will discuss shortly, it may not be.

Furthermore, the attitude which the actor takes towards the character is a more complicated matter than the authors imply. They concern themselves with the actor's decision to execute the characterisation in a certain way. There is also an affective attitude which the actor takes towards the character, namely, whether or not one 'likes' the character or, more realistically, the sort of person that this character represents. It is clear from the interview material that this affective attitude can influence the actor's decision to play the part, the ease and success with which this is done if the part is accepted, and the evaluation of the job as pleasurable or unpleasurable, once having done so. Finally, the actor as actor may assess the personal or occupational value of the production which, while distinct from the attitude towards one's character, can nevertheless influence characterisation work.

Messinger et al. have perhaps contributed to our understanding of everyday interaction or mental illness by taking as their point of departure what is essentially an inaccurate depiction of dramatic actors. The dramaturgical analogy is based on the assumption that the occasionally deliberate or self-conscious quality of everyday behaviour parallels interaction on the dramatic plane; social actors sometimes monitor their performances to produce desired effects in the same way that dramatic actors are purported to do as a matter of course in conveying dramatic characters. This assumption is evident in Mead's writings:

> if [the actor] assumes a certain attitude he is, as we say, aware that this attitude represents grief ... [however], one is not an actor all of the time. We do at times act and consider just what the effect of our attitude is going to be, and we may deliberately use a certain tone of voice to bring about a certain result. (emphasis added)[45]

Thirty-eight years later, Burns, in her work, Theatricality [46], the aim of which is to 'explore the significance and meaning'[47] of the dramaturgical analogy, finds theatricality in everyday life to the extent that the behaviour is 'composed'[48] or deliberately chosen to produce a particular effect upon its audience. And, despite the overwhelming similarity between the two writers' views, we know that the latter author's attempt to pinpoint the differences between everyday and dramatic interaction in fact emanates from the great interest aroused by Goffman's The Presentation of Self in Everyday Life [49]. Here, rather than merely alluding to the nature of dramatic acting, Goffman clarified its components of presentation in his attempt to analyse systematically the theatrical features of everyday interaction.

The view of dramatic acting implicit in these writers' conceptions of everyday life stems from their audience standpoint; their analogy rests on the staged quality of theatrical productions for it is the production which, as audience, they view. Investigating acting from the standpoint of the _actor_ requires one to pose questions overlooked by these writers. Is the action deliberate or composed in rehearsal as well as performance? Can it be deliberate or spontaneous, at varying times, in rehearsal and performance? Does the intended or composed quality of the production as a whole obscure the mode of consciousness employed by the actor? The following discussion will show that conventional psychological and sociological approaches manage to obscure the true and varied relations between self-identity and character in rehearsal and performance.

INVOLVEMENT WITH ROLE

In order to understand the actor's variable involvement with role, we need concepts which differentiate varieties of consciousness of role behaviour. Sarbin[50] provides a continuum of 'organismic involvement' with role, contrasting two levels of dramatic acting in the process. He calls the first 'ritual acting':

> This level of organismic involvement has as its point of reference the stage actor who performs the motoric actions necessary for the portrayal of the role assigned to him. This type of acting is frequently alluded to as mechanical acting, or push-button acting. On cue, the actor "pushes the button" to depict anger, lust, vanity, or whatever is called for. On self-examination, the actor will report some involvement of self in the assigned role. He must maintain a certain degree of consistency in the role enactment, which engages more of the self than in casual roles ... Archer's classic study (1889) contained self-reports of competent stage actors who reported that under some conditions the actor does not get involved but maintains his identity, giving service to the stage role only through stylized gestures, intoned sentences, sham effect.[51]

This is the kind of dramatic acting Mead referred to, in which the actor selects a set of gestures which express a particular attitude. It is quite likely that Mead's notion of dramatic acting stemmed from the prevailing dramatic style of the late nineteenth and early twentieth centuries. Stanislavsky, a contemporary of Mead's, described the representational school of acting which his own teachings later overshadowed:

- 155 -

At first they feel the part, but when once they have done so
they do not go on feeling it anew, they merely remember and
repeat the external movements, intonations, and expressions
they worked on first.[52]

Sarbin contrasts ritual or representational acting with 'engrossed'
or 'heated' acting, a style whose origins are found in
Stanislavsky's writings and which were later codified in the school
known as 'The Method':

This level of involvement is noted in the stage actor who
'takes the role' literally. He throws himself into the action,
temporarily separating himself from his own identity and taking
on the identity of the character.[53]

This approximates the model associated with psychological
conceptions of dramatic acting. Of paramount importance, however,
are Sarbin's immediately following remarks:

The successful stage actor who engages in engrossed acting does
not surrender his entire identity to the part. In order to
change his tempo, intensity, and amplitude commensurately with
changing and unforeseen conditions, he must maintain some
contact with his role as actor ...(emphasis added)[54]

This is the crux of the matter: to be in character, even with
maximal involvement (short of insanity) is not the same as to
become the character. For this reason, the enactment of a dramatic
character exerts a limited influence on its player, as the
following professional actors' comments make clear:

And the actor's own perceptions - does the character he is
inhabiting (his [Paul Schofield's] word) change his own?
Playing Macbeth, say, did he feel an evil man himself? "No" -
quickly. "One's perception of the mentality of a cold-blooded
murderer is heightened. You see things in the way those people
would. But one's got to take sides. One's got to have one's own
private censorship rejecting those perceptions, and saying
that's something that human beings don't do - mustn't do. You
are still inside yourself and you have the web of your own life
to return to."[55]

In some ways ... acting is a slightly disheartening process,
because one is usually measuring up to personalities which one
has got very little chance of being. Consider some of the
parts I have played, and the qualities that in their nature
Shakespeare had given them, his creatures, these extraordinary
people. The insights they have and observations they make about
life, you are playing. You are being the medium for them, and

it's you, and then when it's over you're back where you were. I like to think, but I doubt, that some of these extraordinary qualities might affect one to make one a bit less selfish, more understanding. But I'm not sure that they do.[56]

The confusion of this relationship between self-identity and character permeates sociological and psychological conceptions of acting. There are in fact a number of relevant variables which influences the degree to which actors become involved in their roles:

(1) A particular style of acting may prevail in a particular historical period. Despite the fact that modern theatre often permits maximal involvement of self in role, minimal involvement may also be employed as a means of creating specific theatrical (and political) effects [57]; this makes it a very different approach from the minimal involvement of the nineteenth century. Moreover, minimal involvement with role may be re-emerging as a modern style because, as we saw in the TV study, the technical medium may preclude maximal involvement.

(2) The choice of minimal versus maximal involvement with role may reflect the actor's preferred working style; a strategy for particular productions (for example, the long run may be endured by relying on mechanical responses) [58]; or the level of interest in the production:

[Sir Herbert Tree] quickly got bored with a part and would 'walk through' it, thinking of something else. I have seen him act greatly and outrageously in the same play within the same week; and when he described one of his productions as 'an obstinate success' he really meant that it was getting on his nerves.[59]

(3) Finally, directorial style may influence the actor's degree of involvement with the role. If the director emphasises physical staging at the expense of emotional interplay between characters, it may be difficult for the actor to achieve maximal role involvement.

Degree of involvement with role may also differ in rehearsal and performance. Generally, rehearsal consists of more conscious experimentation, self-observation and reflection than does performance. Even here, though, we can distinguish varieties of activity necessitating varying degrees of involvement. The director may communicate this to the actors by saying, 'Let's run this scene and see how you feel [about enacting the role in this particular way]' or by saying, 'Okay, now [that we've got that straight] let's run the scene'. In the first instance, the director implicitly asks the actors to monitor their own performances while in the second the director implies that they should treat the rehearsal like an actual performance. To refine (or confuse!) matters further, given that the performance of the scene occurs in rehearsal no matter which cue the director gives, we can see that in the first case the actors maintain awareness of their performance while enacting their roles, whereas in the second case they are likely to report on the effect which their relatively unselfconscious enactment had on them - upon reflection, that is, or one step removed from the event itself.

Moreover, where the rehearsal has been relatively reflective but maximal involvement is expected in performance, the actor has the problem of keeping the performance fresh. Reactions to the repeated actions of others must be continually renewed. Maintaining spontaneity is only a problem because it is normatively required by mainstream, modern Western theatre culture. Although members of that culture concede that 'actors differ in the extent to which they are involved in the emotions that they are playing' [60], the value of spontaneity underlies another writer's comment that 'automatically' played parts take on a quality of 'lifelessness' [61]. The normative standpoint is evident in a Drama School student's descriptions of the relations between self and character in performance:

> You're no longer yourself, you're using yourself. You are the medium of the character you're playing, but theoretically you're no longer yourself so you shouldn't be looking at yourself. Of course you can if you're not quite in it.

It is also evident in professional actors' descriptions of successful acting:

> The best performances are those performances in which you remain unaware of what you're actually doing.

> You know it's working when you not only say the lines right, but you're not thinking about how you feel.[62]

Paradoxically, spontaneity must be worked for. Actors may offer insipid deliveries of lines when starting work on a script; with discussion and rehearsal, those lines may come to life. Moreover, through rehearsal and involvement with the role, those lines may come to mean, authentically, what they do to the actor as character, bringing the actor to the stage where he or she ceases to think about the lines. Insufficient involvement with role may make for an artificial distance between the character and its utterances which the audience will sense. This is implied in one director's note to an actor, following a rehearsal, that 'there were too many internal thought pauses rather than it happening on the line'. The problem of being inadequately involved in the reality of the play is also called not being 'in the moment' or being 'behind the line'. These phrases denote disruptive awareness of self as actor when awareness of character as self is required.

Lawrie[63] takes up this problem of awareness of self and others by noting that being oneself or being one's true self is not always identical with being one's usual self [64]. He exemplifies his point with a psychiatric case study reported by Laing[65] in which a woman:

> tried to become the person she imagined her parents, and in particular her mother, wanted her to be. This imaginary person, it seems, was virtually a duplicate of her mother. But if one forces oneself into the mold of an imaginary person, one cannot be one's real (or true) self. (emphasis added)[66]

For the actor, forcing oneself 'into the mold of an imaginary person' (the character) is something which must be done while remaining one's true self (the actor). The actor and Laing's mental patient are certainly not equivalent cases. Whereas the patient described may require the psychiatrist's skilful therapy in order to achieve even the awareness of this discrepancy between her usual and true selves, the actor is always, even if minimally, aware of this distinction between self and character. On this point, Shank writes:

> In order for the actor to actually experience the character's emotions it would be necessary for him actually to believe himself to be the personage he is creating ... [Yet], too many actors insist that they 'feel their parts' for us to assume that they do not feel something which is related to the roles they act. It is probable that what the actor feels stems from the mental image he forms of the character and his surroundings, which may be very detailed.[67]

The actor who enters the mould of an imaginary person, does so consciously, intentionally, and, above all, within the confines of a theatrical frame [68]. This frame limits the effects of such role playing on the everyday fate of its player, whereas the mental patient's usual self, inauthentic as it may be, can exercise monumental effects upon the true self of its real life player. Where this particular mental patient and the actor converge is at the point where awareness of self is at its lowest; disattention to self entails direct awareness of an other. In this very limited sense, the job of acting requires a dual self.

- 159 -

As Lawrie examined the 'true self', Turner examines the 'real self', arguing that it has become increasingly common for people to locate their true selves in impulsive behaviour rather than in the pursuit of institutionalised goals. 'The self as impulse means a present time perspective, while the self as institution means a future time perspective' [69], with a meaningful world being built through commitments. Where is the dramatic actor more likely to locate the true self? While the ideology of acting - professed by actors and believed by others - may favour a 'self as impulse' perspective, the issue is once again that of misunderstanding the professional's advice to the novice which I quoted earlier. The actor in rehearsal and performance may adopt a present perspective, but the actor as professional requires a future perspective, without which the occasions for 'impulse' - which acting never fully is - will be few.

Finally it would be interesting to determine empirically whether actors are, in Snyder and Gangestad's terms, 'high self-monitoring individuals [who] chronically strive to appear to be the type of person called for by each situation in which they find themselves' or 'low self-monitoring individuals [who] strive to display their own personal dispositions and attitudes in each situation in which they find themselves' [70]. It could be argued that the paradoxical art of acting requires both dispositions.

THE DRAMATURGICAL ANALOGY RECONSIDERED

As we have seen, the actor's relationship to the dramatic role is too varied to be invoked unreservedly as a model of dramaturgically based everyday behaviour. Undeniably, however, dramatic performances have features which are 'dramaturgical' in the sociological sense of the word. Messinger et al. provide an interesting description of what a dramaturgical explanation of a theatrical performance would entail [71]; in brief, it would consist of an explanation of how the worlds of theatre and reality are kept distinct - how the actors convince the audience that what they are watching is indeed a play. These have not been my predominant concerns. What I have included in my analysis of theatrical interaction, however, is first of all the way that dramaturgical concerns influence dramatic actors' behaviour on several levels. They may, in attempting to interpret the dramatic reality before them, evaluate their characters' dramaturgical concerns, incorporating these into the performance. Secondly, I have devoted considerable discussion to the dramatic actors' own dramaturgical concerns as social actors who happen to be engaged in dramatic acting, observing their attempts at impression management in a variety of work settings. Once again, then, the case of the dramatic actor has necessitated an expansion of the discussion on several levels. I have also shown that dramatic actors do not always stand outside their characters any more than they completely become their characters. They operate simultaneously on two levels and can thus at times authentically participate in the dramatic reality as though it were real, rather than merely indicating in almost Brechtian fashion that it is less than real.

Only later refinements to the dramaturgical analogy mirror the variable theatrical basis of the analogy. Part of the difficulty in evaluating the dramaturgical analogy stems from the ambiguity in deciding just whose perspective it is - ego's perspective on ego's own actions, alter's perception of ego's actions, or the observer's (sociologist's) description of the naive actors' actions? Cicourel criticises Goffman for failing to make explicit in his early work how the actor's perspective differs from the observer's [72]. The problem of specifying whose perspective we are discussing was pointed out by Messinger et al. who argued that the dramaturgical perspective was not the actor's perspective [73]. Later writers have taken a more balanced view, indicating that the dramaturgical perspective may be held by the actor or by others [74]. This position is most clearly articulated by Harre and Secord[75] who note the double role of the dramaturgical standpoint, in that it can be applied to and derived from the observation of interaction. They characterise as the 'explanatory principle', which is a methodological principle, the fact that:

In order to understand, that is to provide a plausible account for the details of what people are doing, one must see their activities in terms of deliberate followings out of one or more rules or conventions of style

and as the 'constitutive principle', which is an empirical hypothesis, the fact that:

For certain purposes people control the style of their actions, sometimes consciously and sometime not, and superimpose this upon other activities.[76]

Brittan likewise observes that 'we assume roles without necessarily being aware that we are doing so' - simply because we are socialised into these roles - and that 'the performance is not perceived as being a performance by the actor - it is regarded as being normal, in the nature of things' [77]. I would disagree that actions could be considered dramaturgically controlled without the actor's awareness of such control, but if performance control may or may not be conscious, we must consider the matter of the actor's motives or intentions.

Unlike the psychologist, the sociologist does not use the concept of motive to refer to innate predispositions to action which inhere in the individual. According to some sociologists - C. Wright Mills, for example - motives are:

> ...words. Generically, to what do they refer? They do not denote any elements 'in' individuals. They stand for anticipated situational consequences of questioned conduct.[78]

This is a view which I shall examine shortly.

The consequences of conduct to which Mills refers are inextricably linked to the identities which we manage to sustain in interaction; in fact:

> To a certain extent, motives are constructed in the interaction process itself, they are part of the process of the negotiation of identity that is central to self-other relationships. In this negotiation, new meanings are established and new meanings are really new motives.[79]

To question the motives for a person's behaviour in a particular situation is to ask who the person is in that situation. To distinguish between true (and possibly concealed) motives and apparent motives thus introduces the question of whether a true self lies behind performance (self as essence) or whether self is nothing more than a collection of situational identities (self as appearance[s]). This problem will be returned to later.

Attention to theatrical action makes it clear that motives are expressed and evaluated equally on the basis of verbal and nonverbal evidence. Within the script, the character may negotiate an identity through verbal and nonverbal gestures. The character may, for example, express anger through hostile words or through friendly words spoken through a tight jaw. But since the script, in this sense, belongs to the character, the dramatic actor's utterances do not communicate the motivational quality of his or her actions. The actor must negotiate an identity by means of expressive, nonverbal gestures. For example, by enacting the part in a certain way, the actor can communicate boredom, confusion, or lack of involvement in the play. Thus, a motive must be distinguished from an 'account' which is:

> a linguistic device employed whenever an action is subjected to valuative inquiry.[80]

Given the nature of modern theatrical conventions, the actor can no more stop the play to give an account to the audience as a means of justifying the performance than the audience can stop the actors in order to substantiate their valuative enquiries regarding the actors' or characters' performances. Interaction between actor and audience is nowadays implicit; actors implicitly offer motives and audiences implicitly assess them. The process only becomes explicit the morning after opening night when the critic's review of the performance is printed and the actor, if he or she chooses, comments on this critique. The same occurs in everyday life. We do not ordinarily conduct social encounters as though they were encounter groups, continually stepping out of the ongoing interaction in order to pass judgement on it. For this reason, it is wrong to conceptualise motives as linguistic statements. We would do well to follow Foote's usage and speak of 'motivated acts' rather than motives [81].

Like the dramaturgical perspective itself, a discussion of motivated acts requires a distinction between the proponent of the motive and its evaluator. In their discussion of awareness contexts, Glaser and Strauss[82] cleverly analyse the permutations made possible by combining the variables of interactants, acknowledgment of awareness (pretence or no pretence), degree of awareness (aware, suspicious, unaware) and identity (other's identity, own identity and own identity in the eyes of others). To rephrase their analysis in the simplified form required for my purposes, an individual's behaviour may be authentic or inauthentic - that is, revealing or concealing of motivation - and the individual's performance may be, in either case, convincing or unconvincing to those who evaluate it [83]. The dramaturgical analogy is based on the assumption that theatrical action is characteristically inauthentic; that the actor appears to be someone (the character) other than he or she really is (the actor); and that the performance may succeed or fail (be convincing or unconvincing). In this light we can view Brecht's acting technique as an attempt to make theatrical action authentic - to reveal to the audience while in performance that one is not pretending to be the character but that one is an actor consciously indicating what the character is [84]. Of course, the alienation technique may be equally convincing or unconvincing, although the criteria of judgement -pleasing or displeasing, being accepted or rejected by the audience - carry different connotations in Brechtian theatre since the audience is not supposed to be mollycoddled. Brechtian theatre aside, the actor's variable involvement with the dramatic role makes authenticity contingent upon a host of factors.

I have explored the ways in which dramatic acting, and so the dramaturgical analogy, have been misconceived. To evaluate the analogy adequately, however, I must raise further questions about the differences between life and theatre.

As the case study of the Theatre Company showed, a good deal of rehearsal time is spent defining the dramatic situation. This process is similar in some respects to reality construction in everyday life. McHugh describes the everyday process in his book, Defining the Situation: The Organization of Meaning in Social Interaction [85], employing the concepts of emergence and relativity :

> As emergence is temporal and involves an event in both the old and the new, relativity is spatial and characterizes an event in its relationship to other events across the boundaries of space. [86]

The following discussion will outline the features of emergence and relativity in everyday life and theatre.

Emergence describes the phenomenon whereby:

> the past influences the symbolic definition of the present, the definition of the present is influenced by inferences about the future, and the events of the future will reconstruct our definition of the past. [87]

The case of dramatic reality is a special one in that it contains two levels of pasts, presents and futures. There is a past, present and future contained within the script, viewed from any one point in time; the present of Act 2 will have been preceded by the past of Act 1 and followed by the future of Act 3. The actors' understanding of the events of the play will be affected, as McHugh predicts, by their symbolic definition and redefinition of events as they rehearse the play. A second level of past, present and future exists within drama in the sense that the whole of the scripted action represents the present, preceded by an imagined sequence of events occurring before the characters appear on stage and another sequence of events which are imaginatively presumed to occur in the lives of the characters after the point at which they leave the stage. Shank, in The Art of Dramatic Art writes:

> the actor must make speeches and physical acts seem to spring spontaneously from thought and feeling, and he must therefore create the illusion of an inward activity issuing in speech and movement. ...all acts - every movement and every utterance - ... must be assimilated into the illusion of the work and through their causal relationship must imply what has preceded and be imbued with the cause of what is to follow. [88]

In attempting to create an illusion, the actors may expand the temporal limits of their interpretive discussion to include these unscripted pasts and futures of their characters' lives. Given that in real life, one's definition of the present is influenced by one's conceptions of the past and future, the actors may assume that the dramatic present will only acquire the appearance of authenticity if they clearly establish in their minds the interpretations of unscripted pasts and futures which their characters can be presumed to have. Not everyone views the inclusion of this temporal level in rehearsal discussion as relevant to the task at hand:

> [The actor] will learn far more of what he needs to know about Iago from studying the movement of the lines Shakespeare has written for him ... than he will from asking Freudian questions about his motives or biographical questions about his off-stage life .. it is the dramatic function which is important, not the personality and not the scenes in the character's life which the writer did not write.[89]

The various properties of emergence are employed by social actors in order to 'create temporal continuity in defining situations' [90]. They begin by assuming that a pattern of meaning will emerge - that there is a theme[91] in the situation which will gradually unfold. This assumption is echoed by a dramatic actor who said:

> What happens is that you just find a certain reality from whatever you can, if you're dealing with something that seems to be - that doesn't make any sense.[92]

Once cognisant of this theme, the actors will use it to connect disparate events into a coherent unity (elaboration) [93]. The same process of elaboration in everyday life has been described by Gergen in his paper, 'Personal Consistency and the Presentation of Self' [94]:

> Noting a person's abrasive speech or brusque treatment of others ... may lead one to conceptualize this person as "aggressive". The concept is thus used to encapsulate a series of observations, and the conceptualization of a body of observations forms the cornerstone for what we know as "understanding" of the other. Once such judgments are formed they tend to remain intact and unchanging. On the one hand, new information about a person may simply be assimilated into the already existing conceptual structure ... On the other hand, if later information grossly violates the once crystallized judgment of the other, it may be distorted or misperceived ...In these ways, persons tend to be seen as stable and consistent.[95]

Gergen concludes that the 'popular notion of the self-concept as a unified, consistent, or perceptually "whole" psychological structure' is 'possibly ill-conceived' [96]. Dramatic characters are even less complete than real selves, but this will be discussed more fully later.

As Gergen noted, some events will contradict or test the developed theme; these require rationalisation as a means of integrating them into the whole of the constructed definition (creating what McHugh calls fit [97]) . The participants author[98] this definition of the situation as, through revelation 'one event connects with another in such a way as to make the first intelligible ...' [99].

Using the raw materials of the dramatic script, actors employ these emergent properties of interaction as a means of defining reality. In dramatic settings, these assumptions are made on two levels: the dramatic actor defines the dramatic situation contained in the script as well as the theatrical situation of staging a play. Just as the actors assume that the playwright has written the play in such a way that a theme will be revealed behind its discrete events as, through discussion and rehearsal, they create the required fit, elaboration, etc., so they assume that, given their understanding and execution of the activities required by a group which defines its work as 'putting on a play', the end result of their endeavours will be a successful production. Thus an assumption of orderly interaction is held by participants on both everyday and dramatic levels.

Regarding relativity, McHugh writes that:

Relativity indicates the absence of an ultimate reality; in this respect it is similar to the notion ... of ... 'multiple realities'.[100]

While dramatic reality may be considered a multiple or 'other reality' in contradistinction to everyday life, we can also view dramatic reality as containing within itself multiple realities, in the sense of infinite variation in the production of a single script. Harley Granville-Barker divided the dramatic action of a play into two categories: the conscious action, belonging to the structure of the play, which allows for no variation and the subconscious action, into which:

we are to bring everything in the play's acting - movement, expression , emotion, thought - which may, without disturbance of the production's structure or to the distraction of fellow actors, be carried forward in any one of fifty different ways. We say fifty, as we might say a dozen or a hundred simply for comparison with the single way of the first category ...[101]

Whereas emergence is assumed, relativity is assessed [102]. This assessment is conducted by means of what McHugh (borrowing from Garfinkel)[103] calls 'conditions of perceived normality' [104]. The description of these conditions (typicality, likelihood, causal texture, moral requiredness, technical efficiency and substantive congruency) systematises what was generally described in the Theatre Company study, namely, the strategies used by dramatic actors to decide on the meaning of the character's actions within the script.

Typicality denotes a process whereby:

When a member interacts with another, he infers whether or not the other's behavior is representative of some group or category membership.[105]

Dramatically, the character's group membership is progressively refined. In the early stages of rehearsal, the category may be so broad as to include only age, sex, occupation and the like; gradually, the character acquires a rough psychological or motivational classification and, as interpretive work on the script continues, this narrows to the point where more and more behavioural choices fall outside the domain of perceived membership. This parallels the process in everyday life in which increased knowledge of a person causes us to refine our conception of the 'type' of person he or she is.

The various other conditions of perceived normality are similarly employed by the actors in their attempts to uncover the meaning behind scripted actions. They decide upon the likelihood[106] of certain actions. In as much as actions, in the sense of events, are laid down in the script, actions in this context refer to motives. They assess the causal texture in that they:

point to some phenomena as the conditions under which still other things will occur.[107]

In assessing the moral requiredness of characters' actions:

Members assert the ontological necessity of some behavior independent of personal circumstance or desire. In the literature, these are usually referred to as values.[108]

Here again, in defining dramatic situations we find several levels of the same process. The assessment of moral requiredness is on one level entirely internal to the script; the actors speculate on their characters' conceptions of the 'ontological necessity' of certain behaviour, given the particular circumstances (age, sex, occupation, personality, historical period, etc.) which the script

- 167 -

dictates. On another level, the actors' understanding of the script and their characters' viewpoints is necessarily influenced by the actors' own conceptions of moral requiredness originating in their everyday reality. Technical efficiency is the term used by McHugh to describe the fact that:

> Members assert that some means are more effective than others in achieving desired ends. They characterize behavior as appropriate or inappropriate, depending upon how it facilitates an objective.[109]

In theatre, such assessments would necessarily concern the unscripted, nonverbal accompaniments to scripted statements or the unscripted expressive reactions to scripted actions. The final condition of perceived normality, that of substantive congruency also has special status in the case of drama. McHugh describes this condition as follows:

> Members determine whether others' substantive assessments of their environments are empirically right or wrong. "Empirically right or wrong" refers to accuracy of judgment rather than moral or normative correctness, so that etiquette or values would not be included in this category.[110]

McHugh gives the example of offering a seat on a bus to a lady: whether or not one does so would be of no concern here, but determining whether the person was indeed a female would be. In everyday life, even such matters of 'fact' ultimately depend upon the acceptance of data afforded by individual perception. On the level of the dramatic, however, the ultimate source of knowledge is the literal text in which the playwright has determined by fiat what is. Even if the required fact can only be deduced from given information, the supreme status of the playwright in defining reality in its most basic sense differentiates it from the case of everyday life.

McHugh maintains that by classifying the environment by means of perceived conditions of normality:

> [The social actors] are enabled to decide that specific standpoints are interchangeable, as role-taking components of the definition of the situation ... Role-taking fails when interactants agree on none of these components. As actors fail to interchange standpoints, they will fail to communicate and become incapable of entering into the concerted actions that are characteristic of social order.[111]

When this occurs, anomie or disorder ensues. In the production of drama, it is clearly the actors' hope that any threat of anomie will be dispelled by the work of rehearsal. Many productions have been threatened by disintegration, only to be successfully reconstructed in time for opening night. Nevertheless, a feeling of anomie may accompany the actors to the live stage, either through a failure to resolve problems originating in rehearsal, as one professional actor described:

> It's a terrifying thing - opening night there were 12 or 13 people on stage who didn't know what they were doing. They knew the story, but they didn't understand anything because the director didn't know what he was trying to say

or, by virtue of innovations in performance and interpretation made only after the phase of live performance has begun. I shall now turn to a discussion of this threat to dramatic order.

Mead's discussion of gesture and meaning raises questions about threats to dramatic order:

> certain parts of the act become a stimulus to the other form to adjust itself to those responses; and that adjustment in turn becomes a stimulus to the first form to change his own act and start on a different one ... The term "gesture" may be identified with these beginnings of social acts which are stimuli for the response of other forms ... the gesture ... can become an expression of emotions, or later can become the expression of a meaning, an idea ... When, now, the gesture means this idea behind it and it arouses that idea in the other individual, then we have a significant symbol ... It is now a significant symbol and it signifies a certain meaning.[112]

While Mead's analysis is useful in explaining how physical, vocal and verbal gestures acquire meanings which then influence behaviour, my present argument requires a description of symbols which is more specific. To take an example from the realm of physical gesture, there is the broad category of the smile which has one or more general meanings (which are surprisingly diverse: to smile means 'to express amusement, slight contempt, favour, pleasure, etc., by a slight drawing up of the corners of the lips' [113]. Yet, when one considers the range of variations possible in the execution of a smile, and their infinite combinations with other physical, vocal and verbal gestures, one begins to realise the extraordinary range of meanings which any particular smile may evoke in an other.

In drama, the general class of gesture is fixed; we know the general sequence of actions to be performed. Yet, it is the particular, idiosyncratic execution of a culturally understood gesture which lends authenticity to behaviour, whether in theatre or everyday life. Any variation in its actual enactment may indicate a lesser or greater shift in the definition of the situation held by the actor. It is these innovations within an agreed interpretation which concern me here.

Actors may alter their performance in ways which co-workers perceive as grounding that performance more fully in the already constructed definition of the situation, thereby strengthening that dramatic reality. The meaning of the newly enacted gesture may be incorporated into a modified construction of the interrelationships between the characters. If the innovation 'works', it means that members of the company have successfully accounted for the other's action and their own novel reactions, given the previous definition of the situation and its present modification. On the other hand, the innovation may be perceived as straying from or contradicting the constructed definition of the situation. An innovation is destructive if it conveys a meaning which cannot be incorporated into the general definition of the situation; if it signifies the introduction of a completely new and individual interpretation of events, it accordingly introduces the possibility of anomie.

The boundaries between constructive and destructive innovations cannot be preordained; they vary with each company's prior construction of the reality and with the faculties of understanding which the members individually bring to the group. Furthermore, these are not necessarily faculties of logical discourse, but interactional faculties. Within rehearsal, decisions are arrived at either through verbalisations on the level of the everyday, or through enacted performances on the level of the dramatic. A parallel to this exists in ordinary interaction; we may jointly discuss hypothetical conduct and decide whether it is congruent with our understanding of the context in which it would occur, or, we may, in the course of the interaction itself, feel that the performances of self and others are either coordinated or discrepant.

Even though the general sequence of dramatic events and individual actions is fixed in rehearsal, the actors must be open to innovations in performance. These innovations are necessitated by (1) novel effects of the actions of some actors upon others in any particular performance (requiring a modified response on the part of the first actor in order to maintain the credibility or authenticity of both performances); (2) reactions to another actor's accidents or mistakes such as forgotten lines ('drying') or jumped or repeated lines, and (3) unanticipated audience response (applause, longer or shorter than expected laughter, heckling, etc. [114]) . In all of these cases, innovations are required in response to human fallibility, the less than perfect control which others have over their own actions, or the more general unpredictability of human behaviour in that some actions are willed by ego but unanticipated by alter. The range of variables affecting any one dramatic performance is so enormous - taking into account the physical and emotional states of actors and audiences, the weather and time of day, the very effect of previous performances on the present one, etc. - that clearly no one performance can be perfectly replicated [115]. For these reasons, actors cannot fix the specifics of their performances but must skilfully manoeuvre their way through unknown circumstances, nightly. If the performance is in any way alive or fresh - if the actors, rather than merely reciting their lines, actually respond to one another - then purposeful innovation will be common.

Except in the case of ceremony or ritual, social interaction is not scripted in minute detail. Working within this everyday reality which is so fundamentally supported by consensus, unexpected events requiring innovation, in the sense of a response not anticipated by ego, are more easily handled. The uncertainty of alter's specific response is inherent in the nature of everyday social interaction; improvisation is the very nature of this 'paramount reality' [116].

Dramatic reality, however, by virtue of its predetermined sequence of events, requires of its actors a special skill in dealing with the innovations of others. This is why we as the audience are made aware of the actor as actor when he or she evidently surmounts an unexpected obstacle, particularly an accident or mistake [117]. While temporarily disengaged from the dramatic reality, we delight in the skilful rescue of dramatic order. Similarly, without the audience knowing, actors may experience such delight when surviving another's attempt to make them 'corpse' or lose composure on stage [118].

Once the play is running and the director ceases to attend the theatre, the stage manager is responsible for preventing innovations in performance from reaching the point where they threaten the collective definition rather than enliven what has already been rehearsed. Interestingly, deviations are measured in terms of total performance length [119]. Some stage managers may call a rehearsal when performances start overrunning by as little as three minutes. Length of performance is affected by the speed with which individual actors execute their actions and by pauses, or the time required by one actor to respond to the actions of others. Timing, which is often referred to in assessments of dramatic performance, particularly comedy, is central to maintaining the definition of the situation because it influences the very meaning attributed to statements and actions. The stage manager allows for a certain amount of deviation, beyond which it is deemed destructive rather than constructive. Viewed from the standpoint of the audience, one can say that when a performance drags, its unreality is revealed. The failure to interact at the culturally expected pace is a clue to deception in dramatic and everyday realities.

ACTORS AND AUDIENCES IN LIFE AND THEATRE

Actors have three audiences: themselves, other actors and theatregoers [120]. Each responds to the action in a different way. The actor serves as the audience for his or her actions as actor; in fact, with a minimal degree of involvement in the dramatic role, an actor may attend wholly to these extra-dramatic concerns. With maximal involvement in the role, the actor may approximate reflexivity from the standpoint of the character; to do so completely would signal a flight from reality, as the stereotype of the dramatic actor suggests. Other actors may similarly provide the audience for ego on both levels, attending to concerns internal to the drama (from the standpoint of their characters) or in ways external to the drama (from the standpoint of the actor - e.g., by attending to accidents and mistakes). The member of the audience also plays a dual role. The social role of theatregoer includes mundane activities like choosing plays and buying tickets as well as participating in an aesthetic event [121]. Examination of the audience's role will clarify the differences between staged and everyday interaction and thus the dramaturgical analogy itself.

What is the difference between the street fight observed by passersby and the stage fight observed by a theatrical audience [122]? The significance of the street fight is usually independent of passerby observation; where this is not the case, we can say that the street fight contains a strong dramaturgical component. Yet, if the passersby choose to intervene, their actions can directly alter the course of events. If, on the other hand, a member of the theatre audience tries to intervene in a stage fight, this will not alter the course of events, but will thoroughly destroy the dramatic reality which is, in Natanson's term, 'inviolable' [123]. This means that although members of the audience may 'join' the stage fight, theatrical reality will be temporarily suspended, collapsing to the everyday level, if they do. In this sense theatrical reality is self-contained and impervious to everyday influence. For this reason, if the real street fighters carried on without acknowledging passerby intervention, someone would soon conclude that this was actually an open air performance. Thus, the important difference between life and theatre is not that everyday life is unscripted in comparison to the theatrical, but that the theatrical has this quality of inviolability.

Goffman speaks of action being 'framed' and therefore appropriately understood and reacted to [124]. When keyed into a theatrical framework, the spectators observe the action before them in the 'epoche of the aesthetic attitude' [125]. Duvignaud is correct in stating that the difference between life and theatre is that theatre is made for seeing [126]. Clearly, some individuals fail to grasp the requirements of the aesthetic attitude; we have all watched drama in the presence of people who oddly overreact to staged events, as though they were real .

Thus, real life is constituted and altered by the interaction of actors and audiences; theatre relegates the audience to a peculiarly non-participatory role. But wherein lies the actual interaction of theatrical events?

Interaction is built up through the fitting together of lines of action. These actions originate in the active part of the self (the 'I') and a course of action is modified by the reflective incorporation of reactions of others to those acts. Yet, actions in theatre are not truly initiated by the actors, for they are scripted. As I will discuss shortly, action cannot be attributed to characters since they are neither initiators nor reflecters. Since the audience cannot. respond to staged action in a way which could alter its course while remaining theatrical, they do not interact with the actors either. Thus an event which so fundamentally depends on interaction, in the sense of playing out the script as well as requiring an audience to bestow upon it the meaning of theatre, is at the same time totally lacking in real interaction. At least it is totally lacking in direct interaction. Each of the participants, whether actor or audience, participates in a fashion once removed from everyday reality. This is the meaning of the epoche of the aesthetic attitude.

At the same time, however, the participants experience a heightened sense of reality. Thus it is only when removed from the real interaction of everyday life that we achieve the most penetrating sensation of that reality. As Wilshire says,

> theatre is a mode of discovery that explores the threads of what is implicit and buried in the world, and pulls them into a compressed and acknowledgeable pattern before us in its "world."[127]

Price, in his paper, 'The Other Self: Thoughts about Character in the Novel' [128], writes that the difference between characters and persons is that characters and readers don't impinge on each other's lives, even if the character seems more real than the real people we know. I believe that this qualification is of greater importance than Price or other writers might allow.

It is the dramaturgical component of everyday interaction which prevents us from feeling this reality. As W.I. Thomas said, deception is an ever present danger in everyday life because social life depends on mutual trust [129]. Yet, dramaturgical concerns are not truly ever present in everyday life. Our trust in the authentic presentations of particular others enables us to act without regard to impression management, even though the people before whom we can afford to be ourselves may be very few indeed. On the other hand, pretence and dissimulation, because they are the basis of theatre, cease to challenge our sense of authenticity. We expect to see a performance which is not really real [130]. Yet, the poor theatrical performance perpetrates its own deception[131] insofar as we come to the theatre to be moved or entertained, not to cringe under the assault of bad acting.

Thus, theatrical action is indirect interaction in which actor and audience do not mutually influence the course of events. Even though the potential for authenticity and deception are equally (but differently) available in everyday life and theatre, being removed from the direct interaction of everyday life paradoxically heightens one's sense of reality in theatre. For this reason, the symbolisation of everyday life in theatre can potentially alter the audience's perception of and action in the real world.

THE REALITY OF SELVES AND CHARACTERS

I said earlier that the dramaturgical perspective could lead to a view of the self as essentially true or real or to a view of the self as mere appearance(s). Brittan writes:

> But what is one's real identity? Is it purely social confirmation from relevant others? If identities are conceived of as masks, is there nothing else but masks? ... Impression-management, while constituting a crucial element in social interaction, is surely not the whole story.[132]

I agree with Brittan's view that this is not 'the whole story' but, even so, we must continually guard against the implication that any acknowledgement of a real, true or essential self indicates acceptance of a reified view of self as a controlling mechanism 'within' the person.

In Stone's paper entitled, 'Appearance and the Self', he writes:

> One's identity is established when others place him as a social object by assigning him the the same words of identity that he appropriates for himself or announces.[133]

Thus, identity depends upon the complementarity between what is projected and what is perceived. Identity can be situational while containing transituational residues which we might consider to be the self. Elaborating on Stone's position, Edgley and Turner note:

> Appearance means identification of another. And no matter how much we claim to know the other, what we "know" are a host of appearances that the person mobilizes toward us.[134]

This again refers back to the position of alter, the evaluator. But what of ego, the actor? Is there, as Brittan questions, 'nothing else but masks', even to oneself ? Brittan remarks that:

> It took a long time for psychologists to rid themselves of the 'essentialist' cast of thought which attributed to the self some kind of inner force and substantive reality. [Yet] with the advent of behaviourism, the self disappeared together with 'subjectivity'.[135]

The important point is that what surely exists is the subjective sense of an essential self. Others may not know us, but we do, at least insofar as we feel that we do. To say that we feel that we exist as an ontological unity, rather than that we really do, is to reject a reified conception of self in favour of the reality of subjectivity. As Turner says, 'there is no objectively, but only a subjectively, true self' [136]. Natanson speaks of the 'essential structure of the self' as being its 'interior form' which the presenting self 'merely hints at' [137]. I would say that we can only hint at to others what we know to be true ourselves. While Strauss says that 'The awareness of constancy of identity ... is in the eye of the beholder rather than "in" the behavior itself' [138], Travisano adds that the beholder may be oneself [139].

Brittan provides the clearest statement of the view of self as more than its appearances:

> It is true that men project different identities in different situations, but surely this is not the same as saying that they are not aware of some type of structure in their self-other systems. Probably it is appropriate to speak of the alternation of identity rather than the full assumption of a new identity ... There is no reason to suppose that a [person] can't assume [two] identities without becoming two different people ... [At times, however], we are faced with the situation in which one set of self-perceptions colours both identities ... Granted that one can only become aware of the self as a result of social interaction, this does not mean that the individual is incapable of experiencing reality except through the eyes of the other. Although difficult to pinpoint, the experiential

self is the focus of the way we define the world and ourselves.[140]

Brittan's use of the term alternation may pose difficulties for those familiar with Travisano's paper on alternation and conversion when applied to the case of the dramatic actor. Travisano distinguishes the two concepts by saying:

> Alternations and conversions, then, are different kinds of identity change. Alternations are transitions to identities which are prescribed or at least permitted within the person's established universes of discourse. Conversions are transitions to identities which are proscribed within the person's established universes of discourse that negate these formerly established ones.[141]

Dramatic actors, like any social actors, experience alternations of identities, even within the dramatic realm. In other words, they take on different characters without losing sight of the self which underlies these enactments. Yet, I argued earlier that the socialisation programme entailed conversion to the occupational identity of the dramatic actor. The two are quite separate problems: conversion to the occupational identity of the actor enables a person to subsequently manage the alternation of dramatic identities.

Natanson states[142] that dramatic actors find themselves in their characters, not in the sense of soul searching (which I take to be comparable to the view put forward by Henry and Sims) but in the sense in which we all find ourselves in others. Like others, actors find themselves or elaborate upon their self-conceptions in interaction with fellow workers - and in interaction with their characters. Actors have a second level of 'persons' in interaction with whom they can elaborate their self-conceptions.

The fact that the work of dramatic actors is extremely reflexive with regard to interactional matters may mean that their experiential selves are more highly developed than most. This does not mean, as I pointed out earlier, that they can provide detailed verbal accounts of self, but we should not assume that they are any less capable of self-description than non-actors; both can and do provide basic classificatory self-descriptions; the non-actor may produce no more fascinating descriptions of self than the actor. Perhaps it is only the proponents of the 'selfless actor' view who, ironically, confuse the depth we may expect from actors with the depth we expect from dramatic characters! Put differently, dramatic actors may, to a greater extent than most, feel that they are, without being able to state exactly who they are - whereas it would seem to be the unfortunate fate of modern individuals that they are provided with innumerable statuses which enable them to clearly state who they are, although the consequent fragmentation prevents them from feeling that they are [143].

I have commented on the ability of actors to assume dramatic characters as a consequence of reformulating personal identity (conversion) and of their ability, to 'hold onto themselves' while doing so (alternation). Having discussed the reality of the experiential self, I must now examine why, in interactionist terms, the dramatic character is not equally real. I will discuss the difference between characters and persons first in terms of reflexivity and then in terms of groundedness.

Mead states very clearly that the self is not defined by its 'bodiedness':

> The body is not a self, as such; it becomes a self only when it has developed a mind within the context of social experience ... a self is not, I would say, primarily the physiological organism. The physiological organism is essential to it, but we are at least able to think of a self without it. Persons who believe in immortality, or believe in ghosts, or in the possibility of the self leaving the body, assume a self which is quite distinguishable from the body.[144]

Thus, the fact that the dramatic character lacks a physical body (or is only brought to life by the body which is 'attached' to the actor's self) is not of major importance:

> Self-consciousness, rather than affective experience with its motor accompaniments, provides the core and primary structure of the self, which is thus essentially a cognitive rather than an emotional phenomenon. The thinking or intellectual process - the internalization and inner dramatization, by the individual, of the external conversation of significant gestures which constitutes his chief mode of interaction with other individuals belonging to the same society [is of primary importance].[145]

Clearly it is this internal conversation which the character distinctly lacks in comparison to the person. The internal conversation is an indication of self-consciousness which is itself a necessary condition for reflexivity. An actor may, in enacting the character, represent the character's reflexivity, but it is meaningless to attribute reflexivity to a character in a real or direct sense. Some plays - for example, Pinter's The Collection - derive their meaning almost wholly from this representation of the character's internal self-conversations; the lines of that particular play fall flat when reflexivity is neglected, for there is little action in any other sense to carry the play. The interpretation and evaluation of one character's accounts by another (for, The Collection is supremely a dramatisation of the communication and interpretation of motives and accounts in everyday situations) is conducted by the actors on behalf of these characters; they cannot do it themselves, for they are not complete selves.

Harre and Secord note that it is crucial to realise that the character corresponds to the role, not to the person [146]; similarly Natanson says that 'it is only persons who see persons' and the 'forces of intersubjectivity' which underlie this depend, of course, on subjectivity itself [147]. The character lacks a self in that it neither truly initiates the actions it performs on stage ('I') nor can it do so since it lacks the self-consciousness which would precede and follow the immediate moment of the act ('me'); in Brittan's terms:

> To act socially is to act dramatically, in the sense that one's behaviour is underpinned by the 'self' monitoring its own performances.[148]

Thus the dramatic character does not act dramatically, for it does not act.

An interactionist analysis of the ontological status of the dramatic character illuminates facets of theatre which are sometimes taken for granted. For example, it is commonly held that actors need directors to monitor their performance since involvement in the dramatic action prevents the actor from doing so. Through identification with their characters, actors can temporarily suspend consciousness of their own selves while approximating consciousness from the standpoint of the character. The director steps in to replace this monitoring of performance which actors temporarily surrender. But the director's role only assumed importance in the nineteenth century with the change in acting style. Previously, when actors merely recited their lines and displayed their character in a literally self-centred way, they had no need for directors. They presented themselves as actors more than they represented characters; and in presenting ourselves, we usually manage without the aid of a guiding onlooker.

Mead writes that:

> The self is essentially a social process going on with these two distinguishable phases [the 'I' and the 'me']. If it did not have these two phases, there could not be conscious responsibility and there would be nothing novel in experience.[149]

Conscious responsibility requires reflexivity which the character decidedly lacks. In noting that there is no novelty without selves, it becomes clear that characters are grounded in the script while persons enjoy a relatively ungrounded existence in multiple situations.

Everyday actors may need to reaffirm their identities continually, but they bargain on behalf of a self which is based in multiple settings. Doubts cast on the essential unity of the self, on the 'really me' [150], in any single arena of social interaction can be dispelled through the legitimation received in others. In other words, our sense of self-identity is rarely tied to a specific situation; there is always another informal encounter, geographical location, job or spouse if one's attempts to sustain credibility in present circumstances fail. Given that the self consists of an acting 'I' and a reflecting 'me', the 'me' being that group of organised attitudes to which the individual responds as an 'I' [151], we can see that through interaction with different others, the self, by means of adaptation, modification and flexibility, can persist. Even within a single situation, the mental backstage we possess as real selves, in which we interpret the indications of others to ourselves, can serve to protectively mediate the judgements which others serve on our claims to particular identities.

Dramatic identities, on the other hand, are relatively grounded. They exist only in the scripted present and to fail here is to fail completely. The character's limited spatiotemporal existence is related to its 'characterological' incompleteness:

> The stage character, as it is in the text, is not really, so to speak, a complete man: not a human being in the ordinary sense, but a complex assortment of verbal clues for a man.[152]

> Creating a character is like reconstructing a fossil in a big archaeological dig, putting one piece in relation to another, leaving spaces between an elbow and a heel; but while one knows the fossil is the remnants of something that was actually there, in a play the character's fragments are remnants of something which was never there, except in the imagination of someone.[153]

Thus, unlike the real self, the dramatic 'self' cannot replenish its reserves of credibility in multiple situations; nor, given its fictitious and script-bound quality, can it buffer the doubts of others (actors and audiences) with 'personal' interpretations of discrediting events. The dramatic character is, not surprisingly, a self totally collapsed into role. If an analogy to particular forms of mental instability is in any way appropriate, it is insofar as this identity (of character, _not_ actor) so precariously depends on the acceptance of others, lacking in any internal self-certainty.

Considering the script-bound nature of characters, we may speculate on the effects of acting on actors. The actor is permitted the luxury of living through situations without personal consequence and of interacting with others in a sphere in which the outcomes, in the sense of events, are known. Moreover, one can retrace one's steps - play out the same sequence of action over and over with different _experiential_ outcomes. Each night, the dialectical process of subtle shift in the definition of the situation and individual performance deepens the actor's awareness and understanding of the character, bringing the actor closer to acting from the character's standpoint, enabling the actor to, as they say, 'live truthfully in the moment' of what is really only a fictitious scene. In real life, the script is ever changing; and while a sense of self is surely gleaned from diverse interactions, the quality of this self-awareness is necessarily extensive, not, as in the dramatic case, intensive. As I showed earlier, the experience of dealing with dramatic characters may lead the actor to perceive real selves in this intensified or objectified way.

We may also speculate that the assuming of dramatic identities gives the actor an opportunity to simultaneously conceal and reveal self-identity in a way that few others enjoy. Henry and Sims quoted Ingrid Bergman who expressed much the same sentiment as Denis Quilley:

I don't mind singing on stage in character, but getting up on a platform as myself and singing songs used to reduce me to absolute jelly.[154]

Again, we need not interpret such statements as a need to hide behind the identity of an other, in the negative sense that Henry and Sims do; rather, they point to the positive sensation of role playing in a framed and non-consequential setting. Taylor and Williams describe how actors enjoy sustaining their identities as actors by risking their identities as characters:

We observed in rehearsals and productions a fondness for "corpsing" - for sending up the other actor in such a way as to make him lose his composure. Corpsing is a form of ranking which the audience is only rarely supposed to see. One actor is, as it were, trying to kill the other's assumed character by certain vocal inflections or actions. The other wins if he successfully remains in character, or if he turns the tables upon the initiator of the action by making him break down. When actors corpse each other without the audience's knowledge, they are providing reassurances of their technique to each other, stressing their competence by departing from the formal lines of their role.[155]

While corpsing may reveal the self concealed behind the character, the very process of successful acting itself reveals self. By using their bodies as tools, actors at least minimally involve themselves in their acting. Alan Howard's comments reject the notion of concealment in favour of revelation:

Acting is much more a matter of exposing oneself than of adopting a mask. The actor performs on his own person, not on some illusion; the illusion springs from performing on himself. An actor is worthless if he cannot reveal himself on the stage. When people say of an actor that he's boring because he's always the same, they mean he's always the same mask.[156]

NOTES:

[1] W. Henry and J. Sims, 'Actors' Search for a Self'.

[2] See E. Erikson, Childhood and Society.

[3] W. Henry and J. Sims, 'Actors' Search for a Self', p. 58.

[4] Ibid., p. 60.

[5] Ibid., p. 61.

[6] Ibid., pp. 61-62.

[7] Ibid., p. 62.

[8] Ibid.

[9] D. Layder, 'Sources and Levels of Commitment in Actors' Careers', p. 154.

[10] W. Henry and J. Sims, 'Actors' Search for a Self', p. 62.

[11] Ibid., p. 60.

[12] Ibid., p. 62.

[13] G. Allport, Becoming, p. 36.

[14] G. Mead, Mind Self and Society, p. 171.

[15] W. Henry and J. Sims, 'Actors' Search for a Self', p. 58.

[16] Ibid.

[17] See ibid., p. 60.

[18] Ibid.

[19] Ibid.

[20] S. Little and A. Cantor, The Playmakers, p. 97.

[21] See H. Becker, 'Personal Change in Adult Life', p. 50.

[22] W. Henry and J Sims, 'Actors' Search for a Self', p. 60.

[23] R. Caillois, Man, Play and Games, p. 78.

[24] W. Henry and J. Sims, 'Actors' Search for a Self', p. 60.

[25] 'Self-resolution' is the term given by Turner to that quality of self-identity which can be expressed as a continuum from 'clear and stable self-conception' to 'vague and uncertain identity.' 'The Real Self: From Institution to Impulse', p. 208.

[26] W. Henry and J. Sims, 'Actors' Search for a Self', p. 60.

[27] See L. Taylor and K. Williams, 'The Actor and his World' and J. Bernard, 'A Little Bit of Drama'.

[28] R. Travisano, 'Alternation and Conversion as Qualitatively Different Transformations', p. 601.

[29] See E. Erikson, 'The Problem of Ego Identity'.

[30] C. Swift, The Job of Acting, p. 56.

[31] A. Pepitone, 'An Experimental Analysis of Self-Dynamics', p. 349.

[32] T. Sutcliffe, 'Giving them Hal', p. 10.

[33] See J. Blake, 'Occupational Thrill, Mystique and the Truck Driver'.

[34] S. Messinger, et al., 'Life as Theater: Some Notes on the Dramaturgic Approach to Social Reality'.

[35] Ibid., p. 99.

[36] See N. Polsky, Hustlers, Beats and Others.

[37] See K. Plummer, Sexual Stigma.

[38] S. Messinger, et al., 'Life as Theater', p. 101.

[39] Ibid., p. 109.

[40] The counterpart for the audience is what Ben Chaim calls a willingness to 'see as'. Distance in the Theatre, p. 73.

[41] T. Sarbin, 'Role Theory', p. 237.

[42] Interview notes.

[43] Robert Duvall, quoted in B. Mills, 'Support Craft', p. 8.

[44] S. Messinger, et al., 'Life as Theater', p. 109.

[45] G. Mead, Mind Self and Society, p. 147.

[46] E. Burns, Theatricality.

[47] Ibid., p. 2.

[48] Ibid., p. 33.

[49] E. Goffman, The Presentation of Self in Everyday Life.

[50] T. Sarbin, 'Role Theory', 2nd ed.

[51] Ibid., p. 493.; W. Archer, quoted in T. Sarbin, ibid.

[52] C. Stanislavsky, An Actor Prepares, p. 20.

[53] T. Sarbin, 'Role Theory', 2nd ed., pp. 493-4.

[54] Ibid., p. 494.

[55] Paul Schofield, in interview with J. Watts, p. 12.

[56] Alan Howard, quoted in J. Sutcliffe, 'Giving them Hal', p. 10.

[57] See B. Brecht, 'The Street Scene; A Basic Model for an Epic Theatre'.

[58] See W. Wheatley, 'Some Problems of Sustaining a Role in Acting'.

[59] H. Pearson, The Last Actor Managers, p. 16.

[60] R. Hayman, Techniques of Acting, p. 22.

[61] W. Wheatley, 'Some Problems of Sustaining a Role in Acting', p. 25.

[62] Interview notes.

[63] R. Lawrie, 'Personality'.

[64] Ibid., p. 310.

[65] See R. D. Laing, The Divided Self.

[66] R. Lawrie, 'Personality', p. 131.

[67] T. Shank, The Art of Dramatic Art, pp. 127, 128.

[68] See E. Goffman, Frame Analysis.

[69] R. Turner, 'The Real Self', p. 207.

[70] M. Snyder and S. Gangestad, 'Choosing Social Situations: Two Investigations of Self-Monitoring Processes', p. 124.

[71] See S. Messinger, et al., 'Life as Theater', p. 106.

[72] See A. Cicourel, 'Interpretive Procedures and Normative Rules in the Negotiation of Status and Role', in Cognitive Sociology, pp. 23-24.

[73] See S. Messinger, et al., 'Life as Theater', p. 105.

[74] See C. Edgley and R. Turner, 'Masks and Social Relations', p. 10.

[75] See R. Harre and P. Secord, The Explanation of Social Behavior.

[76] Ibid., pp. 215-16.

[77] A. Brittan, Meanings and Situations, pp.116-17.

[78] C. Mills, 'Situated Actions and Vocabularies of Motive', p. 905.

[79] A Brittan, Meanings and Situations, p. 97.

[80] M. Scott and S. Lyman, 'Accounts', p. 46.

[81] See N. Foote, 'Identification as the Basis for a Theory of Motivation', p. 15.

[82] See B. Glaser and A. Strauss, 'Awareness Contexts and Social Interaction'.

[83] See R. Cuzzort, 'Humanity as the Big Con: The Views of Erving Goffman', p. 177.

[84] According to Ben Chaim, Brecht 'wanted to create an awareness in the spectator of the characters' emotions and of the spectator's own emotions in response to the events on stage.' Distance in the theatre, p. 72.

[85] P. McHugh, Defining the Situation.

[86] Ibid., p. 28.

[87] Ibid., p. 24.

[88] T. Shank, The Art of Dramatic Art, p. 76.

[89] R. Hayman, Techniques of Acting, pp. 68, 66.

[90] P. McHugh, Defining the Situation, p. 36.

[91] Ibid., p. 37.

[92] Interview notes.

[93] P. Mc Hugh, Defining the Situation, p. 38.

[94] K. Gergen, 'Personal Consistency and the Presentation of Self'.

[95] Ibid., p. 299.

[96] Ibid., p. 306.

[97] See P. McHugh, Defining the Situation, p. 39.

[98] Ibid., p. 40

[99] Ibid.

[100] Ibid., p. 28.

[101] T. Cole and H. Chinoy (eds.), Directors on Directing, pp. 203-4.

[102] See P. McHugh, Defining the Situation, p. 107.

[103] Who borrowed the idea from Karl Mannheim.

[104] P. McHugh, Defining the Situation, p. 43.

[105] Ibid.

[106] See Ibid.

[107] Ibid.

[108] Ibid.

[109] Ibid.

[110] Ibid.

[111] Ibid., pp. 43, 45.

[112] G. Mead, Mind, Self and Society, pp. 43-46.

[113] Chambers 20th Century Dictionary, p. 1276.

[114] See T. Shank, The Art of Dramatic Art, p. 91.

[115] Expressing the same idea, but on the level of everyday reality, Brittan writes that: "Each new situation or context that the individual encounters is obviously like some situations in some respects; it is also different in other respects. Symbolization or interpretation of the situation in terms of past cultural prescriptions does not proceed automatically. If it did, then we could not account for novelty in human affairs. Each new situation is a compound of old and new understandings - it is never a carbon copy of the past." Meanings and Situations, p. 91. Wilshire points out that in both theatre, and everyday life, the participants may surprise themselves and each other 'with what emerges through their spontaneous interaction and involvement'. Role Playing and Identity, p. 17.

[116] See A. Schutz, 'On Multiple Realities', p. 226.

[117] Mangham and Overington write that 'any suggestion that there is an actor present in a character ... will erode the taken-for-granted nature of this special form of consciousness' ('Performance and Rehearsal: Social Order and Organizational Life,' p. 208), whereas Wilshire asserts that 'We are always aware of Hamlet-played-by-this-actor'. Role Playing and Identity, p. 275.

[118] See L. Taylor and K. Williams, 'The Actor and his World', p. 189. By contrast, Layder considers corpsing a manifestation of interpersonal conflict. See Structure, Interaction and

Social Theory, p. 126.

[119] See S. Little and A. Cantor, The Playmakers, p. 108.

[120] Wilshire takes this further by writing that 'The actor onstage is engaged not only in a "conversation" with the audience but in a three-way dialogue between himself as person, himself as artist and himself as character'. Role Playing and Identity, p. 267.

[121] E. Goffman, Frame Analysis, pp. 129-31.

[122] I am grateful to Edward Sagarin for this concrete formulation of the problem.

[123] See M. Natanson, Phenomenology, Role and Reason, pp. 140-41; also, B. Wilshire, 'The Dramaturgical Model of Behavior: Its Strengths and Weaknesses', p. 289.

[124] See E. Goffman, Frame Analysis.

[125] See M. Natanson, Phenomenology, Role and Reason, pp. 140-41.

[126] See J. Duvignaud, 'The Theatre in Society: Society in the Theatre', p. 85.

[127] B. Wilshire, Role Playing and Identity, p. xiv. See also ibid., pp. 32, 90.

[128] M. Price, 'The Other Self: Thoughts about Character in the Novel'.

[129] See C. Edgley and R. Turner, 'Masks and Social Relations', p. 7.

[130] M. Mauss, mentioned in J. Duvignaud, 'The Theatre in Society', p. 89.

[131] See G. Simmel, 'The Dramatic Actor and Reality', p. 93.

[132] A. Brittan, Meanings and Situations, p. 152.

[133] G. Stone, 'Appearance and the Self', p. 93.

[134] C. Edgley and R. Turner, 'Masks and Social Relations', p. 7.

[135] A Brittan, Meanings and Situations, p. 182.

[136] R. Turner, 'The Real Self', p. 219. Wilshire, too, argues that, 'One is one's roles but not just one's "roles", for

one is also an unobjectifiable consciousness of "roles" actual and possible - even roles as yet unimagined.' Role Playing and Identity, p. 227.

[137] M. Natanson, Phenomenology, Role and Reason, p. 144.

[138] A. Strauss, Mirrors and Masks, p. 147.

[139] R. Travisano, 'Alternation and Conversion as Qualitatively Different Transformations', p. 594.

[140] A. Brittan, Meanings and Situations, pp. 155, 176.

[141] R. Travisano, 'Alternation and Conversion as Qualitatively Different Transformations', p. 601.

[142] See M. Natanson, Phenomenology, Role and Reason.

[143] The alienating consequences of modern life are dealt with by A. Weigert in Sociology of Everyday Life.

[144] G. Mead, Mind, Self and Society, pp. 50, 139-40.

[145] Ibid., p. 173. Wilshire, who acknowledges some points of agreement between Mead's approach and his own phenomenological approach (See Role Playing and Identity, p. 166), characterises the self-body relationship thus: 'It is a conscious, or potentially conscious, body which must be identified as a self, and it is so under the following conditions: when it can experience objects or persons which are in fact other than itself - but with whom it is mimetically involved - and then can reproduce them as other in their absence'. Ibid, p. 152. Clearly, in these terms the character cannot be a real self.

[146] See R. Harre and P. Secord, The Explanation of Social Behavior, p. 214.

[147] M. Natanson, Phenomenology, Role and Reason, p. 162.

[148] A. Brittan, Meanings and Situations, p. 116. Perinbanayagam also argues that drama is something that occurs equally in theatre and everyday life, but attributes this to the fact that in each case, one finds 'the utilization of act, scene and agency by humans trapped in the temporal dimension to create meaning, demonstrate purpose.' 'Dramas, Metaphors and Structures', p. 262.

[149] G. Mead, Mind, Self and Society, p. 178.

[150] E. Tiryakian, 'The Existential Self and the Person', p. 77.

[151] See G. Mead, <u>Mind, Self and Society,</u> p. 186.

[152] G. Simmel, 'On the Theory of Theatrical Performance', p. 304.

[153] Jonathan Miller, quoted in J. Watts, 'Diagnosing the Doctor', p. 8.

[154] G. Gow, interview with Denis Quilley, <u>Plays and Players,</u> p. 11.

[155] L. Taylor and K. Williams, 'The Actor and his World', p. 189.

[156] T. Sutcliffe, 'Giving them Hal', p. 10.

5 Conclusion

Theatrical acting is a vicarious freedom of <u>acting control</u> of a
situation.   It demonstrates perfectly how control can be gained
merely by properly saying the right things. Perfect acting is a
unique exercise in omnipotence,   gained simply by infallible
command of the script. By impeccable wielding of deference and
demeanor the actor   is at the same time   undisputed director of
his destiny...[1]

The dramaturgical perspective contains the paradoxical elements
of freedom and constraint; although social reality is construed as
a monolith of rules which govern social encounters,   each player
exercises considerable skill and   ingenuity in turning these
constraints to his or her advantage. Still, the perspective lends
itself to a more constraining than liberating view of social
reality for, as Brittan remarks:

We can,   like Goffman, describe action as being an essay in
self- and impression-management and, in so doing, place action
in a context which is taken for granted. <u>The system is there</u>
<u>for the purposes of men so that they can realize these purposes</u>
...Ultimately, Goffman, while mapping out the intricacies of
'face work',   etc., is committed to a view of action which
places the actor very much at the mercy of the script. He
cannot get beyond the script because, by definition, the script
is the total world - the stage on which his performance is
validated. (emphasis added)[2]

Of course, outcomes (events) in drama are undeniably scripted, predictable and known. It is equally undeniable that social actors' real performances:

> are not set or prescribed for all time...They literally can act in the strongest sense of the term - they can choose to perform and interpret the behaviour in a context in symbolic indications which are not circumscribed by the role-script.[3]

Yet, while drama is usually scripted, the theatrical production or enacted drama is much more than the script. The true equivalent of social life is the enacted drama, not the scripted drama which provides mere guidelines. If theoretical statements about social life are empirically grounded - and if not, are empty speculation - then I am correct in my choice of equivalent [4].

Although the production viewed by the member of the audience is in its own way real theatre, we sacrifice a great deal by examining interaction from the audience standpoint only. The dramaturgical analyst relies on a familiarity with theatre from this standpoint in formulating conceptions of theatre and real life; yet, it is dramaturgically far more orthodox to inspect the means by which these performances are created. Observation of theatre in the making must lead us to question Burns' statement that:

> The fact that the theme of a play is in most cases (except in improvisation) already part of a predetermined pattern and that the action is only animated by the actors means that a selection has taken place which constrains the possible forms of action which may emerge.[5]

Only animated? 'Themes' are abstractions from meaningful expressions and, as audiences know, a theme is only as evident as its credible portrayal allows. I have attempted to show throughout this study that dramatic meaning is constructed in interaction. As Brittan contends, with regard to everyday action which is essentially dramatic in nature, 'Dramatically action is not scripted by hidden manipulators but is constructed by the actors themselves' [6]. And, carrying this idea further, I quote Berger:

> If social reality is dramatically created it must also be dramatically malleable. In this way, the dramatic model opens up a passage out of the rigid determinism into which sociological thought originally led us.[7]

If the preceding study has successfully demonstrated the interpretive, socially constructed nature of dramatic reality, it must also support a view of social reality which emphasises its interpretive rather than constraining features. While the interactionist perspective has often been accused of neglecting the structural features of social interaction [8], I merely wish to stress that the structural is not all, that it is only constructed from individual action and, moreover, that even the structural must be interpreted in order to be acted upon in a reinforcing or modifying way.

Once we focus on social and dramatic actors, rather than on social and dramatic roles, as well as on the unscripted potential of drama rather than its scripted givens, we find some of the purported differences between life and drama to be untrue. Gurvitch, for example [9], depicts real life as a sphere in which, unlike theatre, the roles of the players are not interchangeable. In theatre, presumably, the actors could stop the play and exchange roles; in social life 'as it really is'[10] this could not be done. Gurvitch thus neglects the inviolability of theatre, characterises social structure as immutable and ignores the capacity of human beings to transcend their given roles [11].

Staged life is pared of irrelevancies or 'condensed' in order to communicate 'paradigmatic values', 'felt life' or the essence of the human condition [12]. This condensed and heightened quality is both found in the scripted drama and reinforced in its enactment through techniques of acting. I have previously referred to the heightened view of reality which continual theatrical experience can induce in its practitioners (and, perhaps, in its devoted audiences). In concluding this study, I would like to emphasise how dramatic acting mirrors the freedom which is potentially available to everyone in everyday life.

First, I examined a case of secondary socialisation in which the self was fundamentally transformed in order that it might be capable, in its peculiarly indirect form, of a greater breadth of experience than that ordinarily contained in everyday experience. The actor transcends the boundaries of everyday life through this strange brand of broadened or heightened participation in varied social worlds. Yet, this can be viewed as the reflection of possibilities available to everyone. For example, in recent decades, ordinary people have borrowed techniques from dramatic acting as a means of enriching their everyday lives. As Strauss writes:

some of the effect of experimental role-dramas is that the drama allows and forces the person to play a range of roles he did not believe himself capable of playing, or never conceived of playing; it brings him face to face with his potential as well as his actual self.[13]

Such dramatic role-playing for non-dramatic ends can also be viewed as an attempt to recapture the dramatic quality of everyday life – to rediscover the feeling <u>that</u> one is, which is muted by the fragmentary nature of modern existence.

Secondly, I focused on the interpretive efforts which are required of dramatic actors, even though they are provided with a script. This finds its parallel in everyday life in the indisputable fact that the givens are merely guidelines, and that we must <u>act,</u> even if only in carrying out what we assume to be the requirements of our roles. I have argued throughout that deterministic views of social life <u>and</u> enacted drama err in their denial of individual imagination, the limits of which are themselves unpredictable. Social life and its dramatic enactment may be overwhelmingly predictable, but they can never be wholly so.

Finally , through the case study of television drama, I analysed a work situation in which broad, constraining factors deny the creative potential of the actor. I examined in detail the ways in which the participants circumvent acknowledgment of this surrender of selfhood. Berger quotes Sartre as saying that we are 'condemned to freedom'[14] and it is the awareness of this potential which underlies the TV actor's role conflict.

Thus the dramatic actor emerges, not as a symbol of the constraints of social life, but instead as a symbol of the potential freedom of human existence which can be ignored but not denied. This is implicit in the ambivalence which underlies the lay reaction to actors [15]. Actors not only hold the enviable position of transcending the mundane; they also serve as a reminder that this transcendence is an intrinsic human quality. In attempting to further our understanding of social reality, the dramaturgical analogy draws upon the apparent constraints of theatrical action. However, an examination of the actualities of the dramatic actor's work and career paradoxically highlights the potentially liberating features of everyday life.

NOTES:

[1] E. Becker, <u>The Birth and Death of Meaning,</u> p. 96.

[2] A. Brittan, <u>Meanings and Situations,</u> p. 86.

[3] Ibid., pp. 118-19.

[4] Overington and Mangham write, 'Clearly, to offer an account of the theater for social scientists one must start somewhere...So it is that we start where we are, from within the world as it is theorized by what we take as symbolic interactionists...As

interactionists we start with the event of theater as it is before us in performance.' 'The Theatrical Perspective in Organizational Analysis', p. 175.

[5] E. Burns, Theatricality, p. 16.

[6] A. Brittan, Meanings and Situations, p. 87.

[7] P. Berger, Invitation to Sociology, p. 160.

[8] See A. Brittan, Meanings and Situations, p. 195.

[9] See G. Gurvitch, 'The Sociology of Theatre'.

[10] Ibid., p. 75.

[11] Overington and Mangham's remarks are also relevant here: 'casting is one more element that helps to demystify the givenness of everyday life. Someone else could have been cast.' 'The Theatrical Perspective in Organizational Analysis', p. 181.

[12] See T. Shank, The Art of Dramatic Art, p. 190; M. Natanson, Phenomenology, Role and Reason, p. 153; E. Burns, Theatricality, p. 39; and Henry James, quoted in T. Shank, The Art of Dramatic Art, p. 32.

[13] A. Strauss, Mirrors and Masks, p. 97.

[14] P. Berger, Invitation to Sociology, p. 165. Lofland makes explicit the connection between Goffman's dramaturgical view of self and Sartre's existentialism in, 'Early Goffman: Style, Structure, Substance, Soul', pp. 46-8.

[15] See M. Goldman, The Actor's Freedom, p. 12.

Research appendix

THE DRAMA SCHOOL

Field work period: January - May 1976

Hours of observation: 50+

Interviews conducted:

2nd term students	7
4th term students	8
Senior students	4
Teachers	12
Principal	1
	--
	32

Interview length: 30-90 minutes

Interview Schedule : *

1. What made you decide to become an actor?

2. Have you ever done any other kind of work or thought of doing anything else?

3. Can you remember your reactions to your audition? Why do you think you were selected?

4. Can you describe your first reactions to the training? How, if at all, has this changed?

5. Could you describe some of the differences you've encountered in working with different directors and your reactions to these differences?

6. Do you ever have difficulty understanding a director's direction? Could you give me an example?

7. What do you think the director's role in a production is/should be? and the stage manager's?

8. As far as the relationship between the different people involved in any one production is concerned, is there anything common to every production regardless of differences in the play, cast, director, etc.?

9. Is there any difference between the way you feel when acting in rehearsal and acting in performance?

10. What are the major differences between student and professional productions?

11. Can you describe your reaction to the way you've been cast for different parts at [the school]?

12. Could you tell me what happens in tutorials?

13. Could you describe the relationships between you, personally, and the other students at [the school]? you and the directors you've worked with? between you and the principal?

14. Can you think of any incident which has involved you at [the school] which seemed to you to be very unusual or important or memorable?

15.

(2nd and 4th term): What do you like most about your training? the least?

(4th and seniors): What changes would you make in the training of actors? Would you do this course if you had to do it all over again?

16. Is there anything else you'd like to say about the training here, generally?

17. Has your view of yourself changed since you first came to [the school] and if so, how?

18. Do you think the training here will influence or contribute to your success as a professional actor? (if so, how?)

19. (2nd term): How do you think your feelings about acting might change by the time you leave here?

(4th and seniors): Have your feelings about acting changed since you first came here?

20. What kind of person would be most likely to succeed in the acting profession?

21. What do you think your first job will be like?

22. What are your ambitions for the future?

23. School experience prior to drama school

24. Acting experience prior to drama school

25. Age

26. Place of birth

27. Parents' occupations

* (for students; teacher and principal interviews were unstructured)

THE THEATRE COMPANY

Field work period: October – December 1975

Hours of observation: 100 +

Interviews conducted: Actors   9
                      Director   1
                      Playwright 1

                                 11

Interview length: 30-120 minutes

Interview Schedule :*

1. Could you describe, in whatever way seems best to you, what happened in this production?

2. How would you describe the way decisions were made in this group?

3. What factors do you think were important in determining the progress of this production?

4. Do you think the production was affected in any way by having rehearsals in a different place from the actual theatre, and if so, how?

5. Do you think the lack of payment had any particular effects?

6. How did this production differ, if it did, from other productions you've been involved in?

7. Did your feelings about the production change throughout the course of the production?

8. Could you describe your relationship to other members of the group?

9. Could you try to assess the others' contributions to the group?

10. Which, if any, of the members of the group did you know before this began?

11. How did this relationship between the members make the atmosphere of this production different from others you've been in?

12. Did you feel that there was any correspondence between the actors' selves and the roles they were trying to play?

13. Do you feel that my presence as an observer affected the group's behaviour in any way? If so, how?

14. Could you briefly summarise what you thought was the meaning or message of the play?

15. At what point in the production did that meaning become clear to you?

16. How do you think that the decisions as to the motivations behind the characters' actions and words are ultimately conveyed to the audience?

17. Do you think that the group was trying to arrive at an objective understanding of life in a mental hospital which it then tried to convey, or do you think they were deciding on their own interpretation, regardless of 'accuracy'?

18. Do you think there can be a conflict between portraying situations realistically and portraying situations in a way that the audience will understand?

19. Could you try to describe how acting is done?

20. How do you learn your lines?

21. When do you feel that you've gotten a lot out of rehearsal?

22. How do you go about developing a character?

23. What qualities would make for the ideal production, from the actor's point of view?

24. What qualities should an actor possess to make for an ideal production?

25. What is it about a part that makes it easy/difficult, enjoyable/unenjoyable?

26. Are there any difficulties in working on two parts at a time?

27. How do you think your thoughts on acting differ now from your thoughts when you first started acting?

28. In what terms do you view the development of your career?

29. Have you ever done any other kind of work, or had you ever thought of doing any other kind of work?

30. Approximately how many weeks of the year do you do paid work? Unpaid work?

31. What made you decide to take a non-paying job?

32. How do you think an actor's performance at an audition is related to his or her actual performance?

33. How do you support yourself, financially?

34. Views on auditions generally, this one in particular?

35. Views on directors and directing generally, this case in particular?

36. Age

37. Place of birth

38. Parents' occupations

39. Training

40. Experience

* (for actors; adapted for director and playwright)

THE TELEVISION GROUP

Field work period: October 1977

Hours of observations: 50 +

Interviews conducted: Actors   5
                   Director   1

                            6

Interview length: 30-60 minutes

Interview Schedule :

1. Twenty I-Am Statements

2. Feelings about this production

3. Comparison of this production to other TV productions

4. Why do you think you were cast for this part?

5. Work relations between members of this production

6. What are the rewards of acting?

7. Acting in theatre: memories of last job, distinctive qualities of medium

8. Acting in TV: memories of last job, distinctive qualities of medium

9. Acting in film: memories of last job, distinctive qualities of medium

10. Could you tell me about relations between actors and actors?

11. Could you tell me about relations between actors and directors?

12. Could you tell me about relations between actors and technicians?

13. Could you tell me about relations between actors and extras?

14. Could you tell me about relations between leads and supporting roles?
    (Questions 10-14: Any differences in different media?)

15. Do you think that your experience of acting in any way influences your dealings with people in everyday situations?

16. Training - and memories of drama school

17. Work experience (what kind, since when, where, how much per year)

18. Development of career (in terms of what? Hopes for the future?)

19. Age

20. Place of birth

21. Parents', siblings' and spouse's occupations

Bibliography

ABC Television Ltd, Armchair Theatre, Weidenfeld and Nicolson, London 1959.

Allison, J., 'Religious Conversion: Regression and Progression in an Adolescent Experience', Journal for the Scientific Study of Religion, vol.8, 1969, pp. 23-8.

Allport, G., Becoming, Yale University Press, New Haven 1955.

Baker, F. (ed), Movie People, Abelard-Schuman, London 1972.

Becker, E., The Birth and Death of Meaning, 2nd ed., Free Press, New York 1971.

Becker, H., Outsiders: Studies in the Sociology of Deviance, The Free Press of Glencoe, New York 1963.

Becker, H., 'Personal Change in Adult Life', Sociometry, vol.27, 1964, pp. 40-53.

Becker, H. and Geer, B., 'Participant Observation and Interviewing: A Comparison', Human Organization, vol.16, 1957, pp. 28-32.

Becker, H. et al., Boys in White: Student Culture in Medical School, University of Chicago Press, Chicago 1961.

Becker, H. et al. (eds), Institutions and the Person: Papers Presented to E. C. Hughes, Aldine, Chicago 1968.

Ben Chaim, D., Distance in the Theatre: The Aesthetics of Audience Response, UMI Research Press, Ann Arbor 1984.

Bentley, E., 'Emotional Memory' in Bentley, E. (ed), The Theory of the Modern Stage, Penguin, Harmondsworth 1968.

Berger, P., Invitation to Sociology, Penguin, Harmondsworth 1966.

Bernard, J., 'A Little Bit of Drama', Sunday Times Colour Magazine, London, 18 Jan.1976, p.31.

Blake, J., 'Occupational Thrill, Mystique and the Truck Driver', Urban Life and Culture, vol.3, 1974, pp.205-20.

Blumer, H., 'Society as Symbolic Interaction', in Rose, A. (ed),
Human Behavior and Social Processes.

Blumer, H., 'The Methodological Position of Symbolic
Interactionism' in Blumer, H., Symbolic Interactionism:
Perspective and Method, Prentice-Hall, New York 1969.

Brecht, B., 'The Street Scene: A Basic Model for an Epic Theatre',
transl. by J. Willett, in Bentley, E. (ed), The Theory of the
Modern Stage.

Brittan, A., Meanings and Situations, Routledge and Kegan Paul,
London 1973.

Broadhead, R., 'Individuation in Facework: Theoretical Implications
from a Study of Facework in Medical School Admissions', Symbolic
Interaction, vol.3, 1980, pp.51-68.

Burke, K., A Grammar of Motives, Prentice-Hall, New York 1945.

Burns, E., Theatricality: A Study of Convention in the Theatre and
in Social Life, Longman, London 1972.

Burns, E. and Burns, T. (eds), Sociology of Literature and Drama,
Penguin, Harmondsworth 1973.

Caillois, R., Man, Play and Games, Thames and Hudson, London 1962.

Cantor, M. and Pingree, S., The Soap Opera, Sage, Beverly Hills
1983.

Carragher, B., 'Does a Smash Hit Guarantee a Performer's Future?',
New York Times, 30 July 1978, sect. 2, pp.1,18.

Cassata, M. and Skill, T., Life on Daytime Television: Tuning-In
Serial Drama, Ablex, Norwood 1983.

Chambers, W. and Chambers, R., Chambers Twentieth Century
Dictionary, Chambers, Edinburgh 1972.

Cicourel, A., 'Interpretive Procedures and Normative Rules in the
Negotiation of Status and Role' in Cicourel, A., Cognitive
Sociology, Penguin, Harmondsworth 1973.

Cole, T. and Chinoy, H. (eds), Directors on Directing, Bobbs-
Merrill, Indianapolis 1963.

Cuzzort, R., 'Humanity as the Big Con: The Views of Erving Goffman'
in Cuzzort, R., Humanity and Modern Social Thought, Rinehart and
Winston, New York 1969.

Davis, F., 'Professional Socialization as Subjective Experience: The Process of Doctrinal Conversion Among Student Nurses', in Becker, H., et al. (eds), Institutions and the Person.

Davis, F., 'The Martian and the Convert', Urban Life and Culture, vol.2, 1973, pp.333-43.

Davis, K., Human Society, Macmillan, New York 1948.

Denzin, N., 'Symbolic Interactionism and Ethnomethodology: A Proposed Synthesis', American Sociological Review, vol.34, 1969, pp.922-34.

Dornbusch, S., 'The Military Academy as an Assimilating Institution', Social Forces vol.33, 1955, pp. 316-321.

Drury, D. and McCarthy, J., 'The Social Psychology of Name Change: Reflections on a Serendipitous Discovery', Social Psychology Quarterly, vol.43, 1980, pp. 310-20.

Duvignaud, J., 'The Theatre in Society: Society in the Theatre', in Burns, E. and Burns, T (eds), Sociology of Literature and Drama.

Edgley, C. and Turner, R., 'Masks and Social Relations: An Essay on the Sources and Assumptions of Dramaturgical Social Psychology', Humboldt Journal of Social Relations, vol.3, 1975, pp.4-12.

Elliott, P., The Making of a Television Series, Constable, London 1972.

Erikson, E., 'The Problem of Ego Identity', Journal of the American Psychoanalytic Association, vol.4, 1956, pp.58-121.

Erikson, E., Childhood and Society, 2nd ed., Norton, New York 1963.

Etzioni, A., Modern Organizations, Prentice-Hall, Englewood Cliffs 1964.

Faulkner, R., Hollywood Studio Musicians, Aldine-Atherton, Chicago 1971.

Fay, S., interview with Albert Finney, The Sunday Times, London, 14 December 1975, p.5.

Fife, S., 'No Place to Be Somebody - Acting Schools; Only the Strong Survive', Village Voice, New York, 13 March 1978, pp.39-43.

Foote, N., 'Identification as the Basis for a Theory of
   Motivation', American Sociological Review, vol.16, 1951,
   pp.14-21.

Fox, R., 'Training for Uncertainty' in R. Merton, et al. (eds), The
   Student Physician, Harvard University Press, Cambridge 1957.

Gans, H., 'The Participant Observer as a Human Being: Observations
   on the Personal Aspects of Field Work', in H. Becker, et al.
   (eds), Institutions and the Person.

Geer, B., et al., 'Learning the Ropes: Situational Learning in Four
   Occupational Training Programs' in I. Deutscher and E. Thompson
   (eds), In Among the People, Basic Books, New York 1968.

Gergen, K., 'Personal Consistency and the Presentation of Self' in
   Gordon, C. and Gergen, K. (eds), The Self in Social Interaction.

Gielgud, J., Distinguished Company, Heinemann, London 1972.

Glaser, B. and Strauss, A., 'Awareness Contexts and Social
   Interaction', American Sociological Review, vol.29, 1964,
   pp.669-79.

Goffman, E., 'On Cooling the Mark Out: Some Aspects of Adaption to
   Failure', Psychiatry, vol.15, 1952, pp.451-63.

Goffman, E., The Presentation of Self in Everyday Life, Doubleday
   Anchor, New York 1959.

Goffman, E., Encounters, Bobbs-Merrill, Indianapolis 1961.

Goffman, E., 'On the Characteristics of Total Institutions: The
   Inmate World', in Cressey, D. (ed), The Prison, Holt, Rinehart
   and Winston, New York 1961.

Goffman, E., Frame Analysis, Penguin, Harmondsworth 1975.

Goldman, M., The Actor's Freedom, Viking Press, New York 1975.

Goldman, W., The Season, Harcourt Brace and World, New York 1970.

Gordon, C. and Gergen, K. (eds), The Self in Social Interaction,
   vol.1, Wiley, New York 1968.

Gow, G., interview with Denis Quilley, Plays and Players, July
   1977, pp.11-13.

Gulbenkian Foundation, UK and Commonwealth Branch, 'Going on Stage': A Report to the Calouste Gulbenkian Foundation on Professional Training for Drama, Gulbenkian Foundation, London 1975.

Gurvitch, G., 'The Sociology of Theatre' in Burns, E. and Burns, T., Sociology of Literature and Drama.

Guthrie, T., Tyrone Guthrie on Acting, Viking Press, New York 1971.

Haas, J. and Shaffir, W., 'Taking on the Role of Doctor: A Dramaturgical Analysis of Professionalization', Symbolic Interaction, vol.5, 1982, pp. 187-203.

Harre, R. and Secord, P., The Explanation of Social Behavior, Rowman and Littlefield, Totowa 1972.

Hayman, R., Techniques of Acting, Methuen, London 1969.

Hayman, R., Playback, Davis Poynter, London 1973.

Hearn, H., et al., 'Identity and Institutional Imperatives: The Socialization of the Student Actress', Sociological Quarterly, vol.9, 1968, pp.47-63.

Henry, W. and Sims, J., 'Actors' Search for a Self', Transaction, vol.7, pp.57-62.

Hiley, J., '"Super! We'll Be In Touch!"', Time Out, London, 24-30 June 1977, pp.14-15.

Hobson, D., Crossroads - The Drama of a Soap Opera, Methuen, London 1982.

Hochschild, A., 'Emotion Work, Feeling Rules, and Social Structure', American Journal of Sociology, vol.85, 1979, pp. 551-75.

Hood, S., A Survey of Television, Heinemann, London 1967.

Kingson, W. and Cowgill, R., Radio Drama Acting and Production, Rinehart, New York 1946.

Klemesrud, J., 'Paul Rudd - Every Inch a King', New York Times, 11 July 1976, sect.2, p.1.

Knapp, M., Essentials of Nonverbal Communication, Holt, Rinehart and Winston, New york 1980.

Laing, R.D., The Divided Self, Tavistock, London 1960.

Lauer, R. and Handel, W., Social Psychology: The Theory and Application of Symbolic Interactionism, Houghton Mifflin, Boston 1977.

Lauritzen, M., Jane Austen's "Emma" on Television: A Study of a BBC Classical Serial, Gothenburg Studies in English Number 48, Goteborg 1981.

Lawrie, R., 'Personality', Philosophy and Phenomenological Research, vol.34, pp.307-30.

Layder, D., 'Notes on Variation in Middle Class Careers', in Field, D. (ed), Social Psychology for Sociologists, Thomas Nelson and Sons, London 1974.

Layder, D., 'Occupational Careers in Contemporary Britain: with Special Reference to the Acting Profession', PhD thesis, University of London 1976.

Layder, D., Structure, Interaction and Social Theory, Routledge and Kegan Paul, London 1981.

Layder, D., 'Sources and Levels of Commitment in Actors' Careers', Work and Occupations, vol.11, 1984, pp. 147-62.

Layder, D., 'Social Interaction and Occupational Organization: The Case of Acting', unpublished paper.

Little, S., and Cantor, A., The Playmakers, Norton, New York 1970.

Lofland, J., 'Early Goffman: Style, Structure, Substance, Soul', in Ditton, J. (ed), The View from Goffman, Macmillan, London 1980.

Lofland, J., and Lofland, L.H., Analyzing Social Settings, 2nd ed., Wadsworth, Belmont 1984.

Loudfoot, 'The Concept of Social Role', Philosophy of the Social Sciences, vol.2, 1972, pp.133-45.

Mangham, I. and Overington, M., 'Performance and Rehearsal: Social Order and Organizational Life', Symbolic Interaction, vol.5, 1982, pp. 205-23.

Manning, P. and Fabrega, H., Jr., 'The Experience of Self and Body: Health and Illness in the Chiapas Highlands', in Psathas, G. (ed), Phenomenological Sociology, Wiley, New York 1973.

Manning, P. and Hearn, H., 'Acting: Selves, Careers and the Social Organization of the Occupation', unpublished paper.

Mast, S., 'Working for Television: The Social Organization of TV Drama', Symbolic Interaction, vol.6, 1983, pp. 71-83.

McHugh, P., 'Social Disintegration as a Requisite of Resocialization', Social Forces, vol.44, 1966, pp.353-63.

McHugh, P., Defining the Situation: The Organization of Meaning in Social Interaction, Bobbs-Merrill, Indianapolis 1968.

Mead, G., Mind, Self and Society: From the Standpoint of a Social Behaviorist, University of Chicago Press, Chicago 1934.

Meltzer, B., et al., Symbolic Interactionism: Genesis, Varieties and Criticism, Routledge and Kegan Paul, London 1975.

Messinger, S., et al., 'Life as Theater: Some Notes on the Dramaturgic Approach to Social Reality', Sociometry, vol.25, pp.98-110.

Mills, C., 'Situated Actions and Vocabularies of Motive', American Sociological Review, vol.5, 1940, pp.904-13.

Mills, N., 'Children's Tears', The Guardian, London, 16 April 1975, p.11.

Mills, N., 'Support Craft', The Guardian, London, 21 June 1976, p.8.

Mortimer, J. and Simmons, R., 'Adult Socialization', Annual Review of Sociology, vol.4, 1978, pp. 421-54.

Natanson, M., Phenomenology, Role and Reason, Charles C. Thomas, Springfield 1974.

Oleson, V. and Whittaker, E., The Silent Dialogue, Jossey-Bass, San Francisco 1968.

Overington, M. and Mangham, I., 'the Theatrical Perspective in Organizational Life', Symbolic Interaction, vol.5, 1982, pp. 173-85.

Pearson, H., The Last Actor Managers, White Lion, London 1950.

Pepitone, A., 'An Experimental Analysis of Self-Dynamics', in Gordon, C. and Gergen, K. (eds), The Self in Social Interaction.

Perinbanayagam, R., 'Dramas, Metaphors, and Structures', Symbolic Interaction, vol.5, 1982, pp. 259-76.

Perry, G., 'The Hindenberg Rises Again', Sunday Times Colour Magazine, London (n.d.) 1977, pp.36-41.

Pirie, D. and Petit, C., 'One Flew Over the Cuckoo's Nest', Time Out, London, 20-26 Feb. 1976, pp.14-15.

Plummer, K., Sexual Stigma: An Interactionist Account, Routledge and Kegan Paul, London 1975.

Polsky, N., Hustlers, Beats and Others, Aldine, Chicago 1967.

Price, M., 'The Other Self: Thoughts about Character in the Novel', in Burns, E. and Burns, T. (eds), Sociology of Literature and Drama.

Rock, P., The Making of Symbolic Interactionism, Macmillan, London 1979.

Rose, A., 'A Systematic Summary of Symbolic Interaction Theory', in Rose, A. (ed), Human Behavior and Social Processes.

Rose, A., Human Behavior and Social Processes: An Interactionist Approach, Routledge and Kegan Paul, London 1962.

Roth, J., Timetables, Bobbs-Merril, Indianapolis 1963.

Ryser, C., 'The Student Dancer', in Wilson, N. (ed), The Arts in Society.

Sarbin, T., "Role Theory', in Lindzey, G. (ed), Handbook of Social Psychology, vol.1, Addison-Wesley, Reading 1954.

Sarbin, T., "Role Theory', in Lindzey, G. and Aronson, E., (eds), Handbook of Social Psychology, vol.1, 2nd ed., Addison-Wesley, Reading 1968.

Sarbin, T. and Adler, N., 'Self-Reconstitution Processes: A Preliminary Report', Psychoanalytic Review, vol.57, 1970-71, pp.599-616.

Schatzman, L. and Strauss, A., Field Research: Strategies for a Natural Sociology, Prentice-Hall, Englewood Cliffs 1973.

Schutz, A., 'On Multiple Realities' in Schutz, A. Collected Papers, vol.1, Nijhoff, The Hague 1962.

Schutz, A., Phenomenology and the Social World, transl. by G. Walsh and F. Lehnert, Northwestern University Press, Evanston 1967.

Sewell, W., 'Some Recent Developments in Socialization Theory and Research', in Stone, G. and Farberman, H. (eds), Social Psychology through Symbolic Interaction, (1970 Edition).

Shank, T., The Art of Dramatic Art, Dell, New York 1972.

Shils, E., 'The High Culture of the Age' in Wilson, R. (ed), The Arts in Society.

Shubik, I., Play for Today, Davis Poynter, London 1975.

Simmel, G., 'The Dramatic Actor and Reality' in Simmel, G., The Conflict of Modern Culture and Other Essays, Teacher's College Press, New York 1968.

Simmel, G., 'On the Theory of Theatrical Performance', transl. by T. Burns, in Burns, E. and Burns, T. (eds.), Sociology of Literature and Drama.

Synder, M. and Gangestad, S., 'Choosing Social Situations: Two Investigations of Self-Monitoring Processes', Journal of Personality and Social Psychology, vol.43, 1982, pp. 123-35.

Stanislavsky, C., An Actor Prepares, transl. by E. Hapgood, Geoffrey Bles, London 1936.

Stebbins, R., 'Career: The Subjective Approach', Sociological Quarterly, vol.11, 1970, pp.32-49.

Stebbins, R., 'The Subjective Career as a Basis for Reducing Role Conflict', Pacific Sociological Review, vol.14, 1971, pp.383-440.

Stone, G., 'Appearance and the Self', in Rose, A. (ed), Human Behavior and Social Processes.

Stone, G. and Farberman, H., (eds), Social Psychology through Symbolic Interaction, Ginn, Waltham 1970.

Stone, G. and Farberman, H., (eds), Social Psychology through Symbolic Interaction, 2nd ed., Wiley, New york 1981.

Strauss, A., Mirrors and Masks, The Free Press, Glencoe 1959.

Sutcliffe, T., 'Giving Them Hal', The Guardian, London, 20 Jan. 1976, p.10.

Sutcliffe, T., interview with Cheryl Kennedy, The Guardian, London, 19 Oct 1977, n.p.

Swift, C., The Job of Acting, 2nd rev. ed., Harrap, London 1984.

Taylor, C., Making a Television Play, Oriel Press, Newcastle 1970.

Taylor, L and Williams, K., 'The Actor and His World', New Society, 29 July 1971, pp. 188-90.

Tiryakian, E., 'The Existential Self and the Person' in Gordon, C. and Gergen, K. (eds), The Self in Social Interaction.

Travers, A., 'Ritual Power in Interaction', Symbolic Interaction, vol.5, 1982, pp. 277-86.

Travisano, R., 'Alternation and Conversion as Qualitatively Different Transformations', in Stone, G. and Farberman, H., Social Psychology through Symbolic Interaction, (1970 edition).

Turner, R., 'Sponsored and Contest Mobility and the School System', American Sociological Review, vol.25, 1960, pp.855-67.

Turner, R., 'Role-Taking: Process vs. Conformity', in Rose, A. (ed), Human Behavior and Social Processes.

Turner, R., 'The Real Self: From Institution to Impulse', in Stone, G. and Farberman, H. (eds), Social Psychology through Symbolic Interaction, 2nd ed.

Watts, J., interview with Paul Schofield, The Guardian, London, 21 May 1976, p.12.

Watts, J., 'Diagnosing the Doctor', The Guardian, London, 9 July 1976, p.8.

Weigert, A., Sociology of Everyday Life, Longman, New York 1981.

Wheatley, W., 'Some Problems of Sustaining a Role in Acting', PhD thesis, New York University, 1965.

Williams, C., Theatres and Audiences, Longman, London 1970.

Wilshire, B., Role Playing and Identity: The Limits of Theatre as Metaphor, Indiana University Press, Bloomington 1982.

Wilshire, B., 'The Dramaturgical Model of Behavior: Its Strengths and Weaknesses', Symbolic Interaction, vol.5, 1982, pp. 287-97.

Wilson, R., (ed), The Arts in Society, Prentice-Hall, Englewood Cliffs 1964.

Worsley, T., Television: The Ephemeral Art, Alan Ross, London 1970.

Zimmerman, D. and Pollner, M., 'The Everyday World as a
Phenomenon', in Douglas, J. (ed), Understanding Everyday Life,
Routledge and Kegan Paul, London 1971.

Index